The Science Fiction Film in Contemporary Hollywood

The Science Fiction Film in Contemporary Hollywood

A Social Semiotics of Bodies and Worlds

Evdokia Stefanopoulou

BLOOMSBURY ACADEMIC
NEW YORK • LONDON • OXFORD • NEW DELHI • SYDNEY

BLOOMSBURY ACADEMIC
Bloomsbury Publishing Inc
1385 Broadway, New York, NY 10018, USA
50 Bedford Square, London, WC1B 3DP, UK
29 Earlsfort Terrace, Dublin 2, Ireland

BLOOMSBURY, BLOOMSBURY ACADEMIC and the Diana logo are
trademarks of Bloomsbury Publishing Plc

First published in the United States of America 2023
Paperback edition published 2025

Copyright © Evdokia Stefanopoulou, 2023, 2025

For legal purposes the Acknowledgments on p. ix constitute
an extension of this copyright page.

Cover design: Eleanor Rose
Cover image: *Interstellar*, 2014, Dir. Christopher Nolan © Warner Bros Entertainment
Inc / Paramount Pictures Corporation / Collection Christophel / ArenaPAL

All rights reserved. No part of this publication may be reproduced or transmitted
in any form or by any means, electronic or mechanical, including photocopying,
recording, or any information storage or retrieval system, without prior permission
in writing from the publishers.

Bloomsbury Publishing Inc does not have any control over, or responsibility for, any
third-party websites referred to or in this book. All internet addresses given in this
book were correct at the time of going to press. The author and publisher regret any
inconvenience caused if addresses have changed or sites have ceased to exist,
but can accept no responsibility for any such changes.

Library of Congress Cataloging-in-Publication Data
Names: Stefanopoulou, Evdokia, author.
Title: The science fiction film in contemporary Hollywood : a social
semiotics of bodies and worlds / Evdokia Stefanopoulou.
Description: New York : Bloomsbury Academic, 2023. |
Includes bibliographical references and index. |
Summary: "Delineates the contemporary American science fiction film using a
social semiotics approach"– Provided by publisher.
Identifiers: LCCN 2022058988 (print) | LCCN 2022058989 (ebook) |
ISBN 9781501380235 (hardback) | ISBN 9781501380204 (paperback) |
ISBN 9781501380228 (ebook) | ISBN 9781501380211 (pdf) |
ISBN 9781501380198 (ebook other)
Subjects: LCSH: Science fiction films–United States–History and criticism. |
Motion pictures–United States–History–21st century. | Semiotics–Social aspects.
Classification: LCC PN1995.9.S26 S74 2023 (print) | LCC PN1995.9.S26 (ebook) |
DDC 791.43/615–dc23/eng/20230119
LC record available at https://lccn.loc.gov/2022058988
LC ebook record available at https://lccn.loc.gov/2022058989

ISBN:	HB:	978-1-5013-8023-5
	PB:	978-1-5013-8020-4
	ePDF:	978-1-5013-8021-1
	eBook:	978-1-5013-8022-8

Typeset by Integra Software Services Pvt. Ltd.

To find out more about our authors and books visit www.bloomsbury.com
and sign up for our newsletters.

To Nikos and Electra

Contents

Acknowledgments ix

Introduction: History, Theory, Science Fiction (SF) Film 1

Part 1 Theory/History

1 Uncovering the Deep and Surface Structures of SF Film 11
2 Conglomerate Hollywood, Technology, and Filmmakers 39

Part 2 The Cycles: SF Bodies/SF Worlds

SF Bodies

3 The Techno-Humans Cycle: The Exceptional and the Ordinary Technological Body 61
4 The Alien Encounters Cycle: The Millennial Ambiguity of the Other 79
5 The Creatures Cycle: The Organic, the Mechanic, and the In-Between 97

SF Worlds

6 The Dystopia/Utopia Cycle: Surviving Ecopolitical Disasters 117
7 The Zones Cycle: The Enclosed Spatiotemporalities of Global Capitalism 137
8 The Fantastic Worlds Cycle: The Spectacular Technoscientific Empire 155

Epilogue 173

Notes 188
Bibliography 195
Index 217

Acknowledgments

First and foremost, I would like to thank Professor Betty Kaklamanidou. Aside from being an inspiring teacher and an excellent scholar, Betty is also a wonderful person who believed in my abilities at a time when I was doubting myself. This book wouldn't exist without her guidance, and I am deeply grateful for her generosity, invaluable advises, and constant support.

The book has also benefited from Sherryl Vint and Mark Bould. Their insightful and detailed comments on early drafts of this manuscript helped me significantly. I thank them both for sharing their in-depth knowledge of science fiction and for their constructive criticism. My deepest thanks also go to Professor Karin Boklund-Lagopoulou for sharing her expertise on the semiotic square.

Katie Gallof has been a supportive and perceptive editor. I am thankful for her professionalism and kindness, and for making this project a reality. Erin Duffy helped at the early stages of the book when it was just a proposal, and I deeply thank her. My sincere appreciation also goes to all the people at Bloomsbury Academic who assisted in the book's production. Finally, I would also like to thank the three anonymous readers for their helpful comments and positive feedback—especially the final review of the completed manuscript still brings me tears of joy when I read it!

On a more personal level, I would like to thank my mother Soula and my father Yorgos, for encouraging my love of learning and for the constant life-support; my sister Nicoleta, my brother-in-law Dimitris, and my nephews Nestoras and Phillipos, for being a wonderful part of my life; my friends, Penny, Maria, Yeoryia, Manos, for their valued friendship and their interest in my book. Special thanks also to Yeoryia Aslanidou for designing the semiotic squares with such patience.

Finally, the book is dedicated to two persons whose importance in every aspect of my life (including this book) cannot be expressed adequately with words: my husband Nikos, who encouraged me to pursue my dreams, watched with me all 204 films (and more than once), and helped me in every possible way; and my daughter Electra, who didn't exist when I submitted my book proposal and now she is an amazing little creature. Thank you both for making reality so fantastic!

Introduction:
History, Theory, Science Fiction (SF) Film

The present book centers on the American science fiction (SF) film in the twenty-first century. Currently, SF is one of the most popular film genres. This is evident not only from the numerous SF films (and television series) and their commercial success but also from the various fandom sites, discussion forums, magazines, conventions, and other virtual or real communities, which discuss passionately their favorite SF texts, be that film, TV series, video games, comics or books. The proliferation of the SF label in the current moment cannot be overlooked. According to IMDb, one of the most popular and legitimate online sources of the film industry, the 100 most profitable movies of all time include 39 films that are characterized as science fiction, rendering the SF genre as the third most popular, after the adventure and action labels. At the time of writing (January 2022), the first place in this list is still occupied by the 2009 epic SF movie, James Cameron's *Avatar*, with a total revenue of $2.84 billion—a position which was briefly overtaken by another SF/superhero spectacle, namely, the latest installment of the "Infinity Saga" of the Marvel Cinematic Universe, *Avengers: Endgame* (now in the second place with a gross of $2.79 billion). Although these films draw on the conventions of other genres and modes, such as action, adventure, and superhero, among others, the science fiction elements are prevalent, situating the genre at the center of Hollywood's production. These numbers confirm the ubiquity of SF conventions in high-profile Hollywood films. Although there are also medium- and low-budget SF films, some of which are discussed in this book, the genre currently is identified with Hollywood's most lucrative product, the blockbuster franchise film. The genre's current status can be attributed both to the industrial/economic parameters and to a variety of social and cultural factors—two aspects that are equally addressed in the present study.

Despite the fact that nowadays the genre enjoys cultural, artistic, and industrial recognition, this was not always the case. The science fiction label first appeared in the pulp magazines, specifically in the inaugural issue of *Amazing Stories* in 1926,[1] and thus was associated with their low cultural status. Even though the label had circulated for a considerable time in the literary sphere, the cinematic genre was not established until the 1950s, when the generic characterization was officially recognized and used by the industry, audience, and critics (Sobchack 1987). The film genre's initial formation was equally marked by this low critical status, since the majority of the films were B-movies targeted for the niche market of adolescents, and therefore the SF film was deemed as a juvenile, unsophisticated genre, unworthy of critical consideration. Despite the multifarious production of films in this first golden age of the genre, which included also big-budget productions, such as *Forbidden Planet* (1956) and the *Day the Earth Stood Still* (1951), among others (Cornea 2007), the disdain for it remained unchanged for the next two decades, and it was only in the second golden age of SF film during the 1980s that a critical reappraisal of the genre began.

The renewed interest in the genre was the result of both a commercial and an artistic growth of SF films, as well as the formation of new critical approaches on film genre theory. Although the release of *2001: A Space Odyssey* in 1968 is considered as a turning point in the genre's reception by both audience and critics, it wasn't until the release of iconic SF films in the late 1970s that the second golden age of the genre began, along with a more systematic academic analysis of cinematic SF. Films such as *Star Wars* (1977), *Close Encounters of the Third Kind* (1977), *Alien* (1979), and *Blade Runner* (1982), among others, rendered the SF film as a major player, especially in the context of New Hollywood that revisited the most neglected genres of the studio era, such as horror, fantasy, and science fiction. These SF films were popular and critical successes, spawning a series of imitators that indicated that the genre necessitated scholarly attention. At the same time, genre criticism had already been established as an important site of academic study. Genre films were no longer considered as unworthy of critical examination, but instead they were deemed as contemporary myths that reflect the beliefs and social values of the era in which they circulate, and/or advance the film industry's ideological messages (the ritual and ideological approaches to genre respectively). This new theoretical context combined with the commercial success of SF films generated an important number of critical essays on key generic examples (mainly *Blade Runner* [1982] and *Alien* [1979]). However, as Annette Kuhn (1990) notes, up until the 1990s, the SF film had rarely been dealt as a genre.

An exception to this theoretical and critical lacuna was Vivian Sobchack's (1987) *Screening Space. The American Science Fiction Film*, which was among the first academic studies that critically engaged with the SF film. The author delineates the genre in relation to the horror film, arguing that it is shaped by the interaction of both scientific and magical elements, and giving the following definition: "The SF film is a film genre which emphasizes actual, extrapolative, or speculative science and the empirical method, interacting in a social context with the lesser emphasized, but still present, transcendentalism of magic and religion, in an attempt to reconcile man with the unknown" (1987: 63). Sobchack continues with the mapping of the visual and aural conventions of the genre, contending that although SF lacks a stable iconography it is still informed by a "consistent and repetitious use … of types of images which function in the same way from film to film to create an imaginatively realized world which is always removed from the world we know or know of" (1987: 63). The author adds that these types of images (and sounds) emerge from the dialectical synthesis of the familiar with the strange, inscribing the distinct audiovisual function of the genre. Sobchack's influential account is reflective of the trends in film genre theory, which, up until that point, favored iconographical and/or structural/ritual approaches. These approaches to genre started to change from the 1990s onward, a shift that also informed the academic criticism of SF film, which begun more systematically after 2000.

The turn of the century saw the publication of important academic accounts of the cinematic genre (see King and Krzywinska 2000; Telotte 2001; Cornea 2007; Johnston 2011; Bould 2012; and others). Although there is a plethora of literary definitions of science fiction, with one of the most influential being Darko Suvin's (1972) theorization of SF as "the literature of cognitive estrangement"—a definition that the present book partially employs—cinematic definitions of the genre are far fewer. Nevertheless, the publications that appeared after 2000 occasionally included a definition for the SF film. For example, Geoff King and Tanya Krzywinska maintain that "science fiction deals with the problems and promises offered by science, technology and rationality in an imaginative context given shape by the aims of film industry" (2000: 2). Christine Cornea (2007), reformulating Tzvetan Todorov's (1975) theorization of the fantastic, defines SF as "a genre that is demonstrably located in between fantasy and reality" (2007: 4). The author selects the word "fantasy" to suggest a wider framework that exceeds the literary bounds of the fantastic, while the term "reality" is described as "the perceived model of the known world as constructed through narratives and through media" (2007: 4). With this reframing of the fantastic, Cornea aims to associate narratives with social reality, thus situating the genre's formal and thematic considerations within its historical and cultural contexts. Keith M. Johnston (2011) offers an open definition, claiming that

> A definition of the science fiction genre from an academic perspective might focus on thematic areas around technology, science, futurism or the figure of "the Other". An equally valid definition might come from popular identification of iconographic elements such as flying saucers, robots, ray guns and aliens. A third discussion of the term, from an industrial perspective, might focus on special effects and spectacle. Any attempt to understand the genre must engage with all three and accept that further viewpoints are equally valid.
>
> (2011: 7)

The above definitions, or, in certain cases the lack thereof, are indicative of the new paradigm in genre theory that was introduced with the work of Rick Altman (1999) and Steve Neale (2000). In his influential "A Semantic/Syntactic Approach to Film Genre," first published in 1984, Altman (2012) reconciled different approaches to genre, arguing that an effective genre criticism should consider both the semantic elements of a genre (common traits, attitudes, characters, shots, locations, sets, etc.) and the way these elements are combined in structures (syntax). Altman (1999) later elaborated on this dual approach, proposing a semantic/syntactic/pragmatic approach. This revision stresses the importance of the multiple uses of the genre, and that different user groups perceive and interpret genres in different and even conflicting ways. Thus, the meaning of genres is not located only within the filmic texts, but mostly it is generated by the way they are perceived and used by various spectator groups, producers, distributors, exhibitors, cultural agencies, and others. In turn, Neale argues that genres do not consist only of films, but also "of specific systems of expectation and hypothesis that spectators bring with them to the cinema" (2012: 179). According to the author, genres can exist under theoretical as well as industrial and institutional labels and are always in excess of a corpus of work. Therefore, both Altman and Neale consider genres not only as collections of films, but mainly as discursive practices that include the shifting exchanges between filmic texts, audiences, industry, and critics. In this new generic paradigm, attention is shifted from issues of classification and taxonomy to the examination of the "historical contexts of genre productions, the forms inherited from other media ... and the institutional practices ... through which genres become available ... to audiences" (Langford 2005: 12).

Another significant aspect of contemporary film genre theory is the issue of genre mixing. Janet Staiger (2012) notes that classical Hollywood never produced pure genres, since the bulk of classical Hollywood production always involved at least two plots for every movie, the one usually being the romantic subplot. Thus, the purity hypothesis in genre analysis is unfounded due to the fact that "every work involves more than one genre, even if only implicitly" (Staiger 2012: 207). Likewise, Altman argues that despite common assumptions of the opposite, "Hollywood prefers romantic genre-mixing to the classical ideal of genre purity" (1999: 129), in order to assure a film's appeal to the widest possible audience. In this way, studios not only produce but also promote mixed genres. Related to genre mixing is the concept of belonging or participating in a genre. Celestino Deleyto maintains that "every text participates in one or several genres, there is no genreless text; there is always a genre and genres, yet such participation never amounts to belonging" (2012: 223). Therefore, one film can participate in several genres, using a variety of conventions and patterns. This process results in the "heterogeneity within individual texts and thus within genres" (Bould 2013: 44). Indeed, the filmic corpus on which the present book is based includes films that, besides the science fiction label, also encompass—according to IMDb—characterizations, such as adventure, action, thriller, drama, comedy, fantasy, horror, mystery, family, romance, crime, and war. Given this heterogeneity, as well as the historical and process-like nature of genres, their theoretical delineation is often avoided since they are fluid, historical processes that always elude fixed meaning.

However, as Altman (1987) notes, theory and history cannot be separated, since the theoretical genres are already historical, and the historical ones emerge, among others, from previous theoretical and critical discourses. The current shift from text to context in genre analysis should not lead to the exclusion of theory, but rather an articulation of theoretical issues with historical, economic, and cultural aspects shaping genres. I believe this articulation is best accommodated by social semiotics, that is, the combination of semiotic theory with the examination of social and historical parameters (Lagopoulos and Boklund-Lagopoulou 2014). This approach informs the present monograph, which focuses on the contemporary American SF film by coupling theoretical and historical considerations. Specifically, the book offers a theoretical map of the genre in the 2001–20 period, while placing it in the current industrial context and locating contextual and thematic concerns. This critical discussion is based on a corpus of 204 films that were produced or co-produced in the

United States and released in the above-mentioned timeframe. In this way, the present book takes a different path from the majority of studies of the genre that discuss selective films that span different time periods and countries. Despite the importance of considering the historical development and transnational dimensions of the genre, a more focused research on specific time period and place can shed light on the particular expression that the genre acquires in a given historical and social context, and thus contribute to the ever-growing scholarship around the SF film. The book is divided into two parts. Part 1 consists of Chapters 1 and 2, charting theoretical and historical aspects of the genre. Part 2 includes Chapters 3–8 and centers on the filmic texts of the genre, which are grouped in six cycles. Below, I provide the chapter outline.

Chapter 1 is the theory/methodology chapter. Here, I develop my own theorization of the genre based on two semiotic tools: Algirdas J. Greimas's semiotic square and narrative grammar. In particular, I delineate the two semiotic squares that describe the genre's deep structure, and I label them "SF bodies" and "SF worlds." The first square describes the genre's other-than-human ontologies, while the second square illustrates SF's imaginative worlds. Each square generates three new positions from the interaction of their basic terms; thus, the two squares create a total of six new terms. These new positions/terms provide the basis for the corpus' division in six cycles. The first three cycles that emanate from the interactions of the first semiotic square (SF bodies) are (1) the techno-humans, (2) the alien encounters, and (3) the creatures. The other three cycles that originate from the second semiotic square (SF worlds) are (4) the dystopia/utopia, (5) the zones, and (6) the fantastic worlds. Next, I examine the surface structure, by combining Greimas's narrative grammar with a theoretical concept of the genre, the "cognition effect" (Freedman 2000). At the end of the chapter, I also include a section about the corpus on which the research is based. I refer to the criteria for the formulation of the initial corpus, and how it was subsequently revised according to the chosen methodology.

After the theoretical formulations of Chapter 1, Chapter 2 moves to the exo-semiotic sphere, examining the genre's historical context—mainly, industrial and economic parameters informing millennial SF films. In particular, the chapter delves into two facets of the genre's production context, which are associated by the central role of technology in both contemporary Hollywood, and the SF film. The first aspect explores how the workings of "Conglomerate Hollywood" (Schatz 2009) inform the contemporary SF film. The second strand delves into a specific industrial discourse, namely how the genre's most prominent directors regard the role of technology, and special effects in particular, in the genre's shaping.

Chapters 3–8 discuss the genre's six cycles, connecting structural, thematic, and contextual analyses. That is, each chapter offers a brief background, situating each cycle in its social and historical context, before moving on to the discussion of narrative themes in relation to particular cultural discourses. Therefore, these chapters tackle issues of the genre's cultural significance. Chapters 3–5 include the cycles of the first semiotic square, addressing the genre's "SF bodies," that is, the other-than-human bodies that populate the genre, relating different thematic concerns with each category. Chapter 3 analyzes the techno-human cycle, arguing that the narratives in this category foreground issues of the technological body and its different expressions. Chapter 4 examines the alien encounters cycle, linking the image of the alien body with racial discourses. Chapter 5 delves into the creatures cycle, exploring how the films negotiate the relationship between humans and their artificial creations. Chapters 6–8 continue with the cycles of the second semiotic square, focusing on the "SF worlds," that is, the genre's imaginary worlds and the cultural discourses that they evoke. Chapter 6 charts the dystopia/utopia cycle, associating its collapsing worlds with the environmental discourses surrounding the Anthropocene era. Chapter 7 examines the zones cycle and its confined spatiotemporal configurations, which I discuss in relation with the limits and impasses of technological progress. Chapter 8 addresses the fantastic worlds cycle, associating the category's grand vistas with notions of the technoscientific Empire. Lastly, the epilogue examines the limits of the proposed theoretical model through two liminal examples—*Avengers: Endgame* and *Black Panther*.

Part One

Theory/History

1

Uncovering the Deep and Surface Structures of SF Film

In order to create a taxonomy and embark on a structural analysis of the SF film, I chose tools from semiotics, which is rather marginalized in film theory today as a theoretical and methodological approach. The reason for this marginal position is that semiotics is usually deemed a method that produces static categories and structures that don't consider questions of history and society. Despite the fact that the first-phase semiotics in the early 1960s was indeed characterized by an exclusive attention to formal issues (Altman 2012: 29), in the following decades post-structuralist critique invigorated semiotics with the fluidity of meaning and more historically situated considerations.[1] Thus, semiotics, far from being the monolithic entity of the past, is updated with historical considerations and provides useful tools.

Such an "updated" approach is social semiotics, advocated by Alexandros Ph. Lagopoulos and Karin Boklund-Lagopoulou (2014). According to this theory, semiotic systems such as texts, ideology, and culture are formed by social reality and fulfill social functions that cannot be absorbed into the semiotic/cultural. Therefore, semiotic systems, although relatively autonomous, always exist in relation to social functions. Lagopoulos and Boklund-Lagopoulou (2014) suggest that the non-textual or the "exo-semiotic" must always be taken into account when cultural texts are examined. Specifically, in order to grasp the bilateral communication between semiotic systems and the exo-semiotic sphere, the analyst should consider other aspects shaping cultural productions that reside beyond the text, such as economic, technological, political, and historical factors. Social semiotics is therefore the articulation of semiotic theory with societal parameters.

In the present study of the SF film, I opt for a social semiotics approach that relates semiotic patterns with their social context of production and draws its methodological tools mainly from the theory of Algirdas J. Greimas ([1966]

2005). Particularly, my methodological arsenal consists of Greimas's semiotic square and narrative grammar. The former uncovers the deep structure of narratives, while the latter consists of six grammar roles (actants) and describes the surface structure.[2] The narrative grammar is discussed in the last section of the chapter along with the cognition effect—an important concept of SF theory—while the semiotic square is presented below and is then applied in the theoretical delineation of the SF film genre.

Greimas laid the foundation for the square's construction in *Sémantique Structurale*, first published in 1966, and then further developed it in the 1968 article "The Interactions of Semiotic Constraints," co-written with François Rastier. The square describes the "elementary structure of meaning" or the deep structure "which define[s] the fundamental mode of existence of an individual or a society and subsequently the conditions of existence of semiotic objects" (Greimas and Rastier 1968: 87). The square is formulated by an initial opposition between two contrary terms that characterizes a semiotic system, be that a book, an author's oeuvre, a genre, and so on. This primary opposition, whose two terms are labeled as s1 and s2 by Greimas, forms the basis of the abstract model of the square (Figure 1.1). In order to simplify the square's presentation, I use Greimas's and Rastier's (1968) example of the binary opposition *life* vs. *death* (Figure 1.2). Starting from the basic s1 vs. s2 opposition, the semiotic square is constructed in the following steps. The first axis (the complex axis)

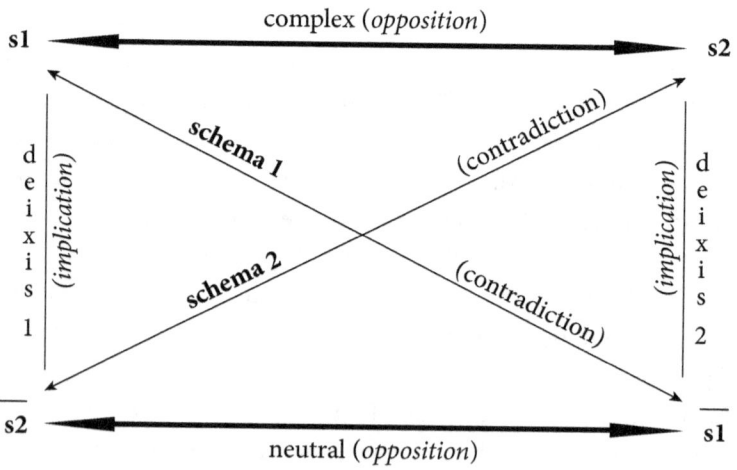

Figure 1.1 The abstract model of the semiotic square.

contains the fundamental elements of the semiotic system, *life* vs. *death*, that are opposite to each other.

1. Parallel and below the complex axis is the neutral axis that consists of the negations of the positive terms, *not-life* vs. *not-death*. Each parallel axis describes a relation of opposition between its terms and is labeled the contrary axis.
2. The diagonal axis (schema) illustrates the contradiction between the complex and the neutral terms. The schema unites the contradictory elements, that is, the elements that the existence of one excludes and contradicts the other. The terms *life* and *not-life* form the first diagonal axis (schema 1) and the terms *death* and *not-death* compose the second one (schema 2).
3. The last association that is depicted in the square is that of implication. This relation combines in a vertical line (deixis) the neutral term whose existence implicates the complex term, and both elements are complementary to each other. Thus, the term *not-death* implicates the term *life* (deixis 1), and the term *not-life* implicates the term *death* (deixis 2) (Greimas and Rastier 1968).

The three relations that the square depicts—opposition, contradiction, and implication—illustrate the axial relations of a semiotic system. In what follows, I analyze the specific forms that the semiotic square takes when used for the description of the SF film genre.

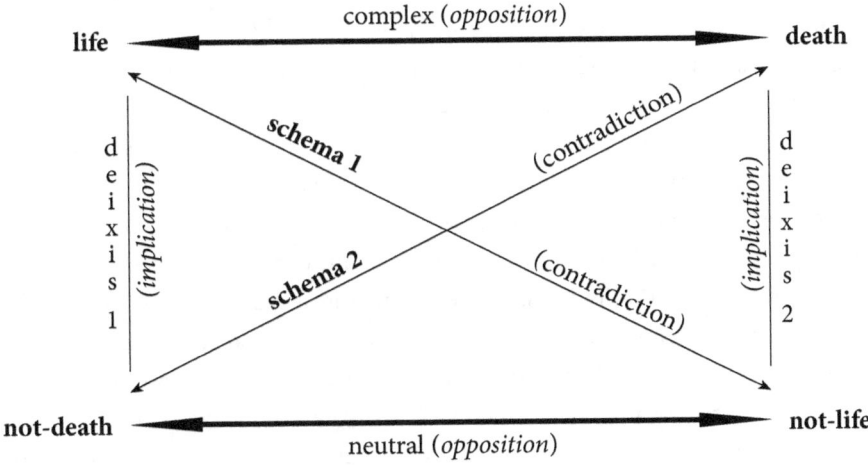

Figure 1.2 An example of the semiotic square: *life* vs. *death*.

The Deep Structure of SF: Two Semiotic Squares

In his foreword on Greimas's (1986: xvi) *On Meaning. Collection of Selected Writings in Semiotic Theory*, Fredric Jameson argues that

> the semiotic square is ... not static but dynamic: The significance of positionality within it is only one index of the way in which it can just as easily be considered to map a temporal process as to register a conceptual blockage or paralysis.

I agree that the square is characterized by a dynamic spatiality; therefore, it is a suitable tool for genre theory because it combines flexibility with stability and eloquently describes the fluctuations that derive from certain basic elements. Applied to SF film, it describes a semiotic system that is structured around two fundamental oppositions. It is important here to note that these two oppositions express a critical choice of the analysis and do not represent a universal or objective category. As Jameson maintains, the choice of the terms of the binary opposition, as well as the order in which they appear, constitutes the "inaugural *decision*" (1986: xv, emphasis added) in the formulation of the semiotic square. Therefore, the following two oppositions are the outcome of a critical consideration of the SF genre based on the specific perspective that the analysis follows and are illustrated in two semiotic squares. I consider that the first basic opposition of the genre is that between human and technology, while the second one is between familiar places and unknown spaces. The human/technology opposition concerns narratives that unfold in the familiar surroundings of Earth, as we commonly perceive it, while the familiar places/unknown spaces dialectic focuses on narratives where the environment is altered either dramatically (e.g., fantastic planets) or slightly (e.g., dystopic Earth).

Although the two oppositions often overlap and/or are combined in SF narratives (e.g., a human/alien conflict taking place in unknown planets), I maintain that when the environment is adhering to social verisimilitude, the genre's unfamiliarity is condensed in a post-/non-human body (alien, cyborg, monster, etc.). In that case, the dominant conflict revolves around the confrontation on a bodily level, between humans and other beings. I label the semiotic square that is based on this first opposition **SF bodies**. In the opposite case, when the surroundings of the narrative are different from our common perception of reality, then the unfamiliarity is dispersed in a wider environment (dystopia, alien planets, etc.) and the dominant conflict is centered on the struggle of an individual with the environment (physical, technological, and social) on a spatial level. I call this second semiotic square **SF worlds**. I argue that the two squares disclose the deep structure of SF and offer a possible genre cartography. In the next sections, I first present the two semiotic squares and the different cycles that emerge from their structural relations, before moving on to examine the genre's syntax.

First Semiotic Square: SF Bodies

The majority of critical studies on SF film point to the genre's preoccupation with the relationship between humans and technology or, in more general terms, between nature and artifice, stressing how the genre is trying to explain what it means to be human in a highly technologized and artificial world (see Kuhn 1990; King and Krzywinska 2000; Telotte 2001; Johnston 2011). Vivian Sobchack (1987: 224–5) condenses this thematic preoccupation by stating that "SF has always taken as its distinctive generic task the cognitive mapping and poetic figuration of social relations as they are constituted and changed by new technological modes of 'being-in-the-world.'" Similarly, Scott Bukatman (1993: 8) argues that "it is not technology per se that characterizes the operations of science fiction but the interface of technology with the human subject." I claim that although it is common to consider the human/technology interaction as genre-defining, this primary opposition has rarely been explored in all its additional dimensions and conceptual formulations that the semiotic square illustrates. The square offers an in-depth analysis of the genre's basic dialectic and its multiple expressions. Not only does it designate the basic opposition that traverses the genre, but it is also a visual articulation of our navigational path through the genre's new positions that the original opposition encompasses.

As seen in Figure 1.3, the first axis of the semiotic square is composed by the antithetical terms human/technology whose selection, as discussed, represents a critical choice of the analysis.[3] The term human is used here with its commonsense meaning, as the unmodified "natural" organism, despite the fact that critical posthumanism (Hayles 1999; Graham 2002; Wolfe 2010; Braidotti 2013) repeatedly suggests that it is rather a historical and ideological construction than a natural category. The opposite term, technology, describes the technics, tools, and generally systems of artificial creation. The neutral terms of human and technology are respectively non-human and non-technology. The contradictory terms human and non-human form the first diagonal axis, while

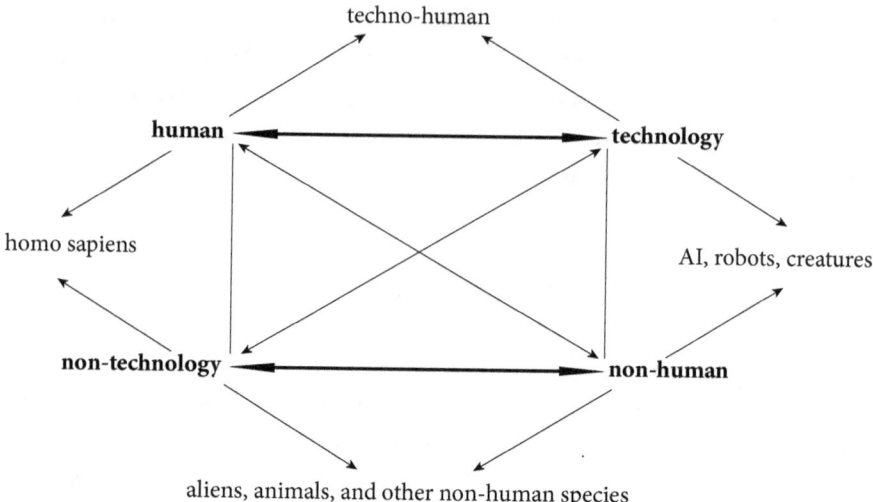

Figure 1.3 First semiotic square of the SF film: SF bodies.

the contradictory terms technology and non-technology illustrate the second one. Moreover, the term non-technology implicates the term human and the term non-human implicates technology. The interactions of the four terms lead to the following new configurations.

The interaction between human and technology produces the intermediate position, which I label the techno-human, a broad category, which entails all kinds of interactions between human bodies and technological/artificial elements, such as cyborgs, genetic posthumans even human/animal hybrids (e.g., the retrofitted bodies of superheroes, such as Iron Man, Captain America, Wolverine, Robocop). It is important to note that the human/technology interaction does not refer simply to technology's impact on human society. The present model is an ontological map of the genre; thus, the human/technology interplay must generate new bodies, and new ontologies. Filmic narratives that don't merge the terms human and technology in a new hybrid organism are not included in this taxonomy. The interplay between non-technology and non-human creates the position of other species, that is, aliens, animals, or other non-human creatures whose physiology is not a product of human technological intervention (e.g., the Heptapods in *Arrival* [2016], the giant aliens Kaijus in *Pacific Rim* [2013]). The synthesis of technology and non-human results in the position of robots, AIs, and other mechanical creations (e.g., the robot boy in *A. I. Artificial Intelligence* [2001], the AIs in *Simone* [2002] and *Transcendence* [2014]). This category also includes non-human creatures whose bodies are the result of a technological/artificial process (e.g., the radioactive monsters like Godzilla or the revived dinosaurs of *Jurassic Park/Jurassic World* film series). Lastly, the reciprocation between human and non-technology creates the position of the homo sapiens—the human as perceived commonly, that is, as a "natural" category.

Second Semiotic Square: SF Worlds

Before moving to the second semiotic square, I want to notice that the importance of space in SF has been emphasized by a number of scholars. For example, Annette Michelson ([1969] 2016) and Scott Bukatman (1993), among others, maintain that SF predicates its narratives not upon psychological motivation and character development, but upon the creation of speculative worlds and alternate topographies that seem to overwhelm and determine the story's development. In a similar note, Fredric Jameson (2005: 306) argues:

> Spatial representation wholly enables, and serves as a pretext for, the more punctual figures, devices and gimmicks touched on above: but it also somehow transcends the SF plot interest in a significantly more general way. The hypothesis is then that, whatever our immediate narrative interest in *this* particular SF plot and its resolutions, we also attend to and derive a readerly gratification from the development of space in SF worlds.

Jameson concludes that SF is less interested in the adventure of a character (individual or collective) than in "a planet, a climate, a weather and a system of landscapes—in short a map" (2005: 313). It is this spatiality of the genre that I want to stress with the delineation of the second semiotic square.

The terms of the second semiotic square are drawn from the seminal phenomenological analysis *Space and Place: The Perspective of Experience* (1977) by Yi-Fu Tuan. In this book the author describes how our known world is experienced as the synthesis of familiar places and unknown spaces. Places consist of familiar topographies that we inhabit and know, while spaces are the uncharted territories that connect the familiar locales. Tuan sums up the dialectic of place and space as "[p]lace is security, space is freedom: we are attached to the one and long for the other" (1977: 3). Abstract space lacks any significance other than strangeness. In contrary, when space starts to acquire definition and meaning, it becomes a place. While a place is a dwelling or residence invested with values and meaning, space provides the ability to move and is experienced as the distance that links or separates places. As the author argues:

> Open space has no trodden paths and signposts. It has no fixed pattern of established human meaning; it is like a blank sheet on which meaning may be imposed. Enclosed and humanized space is place. Compared to space, place is a calm center of established values.
>
> (Tuan 1977: 54)

I claim that we can apply this description of the known world as a dialectic of place and space to the realm of SF film, since its imaginary worlds also consist of these complementary topographies that take on specific generic meanings.

For this reason, I choose these two terms for the second semiotic square. On the one hand, place is identified with the term human of the first semiotic square and bears connotations with the natural, familiar, and known. The term place in SF bears resemblance to our common perception of reality and has a social verisimilitude (e.g., the familiar places of Earth in narratives about alien invasion/encounters, such as *War of the Worlds* [2005], *Signs* [2002], *Super 8* [2011]). On the other hand, space is identified with the term technology of the first semiotic square and is associated with the artificial, the unfamiliar, or the strange. The term space in SF connotes the unknown geographies and fantastic locales, which are characteristic of a generic verisimilitude (e.g., the altered topographies in dystopic narratives, such as *Minority Report* [2002], the fantastic and unfamiliar worlds in space operas, such as *Star Trek* [2009]). Hence, the two squares are homologous and the basic opposition between human and technology of the first semiotic square is transcribed as the opposition between place and space in the second one.

The square's complex axis inscribes the contrary relation between place and space. This relation is then inversely projected in the neutral axis, which includes the negative terms, non-place and non-space. Subsequently, the first diagonal axis unites the contradictory terms place and non-place, while the second one maps the contradiction between space and non-space. The final structural relation is that of implication illustrated in the two vertical axes. The first one registers the implication between non-space and place, while the second depicts how non-place implicates space. This initial formation generates new positions, as described below.

As illustrated in Figure 1.4, the merging of familiar places and strange spaces creates the position of dystopia/utopia. This position refers to the familiar topos of Earth, diffused with semantics of unfamiliarity and strangeness (technology, infrastructure, urban planning, political systems, etc.), such as the simulated reality in the *Matrix* trilogy, the ruined Earth in *Elysium* (2013), and so on. The second position emerges from the interplay of the terms non-space and non-place of the neutral axis. The term non-place is delineated in relation to Tuan's (1977) definition of place as an accretion of established values and familiarity. Therefore, this negative term connotes unfamiliarity and strangeness. Conversely, non-space signifies the negation of space, that is, the negation of open, uncharted territory. I label the square's intersection of the two neutral terms as zones. The etymology of the word derives from the Greek verb ζώνυμμι, which means to gird, to encircle, to fortify. Thus, the term combines the notion of a restricted geographical area imbued with a sense of danger. In other words, zones refer to geographical enclosures, characterized by a threatening and destabilizing spatiality. This position describes locales that are both non-places (unfamiliar) (e.g., the indestructible vessel in *The Core* [2003], the labyrinthine spaceship in *Pandorum* [2009], the confined habitat in the surface of Mars in *The Martian* [2015]), and non-spaces, that is, confined districts that are not characterized by the openness of uncharted territories that the term space signifies (e.g., in *Pandorum*, the unfamiliar topography remains restricted inside the spaceship, while in *The Martian*, the main action is unfolding

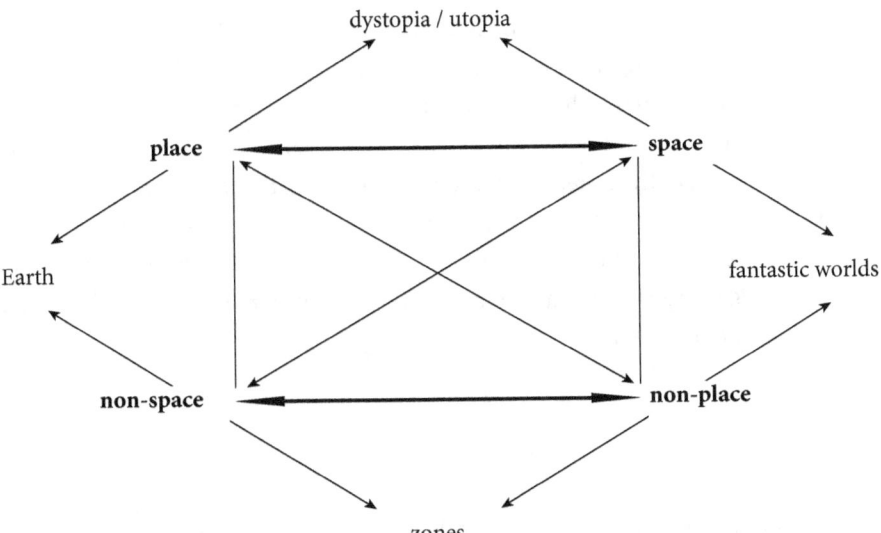

Figure 1.4 Second semiotic square of SF film: SF worlds.

inside the contained zones of the crew's habitat and in other limited areas, such as vehicles, despite the fact that the film takes place on the surface of Mars). Here, I also include the time zones, where the confinement and unfamiliarity are registered not in space but in time and is exemplified in the time displacements and alternate realities in films, such as *Looper* (2012), *Source Code* (2011), and *Edge of Tomorrow* (2014), among others. Hence, this position in the square is exemplified not only by the existence of strange enclaves, such as spaceships and other futuristic and alien zones, but also by distorted temporalities, such as time-loops, parallel worlds/dimensions, and alternate realities/histories. Lastly, the combination of space and non-place produce what I term fantastic worlds, where the unfamiliarity of non-places is extended in the vast unknown spaces outside Earth. The vast dimension that the term space implies manifests in the form of non-human civilizations and unknown worlds that expand throughout the universe (e.g., the moon Pandora in *Avatar*, the different planets and civilizations in the *Star Wars* and *Star Trek* franchises).

The genre's two fundamental oppositions of human/technology and place/space constitute the basis of the two homologous semiotic squares. The human is analogous to place, and they are both associated with the natural, the known, the familiar, while technology is similar to space in that it bears connotations with the artificial, the unknown, the strange. As the narratives shift their attention from bodies to worlds, the central conflict is displaced from the bodily to the spatial level. Furthermore, the squares' intermediate positions function as the basis for the genre's cycles, creating the basic map of the genre.

The SF bodies square illustrates an ontological map of the genre, including cyborgs, genetic posthumans, mutants, robots, aliens, and other more-than-human entities. On the other hand, the SF worlds square creates a topographical chart of SF and reveals the genre's unknown geographies. The synthesis of the two squares discloses the deep structure of the genre and its basic syntax. The deep syntax generates all surface syntaxes we encounter in the films, as discussed in detail in the next section.

SF Syntax and Cycles

The deep syntax that emerges from both squares can be described as the quasi-rationally explained encounter of the human with the non-human that takes place at a bodily or spatial level and aims at the survival, rescue, or reinvention of the human world. In the first square (Figure 1.3), the syntax takes the expression of the struggle of an individual or a group to save or change humanity during their encounter with post-/non-human beings (alien, cyborgs, monsters). In the second square, the syntax designates the struggle of an individual or group to survive in or change an unfamiliar environment (alien, dystopic, etc.). In this way, the SF syntax acquires two complementary expressions; the syntax that describes the struggle against a post-/non-human body is translated in the second square as the combat against an unknown environment, in order to preserve or re-imagine humanity. Although these two syntactic versions can occur simultaneously, I argue that only one dominates each narrative and forms its structure. Hence, if the two syntactic expressions overlap, then the analysis is focused on the dominant one.[4]

The SF bodies square, which describes the encounter of the human with the non-human Other, provides the basis for three different cycles. Each cycle is based on the interaction of two terms of the square and inscribes a different version of the human/non-human structure. I should stress that the following cycles are theoretical constructions based on my proposed model and not industrial formulations. Furthermore, as products of a discursive process, some cycles share certain characteristics that I address in each cycle's analysis. The three cycles that emerge from the SF bodies square are as follows:

1. **The techno-humans cycle.** The first cycle is formulated from the intermediate position of the techno-human and includes the superhero narratives, among others (e.g., *Iron Man* [2008], *Spider-Man* [2002], the *X-Men* film series).[5] In this cycle the basic conflict is centered on enhanced, technologically altered, or (re)created humans.
2. **The alien encounters cycle.** In the second cycle, the human/non-human structure is articulated in the conflict between humans and other species (e.g., aliens). Films included in this cycle are *District 9* (2009), *Arrival* (2016), *Independence Day: Resurgence* (2016), and others.
3. **The creatures cycle.** In the third cycle, the merging of non-human and technology produces the robot/machine/AI narratives (e.g., *Simone* [2002], *Transcendence* [2014], *Her* [2013]), as well as the creatures narratives. (e.g., *Godzilla* [2014], *Jurassic World* [2015], *Splice* [2009]). This cycle describes the conflict between humans and their artificial creations, be that silicon- or carbon-based.

Likewise, the in-between positions of the SF worlds square lead to the following three cycles:

1. **The dystopia/utopia cycle.** Here, the syntax revolves around an individual who struggles to survive in and/or change a social system (e.g., *The Island* [2005], *The Hunger Games* film series, *Elysium* [2013]) or survive in an environment that lies on the verge of extinction due to an ecosocial collapse (e.g., *Children of Men* [2006], *I Am Legend* [2007], *Daybreakers* [2009]). Also included are narratives whose central focus is the unsettling of familiar places due to natural disasters (e.g., *The Day after Tomorrow* [2004], *The Happening* [2008]), since they similarly describe the struggle of an individual to survive in an endangered environment.
2. **The zones cycle.** These narratives include both the space and the time zones. The space zones include films that take place in enclosed areas characterized by unfamiliarity and strangeness (spaceships, futuristic vehicles or alien zones) (e.g., *Gravity* [2013], *Sunshine* [2007], *The Core* [2003]). In the time zones narratives, the unfamiliarity is inscribed not in space but in time, and it is expressed as time displacements, loops, and other time paradoxes, evident in films such as *Inception* (2010), *Source Code* (2011), *Looper* (2012), *Edge of Tomorrow* (2014). Similar to the dystopia cycle, the main conflict is between an individual and the environment, which is depicted here as an encased, looped, displaced, or otherwise contained and convoluted spacetime configuration.
3. **The fantastic worlds cycle.** These films are characterized by the vastness and unfamiliarity of spaces that are far removed from our known reality. The structure in this cycle acquires epic dimensions and is diffused with fantastic elements. Here, the conflict of the human with the unknown cosmic environment is depicted as the struggle to save the planet or galaxy from a destructive force (e.g., the *Star Wars* film series, the *Star Trek* film series, *Avatar*).

As evident from the above, the genre's syntax presupposes vast dimensions, since to save or change the world is a task of cosmic importance. This cosmic scope may take many different forms. For example, SF narratives usually depict global phenomena, such as alien encounters, natural disasters, or oppressive futuristic or postapocalyptic societies, and their protagonists' objectives are equally ambitious (e.g., save the world). Even if the events seem to concern a single individual, his or her actions still have a global impact and are literally placed in a space of comic dimensions (e.g., the abysmal space in *Gravity*), or they change the course of future events that affect the lives of a wider community (e.g., *Source Code*). Therefore, the resolution of conflict in SF narratives invariably acquires a cosmic dimension, since it usually involves a larger community, be that a city, a world, a galaxy, or even the universe. It is precisely this cosmic dimension that I consider as a prerequisite for SF narratives. Hence, in order for a narrative to be considered SF, it must be structured around a dimension of cosmic significance and not be restricted to interpersonal relationships. In the following section, I discuss the genre's surface structure based on Greimas's narrative grammar and in relation with a theoretical concept of the SF genre—the cognition effect.

Narrative Grammar and the Cognition Effect as Actant

Drawing from Vladimir Propp's analysis of the Russian folk tale,[6] Greimas ([1966] 2005) claims that each narrative comprises six grammar roles that can be grouped in three dyads: the Subject/Object, the Sender/Receiver, and the Helper/Enemy. Each grammar role or actant not only represents characters but encompasses a larger category of action and can equally be occupied by persons, things, or even concepts that perform a specific action in the narrative structure (Kaklamanidou 2016: 18). Furthermore, one character can occupy different roles. The grammar roles represent the surface structure of the narrative (Figure 1.5).

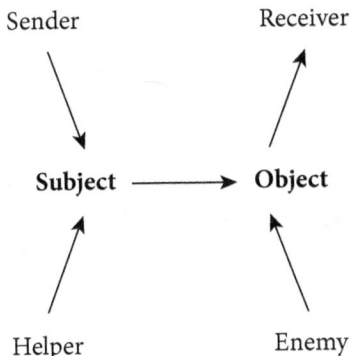

Figure 1.5 The six grammar roles.

The grammar roles Subject vs. Object describe the main subject of action and the object that it desires or pursues. The category of Sender vs. Receiver delineates what causes the initial unfolding of action and the recipient of this chain of events. The last category of action is articulated by the Helper vs. Enemy dichotomy, which entails provision of help toward the fulfillment of the Subject's objective vs. obstacles against the mission. Greimas's model of action is the theoretical transcription of the syntax and reveals the surface structure of the text. The present thesis uses this model in order to examine the surface structure of the SF film. Furthermore, it is applied so as to locate the structural role of the cognition effect, a term which I discuss below.

The imaginary worlds depicted in SF are of a technological/scientific/rational nature, as opposed to the magical or religious realms of fantasy. Although these modes of expression intertwine in many instances, as, for example, when scientific tropes are imbued with religious connotations, and futuristic technologies function like magical artifacts, there is still a liminal differentiation between them. But how is this difference articulated in the narratives? The answer to this question entrenches the famous debate of SF/fantasy distinction. Darko Suvin, one of the first scholars to establish literary SF as a genre worthy of academic consideration, separates SF from other fantastical forms and terms it as the "literature of cognitive estrangement" (1972: 372). It is the role of cognition that differentiates SF from other fantastic forms, since SF is a "literary genre whose necessary and sufficient conditions are the presence and interaction of cognition and estrangement" (Suvin 1972: 375). The estrangement produced by the "novum" in SF texts is bound to rational explanations. With the use of this distinction, Suvin tries to inaugurate SF as a "serious" genre by associating it with acclaimed literary works (e.g., Kafka's) that had little to do with the SF pulp tradition. The Suvinian paradigm is still a major influence and shapes current perceptions of the genre.

More recently, Freedman (2000) pointed to the limitations of Suvin's thesis, arguing that the operation of cognition in literary texts is elusive as the distinctions it presupposes are far removed from issues of genre and literature. Instead, Freedman proposed the more flexible term of "cognition effect" that is not bound to any external epistemological consideration but only "to the attitude of the text itself to the kind of estrangements being performed" (2000: 18). Relevant to this discussion is Jameson's (2005: 58) study of Utopia as a literary form. Although Jameson did not discuss the cognition effect per se, he made a relevant contribution, by proposing a distinction between SF and fantasy in terms of the latter's structural organization around the ethical binary of good and evil and the central role of magic. Jameson remarked that magic reawakens all the inherent problems between fantasy and SF and while some of SF's futuristic technologies seem equally impossible as the existence of dragons and magicians, they do seem to be bound by "the speculations of a rational and scientific age" (Jameson 2005: 63).

China Miéville went a step further by expanding the Suvinian paradigm to its logical end, maintaining that not only is the cognition effect separated from cognition because it concerns a "putatively logical way of thinking and not a function of it" (2009: 239), but it is also a trickery performed by the author-function, a form of persuasion. For Miéville, the cognition effect is "a function of (textual) charismatic authority" (2009: 238), and this dependence on external authority renders it not only "a-rational but intensely ideological" (2009: 239). On this basis, Miéville eschews the category of cognition altogether, claiming that the distinction between SF and fantasy should not revolve around a "fundamental epistemological firewall," but should be understood as "different ideological iterations of the 'estrangement' that ... both sub-genres share" (2009: 243). Thus, attention should be shifted from the differences between fantastic genres to "the fundamental alterity-as-estrangement shared across the field" (2009: 244). Similarly, Mark Bould (2012: 10) supports that "the cognition effect does not necessarily depend upon scientific accuracy but on various forms of persuasion," such as dialogue, visual and aural design. Bould adds that the cognition effect concerns a generic verisimilitude that "builds upon earlier representations rather than upon scientific accuracy" (2012: 12) and that "all scientific explanations are metaphorical, ... [and] even in science there is no direct relationship between sign and referent" (2012: 17).

I agree with Bould and argue that it is the cognition effect as a generic convention and not as actual indication of science and perception that characterizes cinematic SF. Furthermore, although the generic boundaries between fantasy and SF are blurred and interpenetrate each other, I claim that the cognition effect helps the theorist draw a line, however small, between the two. This minimum limit serves not so much to form strict generic boundaries, which is, after all, an elusive task, but is a way to better elucidate the genre's characteristics and functions. Thus, as a broader generic convention, the cognition effect relays materialistic and rational discourses, scientific paradigms, and even commonsense explanations to the audience, through different semantic elements (dialogue, characters, settings, technological artifacts, etc.) and possesses a central role in the structuring of the genre.

I maintain that the cognition effect has a structurally important role in every SF narrative as an actant. As already mentioned, an actant is an abstract category and "must before all else be distinguished from traditional or intuitive notions of character, protagonist, hero, actor, or role" (Fontanille 2006: 96). In other words, the actants must be understood as wider categories of different forms, such as "characters, animals, objects, even sentiments" (in Kaklamanidou 2016: 18) that perform certain functions necessary to narrative development. For example, in *Gravity*, the cognition effect takes the form of the scientific expertise and knowledge that the protagonist (Subject) uses in order to survive (Object). Hence, the abstract category of scientific knowledge, which is represented in a series of textual effects, such as scientific-sounding language, handling of machinery, and in general "the appearance of command over the language of science" (in Bould 2012: 8), occupies a structural role (Helper), thus confirming the film's labeling as SF. Even in films, which are not so scientifically looking or sounding as *Gravity*, we can similarly trace the structural role of the cognition effect. For example, in *Spider-Man* (2002), the protagonist acquires superpowers after he is bitten by a genetically modified spider. Spider-Man (Tobey Maguire/Subject) uses his technologically acquired powers (Helper) in order to prevent Dr. Norman Osborn/Green Goblin (Willem Dafoe) (Enemy)—who is similarly genetically transformed posthuman—from destroying New York City (Object). The cognition effect here occupies two structural roles (Helper/Enemy) and is represented in a series of artifacts, technologies, chemical formulas, and technologically induced powers that try to persuade the viewer that the film has a quasi-rational premise. I believe that even minimum explanations imbued with a pseudoscientific aura and dependent upon previous generic representations can account for the cognition effect as long as they occupy an actantial role in a filmic text. Therefore, I argue that in order for a narrative to be characterized as SF, cognition effect (in whatever generic form it is represented) must assume the role of an actant, that is, one of the six grammar roles in the filmic narrative. Hence, fantastic technologies are not sufficient for a text to be characterized as SF; they must also have an energetic role in the text's structure. If the cognition effect does not assume one of the six grammar roles in the filmic text, the title is not included in the genre's mapping.

The illustration of the two semiotic squares along with the consideration of the six grammar roles created the final mapping and taxonomy of the genre. The surface syntax was illuminated by the additional role of the cognition effect as actant. The human/technology interaction of the first semiotic square, which is transcribed in the place/space opposition of the second square, is operative when the text's cognition effect functions as an actant. In other words, the genre's two elemental oppositions are constitutive of the genre when they are premised in a quasi-rational discourse. Thus, I claim that there are three criteria that delineate the genre:

1. The basic oppositions of the SF narrative are placed in the human/technology and/or the place/space dichotomy.
2. The SF narrative is framed within a cosmic perspective (events, protagonist's goals, places of action).
3. The cognition effect as a generic convention occupies a structural role that is reflected in one of the six grammar roles of the SF narrative.

Concluding, my proposed definition is: a SF film is a narrative that depicts a conflict between human and non-human actants, situated in a body or environment and premised on discourses that originate from the cognition effect.

The proposed definition and taxonomy of the genre are based on an initial corpus of films, which was subsequently revised according to the findings of the research, as discussed below.

Assembling a Corpus for the SF Film

In order to delineate the structures and functions of the genre discussed above, I first constructed a corpus of films so as to operate as the basis for the generic examination. Basing my methodology on both Rick Altman (1987), who was one the first film theorists to stress the importance of the corpus in genre studies, and Betty Kaklamanidou (2016), who more recently elaborated the corpus construction, I delimited a corpus for the millennial SF film. Before discussing further details, I must stress that the following corpus is provisional, contingent, and does not claim a universal consensus. Instead, it is the outcome of a discursive process based on certain criteria, which are set by the researcher and are presented below.

Initially, I formulated a preliminary, broad corpus based on media and industrial labels. Specifically, the broad corpus was compiled by data drawn by two major online sources: IMDb and Box Office Mojo, which comprise the two largest and most legitimate online sources that are recognized and used equally by the press, academia, and audience, shaping general generic perceptions. The initial corpus included 244 movies that fulfilled the following criteria: (a) the films were released between 2001 and 2020, (b) the films were produced or coproduced in the United States,[7] (c) the films were labeled as science fiction by IMDb and/or Box Office Mojo,[8] (d) the films were included in the top-150 of annual worldwide grosses, as drawn from Box Office Mojo,[9] and (e) the films must include live-action scenes, that is, the films were not exclusively animated.[10]

The last criterion (e) was added due to the growing significance of animation in SF films. Since the establishment of the SF label in the film industry during the 1950s, many films have incorporated animation techniques that together with other special effects assisted in the visualization of fantastic worlds, futuristic technologies, and alternate realities (e.g., *Destination Moon* [1950], *Forbidden Planet*, [1956], *Dinosaurus!* [1960]). The role of animation became more prominent in the 1980s with the wide circulation of Japanese animated films (anime) that influenced the genre with various techniques and tropes (Telotte 2001). From the 1990s onward, new digital technologies advanced animation techniques with the use of computer software, thus proliferating the exchanges between SF live-action film and animation. The SF films of the twenty-first century depend heavily on digital technologies and computer animation techniques, further obscuring the boundaries between live action and CGI. The success of films such as *Avatar* that according to director James Cameron is "sixty per cent animation and forty percent live action" (Giardina 2008) indicates the blurring of these boundaries in SF films and the significance of animation in them. My decision not to include exclusively animated films is based on two reasons: (a) the contribution and role of animation in the shaping of the genre should be properly examined in a separate study and is beyond the focus of the present book, and (b) despite the convergence of different media in current cinematic practices, "animation is a medium in itself, not simply a genre of live action cinema. As such, it develops and plays by its own generic restrictions and capabilities" (Napier 2016: 297).

After the setting of the above criteria, a preliminary corpus was formulated and served as the basis for the observations about the genre. Subsequently, it was revised according to the proposed definition. That is, the films that were not explained by the specific definition were excluded. This process resulted in a final corpus of 204 films (see Table 1). These films were then grouped into different generic cycles that emerged from the particular methodological approach, as alternative expressions of the SF syntax.

Table 1 The final corpus (2001–20)

TITLE	YEAR	DIRECTOR
2012	2009	Emmerich, Roland
A. I. Artificial Intelligence	2001	Spielberg, Steven
Ad Astra	2019	Gray, James
Aeon Flux	2005	Kusama, Karyn
After Earth	2013	Shyamalan, M. Night
Alien: Covenant	2017	Scott, Ridley
Alien Vs. Predator	2004	Anderson, Paul W.S.
Alien Vs. Predator: Requiem	2007	The Brothers Strause
Alita: Battle Angel	2019	Rodriguez, Robert
Annihilation	2018	Garland, Alex
Apollo 18	2011	López-Gallego, Gonzalo
Arrival	2016	Villeneuve, Denis
Avatar	2009	Cameron, James
Avengers: Age of Ultron	2015	Whedon, Joss
Avengers: Endgame	2019	Russo, Anthony and Russo, Joe
Avengers: Infinity War	2018	Russo, Anthony and Russo, Joe
Batman V Superman: Dawn of Justice	2016	Snyder, Jack
Battle: Los Angeles	2011	Liebesman, Jonathan
Battleship	2012	Berg, Peter
Black Panther	2018	Coogler, Ryan
Blade Runner 2049	2017	Villeneuve, Denis
Bloodshot	2020	Wilson, Dave
Bumblebee	2018	Knight, Travis
Captain America: The First Avenger	2011	Johnston, Joe
Captain America: The Winter Soldier	2014	Russo Anthony, Russo Joe
Captain America: Civil War	2016	Russo Anthony, Russo Joe
Captain Marvel	2019	Boden, Anna and Fleck, Ryan
Chappie	2015	Blomkamp, Neill
Children of Men	2006	Cuarón, Alfonso
Chronicle (2012)	2012	Trank, Josh
Cloud Atlas	2012	Tykwer Tom, Wachowskis, The
Cloverfield	2008	Reeves, Matt
Cowboys & Aliens	2011	Favreau, Jon
Dark Skies	2013	Stewart, Scott
Dawn of the Planet of the Apes	2014	Reeves, Matt
Daybreakers	2010	The Spierig Brothers
Déjà Vu	2006	Scott, Tony
District 9	2009	Blomkamp, Neill
Divergent	2014	Burger, Neil
Doom	2005	Bartkowiak, Andrzej
Downsizing	2017	Payne, Alexander
Dreamcatcher	2003	Kasdan, Lawrence
Earth to Echo	2014	Green, Dave
Edge of Tomorrow	2014	Liman, Doug
Elysium	2013	Blomkamp, Neill
Ender's Game	2013	Hood, Gavin
Evolution	2001	Reitman, Ivan
Fantastic Four	2005	Story, Tim
Fantastic Four	2015	Trank, Josh

(Continued)

TITLE	YEAR	DIRECTOR
Fantastic Four: Rise of the Silver Surfer	2007	Story, Tim
Gamer	2009	Neveldine Mark, Taylor Brian
Geostorm	2017	Devlin, Dean
Ghost in the Shell	2017	Sanders, Rupert
Godzilla	2014	Edwards, Gareth
Godzilla: King of the Monsters	2019	Dougherty, Michael
Gravity	2013	Cuarón, Alfonso
Green Lantern	2011	Campbell, Martin
Guardians of the Galaxy	2014	Gunn, James
Guardians of the Galaxy Vol. 2	2017	Gunn, James
Her	2013	Jonze, Spike
Hulk	2003	Lee, Ang
I Am Legend	2007	Lawrence, Francis
I, Robot	2004	Proyas, Alex
In Time	2011	Niccol, Andrew
Inception	2010	Nolan, Christopher
Independence Day: Resurgence	2016	Emmerich, Roland
Interstellar	2014	Nolan, Christopher
Iron Man	2008	Favreau, Jon
Iron Man 2	2010	Favreau, Jon
Iron Man 3	2013	Black, Shane
Jupiter Ascending	2015	Wachowskis, The
Jurassic Park 3	2001	Johnston, Joe
Jurassic World	2015	Trevorrow, Colin
Jurassic World: Fallen Kingdom	2018	Bayona, J. A.
Justice League	2017	Snyder, Zack
Life	2017	Espinosa, Daniel
Limitless	2011	Burger, Neil
Logan	2017	Mangold, James
Looper	2012	Johnson, Rian
Man of Steel	2013	Snyder, Jack
Marvel's The Avengers	2012	Whedon, Joss
Maze Runner: The Death Cure	2018	Ball, Wes
Maze Runner: The Scorch Trials	2015	Ball, Wes
Men in Black II	2002	Sonnenfeld, Barry
Men in Black: International	2019	Gray, F. Gary
MIB 3	2012	Sonnenfeld, Barry
Minority Report	2002	Spielberg, Steven
Oblivion	2013	Kosinski, Joseph
Pacific Rim	2013	del Toro, Guillermo
Pacific Rim: Uprising	2018	DeKnight, Steven S.
Pandorum	2009	Alvart, Christian
Passengers	2016	Tyldum, Morten
Paycheck	2003	Woo, John
Planet of the Apes	2001	Burton, Tim
Power Rangers	2017	Israelite, Dean
Predators	2010	Antal, Nimród
Project Almanac	2015	Israelite, Dean
Prometheus	2012	Scott, Ridley
Push	2009	McGuigan, Paul
Rampage	2018	Peyton, Brad

TITLE	YEAR	DIRECTOR
Ready Player One	2018	Spielberg, Steven
Repo Men	2010	Sapochnik, Miguel
Resident Evil	2002	Anderson, Paul W.S.
Resident Evil: Afterlife	2010	Mulcahy, Russell
Resident Evil: Apocalypse	2004	Witt, Alexander
Resident Evil: Extinction	2007	Mulcahy, Russell
Resident Evil: Retribution	2012	Anderson, Paul W.S.
Rise of the Planet of the Apes	2011	Wyatt, Rupert
Robocop	2014	Padilha, José
Rogue One: A Star Wars Story	2016	Edwards, Gareth
Self/Less	2015	Singh, Tarsem
Serenity	2005	Whedon, Joss
Signs	2002	Shyamalan, M. Night
Simone	2002	Niccol, Andrew
Sky Captain and the World of Tomorrow	2004	Conran, Kerry
Skyline	2010	The Brothers Strause
Solaris	2002	Soderbergh, Steven
Solo: A Star Wars Story	2018	Howard, Ron
Source Code	2011	Jones, Duncan
Spider-Man	2002	Raimi, Sam
Spider-Man 2	2004	Raimi, Sam
Spider-Man 3	2007	Raimi, Sam
Spider-Man: Far from Home	2019	Watts, Jon
Spider-Man: Homecoming	2017	Watts, Jon
Splice	2010	Natali, Vincenzo
Star Trek	2009	Abrams, J.J.
Star Trek Beyond	2016	Lin, Justin
Star Trek Into Darkness	2013	Abrams, J.J.
Star Trek: Nemesis	2002	Baird, Stuart
Star Wars: Episode II: Attack of the Clones	2002	Lucas, George
Star Wars: Episode III: Revenge of the Sith	2005	Lucas, George
Star Wars: Episode VII: The Force Awakens	2015	Abrams, J.J.
Star Wars: Episode VIII: The Last Jedi	2017	Johnson, Rian
Star Wars: Episode IX: The Rise of Skywalker	2019	Abrams, J.J.
Stealth	2005	Cohen, Rob
Sunshine	2007	Boyle, Danny
Super 8	2011	Abrams, J.J.
Superman Returns	2006	Singer, Bryan
Surrogates	2009	Mostow, Jonathan
Tenet	2020	Nolan, Christopher
Terminator: Dark Fate	2019	Miller, Tim
Terminator: Genisys	2015	Taylor, Alan
Terminator 3: Rise of the Machines	2003	Mostow, Jonathan
Terminator Salvation	2009	McG
The 5th Wave	2016	Blakeson, J
The Adjustment Bureau	2011	Nolfi, George
The Amazing Spider-Man	2012	Webb, Marc
The Amazing Spider-Man 2	2014	Webb, Marc
The Animal	2001	Greenfield, Luke

(Continued)

TITLE	YEAR	DIRECTOR
The Core	2003	Amiel, Jon
The Darkest Hour	2011	Gorak, Chris
The Day after Tomorrow	2004	Emmerich, Roland
The Day the Earth Stood Still	2008	Derrickson, Scott
The Divergent Series: Allegiant	2016	Schwentke, Robert
The Divergent Series: Insurgent	2015	Schwentke, Robert
The Fourth Kind	2009	Osunsanmi, Olatunde
The Giver	2014	Noyce, Phillip
The Happening	2008	Shyamalan, M. Night
The Hitchhiker's Guide to Galaxy	2005	Jennings, Garth
The Host	2013	Niccol, Andrew
The Hunger Games	2012	Ross, Gary
The Hunger Games: Catching Fire	2013	Lawrence, Francis
The Hunger Games: Mockingjay-Part 1	2014	Lawrence, Francis
The Hunger Games: Mockingjay-Part 2	2015	Lawrence, Francis
The Incredible Hulk	2008	Leterrier, Louis
The Invasion	2007	Hirschbiegel, Oliver, McTeigue, James
The Island	2005	Bay, Michael
The Last Mimzy	2007	Shaye, Robert
The Lazarus Effect	2015	Gelb, David
The Martian	2015	Scott, Ridley
The Matrix Reloaded	2003	Wachowskis, The
The Matrix Revolutions	2003	Wachowskis, The
The Maze Runner	2014	Ball, Wes
The Meg	2018	Turteltaub, Jon
The Mist	2007	Darabont, Frank
The New Mutants	2020	Boone, Josh
The Predator	2018	Black, Shane
The Stepford Wives	2004	Oz, Frank
The Thing	2011	van Heijningen Jr., Matthijs
The Time Machine	2002	Wells, Simon
The World's End	2013	Wright, Edgar
Timeline	2003	Donner, Richard
Tomorrowland	2015	Bird, Brad
Total Recall	2012	Wiseman, Len
Transcendence	2014	Pfister, Wally
Transformers	2007	Bay, Michael
Transformers: Age of Extinction	2014	Bay, Michael
Transformers: Dark of the Moon	2011	Bay, Michael
Transformers: Revenge of the Fallen	2009	Bay, Michael
Transformers: The Last Knight	2017	Bay, Michael
Tron Legacy	2010	Kosinski, Joseph
Ultraviolet	2006	Wimmer, Kurt
V for Vendetta	2006	McTeigue, James
Venom	2018	Fleischer, Ruben
Victor Frankestein	2015	McGuigan, Paul
War of the Worlds	2005	Spielberg, Steven
War for the Planet of the Apes	2017	Reeves, Matt
X-Men: Apocalypse	2016	Singer, Bryan
X-Men: Dark Phoenix	2019	Kinberg, Simon

TITLE	YEAR	DIRECTOR
X-Men: Days of the Future Past	2014	Singer, Bryan
X-Men: First Class	2011	Vaughn, Matthew
X-Men: The Last Stand	2006	Ratner, Brett
X-Men Origins: Wolverine	2009	Hood, Gavin
X2: X-Men United	2003	Singer, Bryan

The films excluded by this process can be grouped into three categories that correspond to the three criteria set in the proposed definition: First, films were excluded because the cognition effect was totally absent or did not assume one of the six grammar roles. As explained above, the cognition effect must assume a structural role in order for a filmic text to be included in the corpus. The films that did not fulfil the above requirement are: *Just Visiting* (2001), *Ghost of Mars* (2001), *K-PAX* (2001), *Blade II* (2002), *Pulse* (2006), *Next* (2007), *Jumper* (2008), *Dragonball Evolution* (2009), *I Am Number Four* (2011), *John Carter* (2012), *I, Frankenstein* (2014), *The Chronicles of Riddick* (2004), *Riddick* (2013), *A Quiet Place* (2018), and *Glass* (2019). In *Just Visiting*, a medieval knight accidentally time-travels to twenty-first-century Chicago, where a series of comic events unfold until he is able to successfully return to his own timeline. The time-travel is described in purely magical ways, since it is achieved with the help of a wizard who gives the protagonist a magic portion. *K-PAX* is about a psychiatric patient named Prot (Kevin Spacey), who claims to be an alien from a distant planet. After a series of ambiguous incidents, which suggest his alien origins, the film concludes by indicating that Prot is actually a human who suffered a traumatic event in the past, thus creating an alternative persona as a copying mechanism. In *Ghost of Mars*, the events unfold in a terraformed Mars, where humans have formed a colony. The story revolves around a police officer and her team, who try to destroy the recently released ghosts of an ancient Martian civilization. These entities are not explained in any rational manner, and the film is overall imbued with horror tropes. In *Blade II*, the human-vampire hybrid Blade (Wesley Snipes) struggles to protect both vampire and human species, from mutant vampires who seek to annihilate both species. Although a quasi-scientific explanation is given for the mutant vampires, the origins of the first vampires are never explained and thus rest in a mythic discourse. Hence, the main Subject's origins and his narrative program are not informed by the cognition effect. *Pulse* is a horror film that narrates the efforts of a young student to survive from evil entities unleashed after a computer virus unlocked a portal leading to the realm of the dead. The world of the dead is a quintessential fantastic element, and is not rationally explained by the filmic text. *Next* tells the story of a man who helps with the prevention of a terrorist attack, due to his ability to see into the very immediate future. The narrative does not justify the existence of such ability and its main conflict concerns a man's effort to protect his loved one. *Jumper* follows a young man who is capable of teleporting as he struggles to survive from a secret group that intends to kill him. Again, no explanation is given for this ability, which is presented as a magical, personal charisma. Furthermore, his actions affect only himself and not a larger community, which means the film does not acquire the genre's cosmic perspective. In *Dragonball Evolution*, a young martial artist is confronted with an evil alien warlord who wants to ravage Earth. The aliens and superpowers are inflected with a mystic atmosphere, and the film provides no quasi-rational explanation of its events and characters. Similarly, In *Number Four* the protagonist's superpowers are not explained, and the narrative is permeated with fantasy tropes. *John Carter* presents an exotic world, where the hero's transportation in the distant planet and the ensuing events are characterized by a rather fantastic tone. *I, Frankenstein* brings Frankenstein's monster, Adam (Aaron Eckhart), vis-à-vis demonic and mythical creatures, which are not rationally explained, thus subsuming a SF character into an overall fantastic narrative. *The Chronicles of Riddick* and *Riddick* narrate the adventures of outlaw Riddick (Vin Diesel) who tries to survive in a fantastic universe filled with multiple threats. In both films, the cognition effect does not assume any structural role. Furthermore, in the second film, Riddick's objective does not have any impact on a wider community, thus limiting the events to an interpersonal perspective. *A Quiet Place* is set in a postapocalyptic world where strange blind creatures with hypersensitive hearing have wiped out most of the human population. Similar to the above examples, the narrative does not hint at the causes for the appearance of the monsters or their origins, and the film adheres mainly to the horror genre. Lastly, *Glass* focuses on three individuals with superpowers who are incarcerated in a psychiatric hospital since the authorities regard them as delusional criminals. Although in the course of the narrative events their superpowers are confirmed, no explanation is given for these extra-ordinary abilities. Overall, the above films avoid any kind of quasi-rational justification for the post-/non-human characters they present and/or the alien/strange environments they describe. Thus, they depict their fantastic worlds in pure magical terms or with no explanation at all.

Second, films whose central opposition is not placed in one of the two semiotic squares—that is, whose central conflict does not concern the encounter with a non-human, posthuman, alien Other and/or the survival in an alien/future world—are also excluded. These are *The One* (2001), *Rollerball* (2002), *The Tuxedo* (2002), *Jason X* (2002), *Ballistic: Ecks vs. Sever* (2002), *The Manchurian Candidate* (2004), *The Forgotten* (2004), *Death Race* (2008), *The X-Files: I Want to Believe* (2008), *G.I. Joe: the Rise of Cobra* (2009), *Dredd* (2012), *G.I. Joe: Retaliation* (2013), *The Purge* (2013), *The Purge: Anarchy* (2014), *The Purge: Election Year* (2016), *American Ultra* (2015), and *Gemini Man* (2019). *The One* and *The Tuxedo* are martial-art films whose science fictional elements do not assume a structural role in the narrative, but rather serve subordinate and decorative functions. Similarly, *Jason X* is a horror film, as its main conflict is structured around the struggle a group of students to survive from a murderous villain. *Rollerball* and *Death Race* use survival in the brutal environment of violent sports as their central theme, while *Ballistic: Ecks vs. Sever, G.I. Joe: the Rise of Cobra, G.I. Joe: Retaliation*, and *American Ultra* are action movies that use high-tech gadgets and weapons as props, but do not involve any encounter with post-/non-human beings and/or alien/altered worlds. *The Manchurian Candidate* (2004) is a political thriller, which narrates a war veteran's effort to uncover a conspiracy in the US government and its main conflict cannot be situated in either of the two semiotic squares (bodies or worlds). *The Forgotten* revolves around a woman who believes that she lost her son in a plane crash. However, her husband and psychiatrist try to convince her that she never had a son. As she tries to find evidence of her son's existence, she manages to expose that his disappearance is a part of a larger alien-government conspiracy. Yet, the film's central conflict is not set around the human/alien encounter—which is never represented in any way and only vaguely suggested—but is structured as a psychological thriller revolving around a mother's effort to find her son. *The X-Files: I Want to Believe* is the second film adaptation of the long-running TV series of the same name. Although the series have many SF elements, the particular film is not included in the corpus, since its main conflict is located in neither of the two semiotic squares. The film is a thriller/mystery where the two protagonists try to find a missing agent, encountering paranormal activity in the process that they cannot rationally explain. Despite taking place in a future postapocalyptic society, *Dredd* was also excluded from the corpus, since the dystopian milieu and the Subject's efforts to transform it are not at the center of the narrative. *The Purge, The Purge: Anarchy*, and *The Purge: Election Year* are thrillers whose central conflict—the protagonists' struggle to avoid the villains/killer(s)—is not located in one of the two semiotic squares that define the genre. Despite the films' representation of a future society, where all crimes are legalized and can be committed without fear of punishment for a single night every year, the films do not focus on society's structure, but rather on a single horrific event. Hence, the narratives are dominated by the horror/action/thriller mode. Furthermore, the Subject's main narrative program in the first two films of the series revolves around his/her own survival, which does not affect the wider community. Lastly, *Gemini Man* is an action film that depicts the effort of a former hitman to untangle a mystery revolving around the existence of a covert military program that creates clones of himself. The narrative is focused not on the encounter with the non-human, but mainly on the resolution of the mystery and the successful ending of the cloning project.

Lastly, I excluded the films that do not involve a cosmic dimension but remain restricted in an interpersonal level. These are *Clockstoppers* (2002), *The Butterfly Effect* (2004), *Eternal Sunshine of the Spotless Mind* (2004), *The Jacket* (2005), *The Prestige* (2006), *Hot Tub Time Machine* (2010), *Paul* (2011), and *The Wolverine* (2013). *Clockstoppers*, *The Butterfly Effect*, and *The Prestige* focus on the protagonist's effort to save a loved person, with no deeper implications on a social level. *Eternal Sunshine of the Spotless Mind* also focuses on the interpersonal level, narrating the story of a former couple who decide to erase each other from their memories, only to meet anew. The narrative objective is the (re)formation of the heterosexual romantic couple, and no wider implications are suggested. In *The Jacket*, a former war veteran blamed for the death of a policeman is incarcerated in a psychiatric hospital. There, he is subjected to experimental treatments and develops the ability to time-travel. However, the Subject's narrative objective is to help a loved person, and his abilities do not affect a wider community. *Hot Tub Time Machine* narrates the adventures of three estranged friends who time-travel back in the 1980s and meet their younger selves. Quasi-rational explanations are given for the time-travel; however, the narrative only describes the implications of personal choices in one's own future life. *Paul* revolves around two science fiction buffs and best friends who meet a cynical alien named Paul, help him to escape from the FBI and to return to his home planet. Despite the fact that the film parodies classical SF films, such as *E. T. The Extra-Terrestrial*, the encounter with an alien being is not focused on the human/Other interaction, but becomes a means to celebrate human friendship. Lastly, The *Wolverine* is also not included in the corpus, despite being an installment of the *X-Men* film series because the main narrative Object does not acquire a cosmic perspective. In contradiction to the other installments, Wolverine's (Hugh Jackman) objective to save one particular person in this film does not implicate a community (i.e., the Receiver is one person and not a community). Finally, in none of the films above are the post-/non-human characters or alien/unknown worlds intertwined in a macroscopic scheme that concerns a community but are used only to narrate a personal story.

The exclusion of films or their inclusion in specific cycles is based on the semiotic methodology discussed in the beginning of this chapter. In other words, the semiotic analysis facilitates the taxonomy of the corpus into the proposed six cycles. However, once this process is complete the variables of history and culture must reappear in the generic equation, in order to grasp the cultural meanings of the genre. The analysis of the six cycles attempts to do precisely this, that is, to articulate the semiotic with the exo-semiotic. But before moving to the discussion of the six cycles, the following chapter further delves into historical and industrial aspects of the genre.

2

Conglomerate Hollywood, Technology, and Filmmakers

In order to complement the genre's theoretical/semiotic analysis, this chapter moves to the examination of certain exo-semiotic aspects that are deemed important for the shaping of the contemporary SF film. These facets are situated in the genre's historical context of production and are connected by the central role of digital technology in the American film industry and SF film in particular. Specifically, the chapter analyzes how the economic imperatives of digital, conglomerate Hollywood influence American SF film in the new millennium. In addition, the chapter examines a specific industrial discourse, namely, how the directors of the genre discuss the role of cinematic technologies—as exemplified in the use of special effects—in the contemporary SF film. This discussion aims to contribute to a pivotal issue in the genre's analysis, that is, the association of SF film and (cinematic) technologies, from a perspective that has not been illuminated before. This twofold research is based on New Film History methods, namely, the "the critical analysis of primary sources" (Chapman, Glancy, and Harper 2007: 1)—that is, non-textual factors relating to the production and reception of the films. In our case, these primary sources include the corpus' data, press interviews, and information drawn online from the economic, industrial, and technological context of the films' production. The two axes of the exo-semiotic analysis unfold in the following sections.

The American SF Film in the Era of Conglomerate Hollywood

In his article "New millennium, New Hollywood," Thomas Schatz (2009) argues that significant structural changes in the US film industry that started from the 1990s onward, and consolidated in the beginning of the new millennium, marked a gradual shift to what the author terms "Conglomerate Hollywood." According to Schatz (2009: 19–20), the main forces that shape Conglomerate Hollywood is "conglomeration, globalization and digitization," which are exemplified in the vertical integration of film, TV, and home entertainment industries into the hands of few global media superpowers that dominate the US media industry. In this transformed landscape, the Big Six Hollywood studios—Warner Bros., Disney, Universal, 20th Century Fox, Columbia, and Paramount—are owned by and serve the interest of media giants WarnerMedia, Disney, Comcast, 21st Century Fox, Sony, and Viacom respectively,[1] which also control the majority of broadcast and cable TV networks (with the exception of Sony), along with media assets such as computer games, music, publishing, electronics, and theme parks. Furthermore, the conglomerate-owned big studios have also incorporated the indie sector by developing subsidiary distribution networks, such as Fox Searchlight (owned by 20th Century Fox), Pixar (owned by Disney), New Line Cinema (owned by Warner Bros.), Focus Features (owned by Universal), and Screen Gems (owned by Sony), in order to cater for niche audiences interested in art house, independent, and genre films (Corrigan 2012: 8) but also to attract artistic personnel and new talent. This strategic movement results not only in more revenue but also in the studio's prestige, thus leading the truly independent sector into marginalization. In this vertically integrated multimedia environment, the films' theatrical release is considered as a showcase window that promotes the DVD or on-demand sales on various media platforms, as well as other ancillary products, such as videogames and toys that comprise the largest source of revenues for the studios and their parent companies (Corrigan 2012: 9).

According to Schatz (2009: 20), Hollywood's major studios are interested in the new type of franchise-spawning blockbusters budgeted between $100 and 250 million—inaugurated by *X-Men* (2000) and *Spider-Man* (2002)—that aim exactly in this "global, digital, conglomerate-controlled marketplace." The franchise trend, although not new in cinema history,[2] has consolidated at the turn of the century and has been significantly augmented by the neoliberal turn in economy from the 1980s onward. In addition, this industrial tendency has been intensified by global digital culture and the concomitant media convergence whose effects are inscribed in the films' production, circulation, and consumption as well as in their formal-aesthetic aspects. The computer-generated imagery (CGI) is pivotal in this regard, since it has become an indispensable aspect not only in the creation of invisible and/or spectacular effects but also in many stages of the film's production (Prince 2012). In particular, the new type of blockbuster is indebted to such digital techniques, and has become distinguished, among others, by the two following traits. First, it exploits or expands an established media franchise (comic book, TV series, video game, etc.) that can be subjected to further continuation in an intertextual, transmedia system. Second, the storyworld is highly complex but also coherent and is realized through digital effects. This rich, computer-generated material can be further elaborated in subsequent films and other media platforms as well (Schatz 2009: 32–3). In this context, fantastic genres, such as SF, become the new major players in contemporary Hollywood since they fulfil the above criteria and are able to provide rich, intricate, and ever-expanding storyworlds that cater to the demands of the conglomerate, media-converging industry as well as the appetites of a global audience that have made these blockbusters[3] a source of staggering wealth for the Hollywood industry to begin with.

A close examination of the corpus reveals how the economic imperatives and strategies of Conglomerate Hollywood, as described above, affect the production, circulation, and reception of the twenty-first-century American SF film. A first observation is that 109 films (53.4 percent) are sequels/prequels/reboots/remakes, while 129 titles (63.2 percent) are adaptations from other sources—many of which are popular novels, videogames, comic-books, and/or other established media franchises. These numbers confirm the industry's interest in serialization and recycling based on popular material that secure pre-established audiences and can be further expanded in other media platforms. Thus, the industry prefers and promotes a specific type of SF story that aligns to the above characteristics. This is evident mainly in three of the genre's six cycles: the techno-human, the dystopia/utopia, and the fantastic worlds, which are also—not coincidentally—the most economically successful cycles. For example, the techno-human cycle (fifty films with a cumulative $29.3 billion gross) consists mainly of the superhero films based on the Marvel/DC comics (thirty-eight titles, 76 percent of the cycle). In the dystopia/utopia cycle (fifty-one titles, $16.9 billion), 78.4 percent of the films (forty titles) are sequels/remakes or adaptations from sources, such as video games, animated television series, books, short stories, novels, graphic novels, and comic books, many of which were quite popular before their cinematic incarnations (e.g., Suzanne Collins', *Hunger Games* novels or Capcom's *Resident Evil* video game series). These numbers underscore the effects of media convergence as a key characteristic of the contemporary digital Hollywood, where films usually "exploit or expand an established entertainment franchise" (Schatz 2009: 32). In the fantastic worlds cycle (eighteen titles, $13.5 billion), the majority of films (fifteen titles, 83.3 percent) are part of a franchise and/or adaptations of previous material. Specifically, the cycle includes phenomenal media franchises (e.g., the *Star Wars* and *Star Trek* films), "signature products" (Elsaesser 2012), such as James Cameron's *Avatar* and other adaptations of popular material (e.g., Douglas Adam's popular SF book series, *The Hitchhiker's Guide to Galaxy*, or the short-lived but cult TV series *Firefly* [Fox, 2002] which is the source material of *Serenity*).

A second observation concerns the films' budgets. More than half of the titles of the corpus (118 films, 57.8 percent) are designed with a "blockbuster mindset"[4] (Schatz 2009), including a budget of $100 million and more. The production of these event films is also accompanied by an extensive media campaign and other promotion strategies that are equally costly. Furthermore, these films are examples of the above-discussed industrial tendency for media franchises and/or adaptation of popular cultural material. There are only few SF blockbusters (seventeen titles, 8.3 percent) based on original scripts (and thus completely unknown material): These are: *Avatar* (2009), *Battleship* (2012), *Jupiter Ascending* (2015), *Pacific Rim* (2013), *Interstellar* (2014), *Inception* (2010), *Stealth* (2005), *After Earth* (2013), *The Island* (2005), *Elysium* (2013), *Passengers* (2016), *Gravity* (2013), *Transcendence* (2014), *Geostorm* (2017), *Rampage* (2018), and *Tenet* (2020). However, even these films confirm the rules of Conglomerate Hollywood in two ways: (1) first, they are based on their directors' reputation, which also functions as a kind of brand-name (e.g,. James Cameron directed and wrote *Avatar*; Christopher Nolan directed *Interstellar*, *Inception*, and *Tenet*, Guillermo del Toro directed *Pacific Rim*, Alfonso Cuarón directed *Gravity*); (2) second, some of these films, such as *Avatar* and *Pacific Rim*, spawned new transmedia franchises. However, it is interesting to note that seven of the above films (*Battleship, Jupiter Ascending, Stealth, After Earth, The Island, Transcendence,* and *Geostorm*) were economic failures or returned far less grosses than expected, thus prompting once again the industry to minimize risks by investing on established material.

Despite the fact that the dominance of big-budget films is expected, since the corpus under examination includes films that are among each years' top-150 box-office entries, and therefore popular productions, there also medium- and low-budget films in the corpus. Of the 204 films of our corpus, sixty-eight titles (33.3 percent) were budgeted between $30 and 97 million, while only eighteen films (8.8 percent) cost between $3 and 27 million. Yet, even in these productions, which are mostly produced/distributed by the big studios as well, we can discern the strategic movements of Conglomerate Hollywood, which provides more modest generic examples designed to cater for niche audiences and/or other media platforms, filling the programming needs of the studios and their parent companies. For example, it is interested to note that eleven films (61.1 percent) from the eighteen films with the lowest budgets are labeled as horror/thriller/mystery (besides SF) by IMDb and Box Office Mojo, thus clearly aiming at a different audience from the mainly action/adventure and mostly family-friendly big-budget SF film (98.3 percent of the 118 big-budget films of the corpus are labeled as action/adventure by the same databases).

Our third observation revolves around the studios' presence in the corpus and, specifically, the dominance of the Big Six and their subsidiary labels in the production and/or distribution of the corpus' films. A staggering 89.2 percent (182 films) were produced and/or distributed by one of the Big Six studios and their parent companies.[5] The only mini-major studio with a noticeable presence was Lionsgate Films and its subsidiary Summit Entertainment,[6] which are responsible for the production and/or distribution of sixteen films[7] (7.8 percent of the corpus). In addition, *The Mist*, *Apollo 18*, and *Dark Skies* were produced and/or distributed by Dimension Films—a label of the mini-major studio The Weinstein Company at the time (2007, 2011, and 2013 respectively),[8] which also coproduced and distributed *The Giver* (2014). Other independent productions include the commercially and critically unsuccessful *The Host* (2013) and the better received *Earth to Echo* (2014), initially developed by Disney, until it was sold to mini-major Relativity Media (Ford 2014), another point that accentuates the major studios' ubiquity. In conclusion, there are only twenty-two titles in the corpus (10.8 percent) where none of the Big Six were involved in their production and/or theatrical distribution in the United States, confirming popular SF film as a staple of Conglomerate Hollywood.

The above industrial strategies that shape SF film also enable Conglomerate Hollywood to diversify its products in relation to the other media platforms, especially television. The new millennium is after all the era of peak TV, which is characterized by a prolific number of high-quality (SF) television shows that also adopt cinematic practices (e.g., *Westworld* [HBO, 2016–22], *Black Mirror* [Channel 4/Netflix, 2011–], *The Expanse* [Syfy/Amazon Prime Video, 2015–22]). As James Fleury, Hikari Hartzheim, and Stephen Mamber argue

(2019), if contemporary television offers shows with intricate narratives and rich characterization or even provides space for the diminishing indie sector, the film industry must compensate with spectacular franchise films that exhibit the latest special effects and promote exhibition innovations such as IMAX screens and Dolby Atmos sound systems. Therefore, the role of Conglomerate Hollywood in this media saturated environment is not only to promote cross-media content and ancillary products, but mainly to become the technological vanguard in the production and exhibition of audiovisual products. Technology thus becomes the key to understanding the workings of Conglomerate Hollywood. Technology is also pivotal in the SF film not only as an integral aspect of the genre's production context but also as the content of its narratives. The next section explores such issues, examining the discourses of those directors most closely associated with the genre, in relation to the role of technology and in particular special effects in contemporary SF film.

Filmmakers and Technology

Cinematic technologies and SF film have a close and mutually shaping relation, since the genre stands, almost by definition, at the forefront of technical innovation exemplified in the design of special effects. This is corroborated by our corpus as from the fifty-four films that have been nominated or won one or more Academy Awards, BAFTA, and/or Golden Globe—that is, one of the most prestigious awards in the industry—the majority (forty-three films, 79.6 percent) include a nomination/win that concerns the Visual Effects category. From these awarded/nominated films, only ten (18.5 percent)[9] include one or more nominations for categories, such as Best Picture, Best Director and/or Best Screenplay. We can thus conclude that although rare are the SF films deemed worthy of an overall artistic recognition, the industry considers the genre as the ideal site for the advancement of cinematic technologies in general, and special effects[10] in particular. Although not all SF films involve special effects in the same degree and scope, they do constitute a fundamental aspect of the genre and how it is perceived. What is more, in the context of the digital turn where all stages of film production—from pre-visualization and cinematography to delivery and reception—have been fundamentally reconfigured, the special effects/SF film relation acquires a new dynamic and is greatly advanced and facilitated. The considerable possibilities that digital media offer to (SF) cinema are exemplified in the use of special effects that have now moved to a central position from the margins of the industry. As Thomas Elsaesser (2015: 205) notes,

> from being an addition and a supplement … [special effects] have become the "digital ground" on which a film is designed, in turn reversing the power relations between production and postproduction, where the latter now determines the former, and software governs not only what is possible but also what feels real.

In this new shift of power relations, the SF film becomes one of the leading Hollywood genres as it prompts, influences, and offers a ground where new cinematic technologies are tested and perfected before being diffused in the media industry. Therefore, there is no doubt that SF film and special effects are interdependent, the one affecting the evolution and transformation of the other. It is exactly this relation that I intend to examine in this section. Specifically, I aim to explore how the prominent directors of the genre perceive and discuss the role of cinematic technologies and special effects in relation to SF film. I do not intend to analyze the aesthetic dimension of special effects, their meaning, or how they function within the SF narrative,[11] but to explore their significance from an exo-semiotic aspect. For this reason, I draw from the filmmakers' discourses, interviews, and relevant articles, in order to illuminate how this relation is comprehended and discussed by the genre's most influential spokespersons. However, a short introduction that presents how film scholars have already analyzed the genre's relation to special effects is necessary.

The fundamental role of cinematic technologies and special effects in particular in SF film has been established from the first days of the medium. The trick films of the early "cinema of attractions" (Gunning 1986), such as Georges Méliès's magical illusions, consist of a series of fascinating views that are enabled by and foreground the technical and aesthetic possibilities of the cinematic medium. These early films can be considered as the predecessors of the SF film, inaugurating the centrality of cinematic technologies for the genre, both in subject matter and in form. This "tradition of trickery" (La Valley 1985) materialized through special effects informs the genre throughout its history and exemplifies "the videology of science fiction"—the genre's inherent inclination to self-reflect on "the fictional or fictive science of the cinema itself" (Stewart 2016). SF film's self-reflexivity regarding its own cinematic technologies has been pointed out by many critics. Kuhn (1990: 7) contends that the cinematic illusion in SF film displays the state of its own art through the use of special effects, making SF the most cinematic of all genres, since "the films themselves are often about new or imagined future technologies"—"a perfect example of the medium fitting, if not exactly being, the message." Brooks Landon ([1992] 2016) describes this technology/SF film relationship as engendering an "aesthetic of ambivalence," where the SF film's production embraces the technologies that the film's narrative often disputes. Hence, production technologies become the genre's central fascination that far surpasses the interest in SF story. Similarly, Telotte stresses SF's interest in "the imagery of film itself" (2001: 30) that constructs the genre's "double vision"—a fascination with cinematic science, exemplified in the use of special effects juxtaposed with a parallel hesitation to embrace such technologies as inscribed in the thematic level. Furthermore, Michelle Pierson (2002: 106–7) argues that

> [e]ven though CGI effects no longer belong to science fiction cinema in the way they did at the beginning of the last decade, it is no accident that this is where audiences first encountered this imagery.... The expectations that audiences have of this cinema put very specific demand on the visual effects imagery in science fiction film.

Pierson maintains that special effects in SF film aim to accommodate the audience's demands for novel attractions, constantly trying to reinvent the genre's "sense of wonder" (Pierson 2002: 156). Stacey Abbott (2006: 89) further underscores the mutually dependent relation between SF and special effects, since "the genre needs special effects to showcase its future worlds and technologies while the imaginative demands of the stories themselves have spearheaded new developments of FX technologies." Lastly, Julie A. Turnock (2015) remarks that the special effects–intensive cinema was first established by landmark SF films such as *Close Encounters of the Third Kind* (1977) and *Star Wars* (1977). This new type of "expanded blockbuster" realized "more intensively manipulated styles of filmmaking that have led to the ability to create infinitely expandable diegetic environments"—a trend evident until the present (Turnock 2015: 5; 15). The above arguments highlight that the genre's scholars regard technology, and special effects in particular, as a quintessential aspect of the genre. Interestingly, the genre's directors promote another view.

In what follows, I examine the discourses of the eight most acclaimed and artistically recognized directors with a strong presence in the genre (as verified by the corpus): Steven Spielberg, George Lucas, Ridley Scott, James Cameron, J. J. Abrams, Christopher Nolan, Alfonso Cuarón, and Neill Blomkamp.[12] These directors function as "concept-authors," a characterization that highlights both "the mode of production as 'high concept,' and … the resulting narrative as (in concept, if not in actuality) a brand or a franchise" (Elsaesser 2012: 288). Thus, they exemplify and embody the ideals of Conglomerate Hollywood, rendering the genre an ideal site where art and commerce, innovation and repetition, technical wizardry and traditional narrative converge. Furthermore, through their public personas and interviews, these filmmakers actively shape the genre's reception and understanding. In this context, they become among the most influential "user groups" (Altman 1999) of the genre. By examining their discourse, in conjunction with the discussion above, I aim to show how contradictory uses are at work and influence American contemporary SF. Although scholarly work considers cinematic technologies and special effects as the genre's raison d' être, the genre's prominent directors usually downplay, bypass, or discuss the fundamental relationship between SF film and cinematic technologies in different terms, while none of them considers technology as the factor that drives and shapes their SF films.

Spielberg and Lucas practically invented the SF/fantasy action blockbuster (Gordon 2008), which was assisted by the deregulation of the film industry under the Reagan administration (Gianos 1999: 5) and played an instrumental role in the transition to Conglomerate Hollywood. Spielberg's influence on the genre from the 1970s onward is remarkable and his twenty-first-century presence includes not only the four films he directed (*A. I. Artificial Intelligence* [2001], *Minority Report* [2002], *War of the Worlds* [2005], and *Ready Player One* [2018]) but also another fourteen films he produced/coproduced.[13] Spielberg's technical wizardry is also well established and evident in the groundbreaking effects of *Close Encounters*, *E.T.* (1982) and *Jurassic Park* (1993), among others, all of which marked a shift in the standards of effects-driven movies. Although the director's trademark is a warm, emotional, and dream-like style of filmmaking that foregrounds familial relationships (Morris 2007; Gordon 2008), his millennial films are imbued with darker tones. The director reflects this "emotional" attitude when discussing the role of special effects, downplaying their technological aspects and accentuating the human or magical element instead. According to Spielberg:

> A special effect is an alternative to making a direct deal with God and asking him … [to] create a fantastic light-show in the sky or to allow us to see spirits of the past floating through space. It's just another way around that. Failing that

you need special effects. I find the most successful special effects are when it appears that you did make some sort of "special arrangement."

(Friedman and Notbohm 2000: 90)

When asked about his films' technology, Spielberg replied: "You know, to me humanity always comes first ... You have to like the people of your story ... if you don't like the people, no matter how technologically superior the film is, it's just not going to succeed" (Friedman and Notbohm 2000: 90). Thus, technology, as a material and mundane aspect of the film industry, is discursively transformed into a magical, ethereal, and delightful element serving only humanist tales. Spielberg's discourse on special effects and cinematic technologies reflects his own cinematic vision, which turns prosaic everyday life into sublime experience and embodies the paradox of a studio mogul who "call[s] attention to the dangers of instrumental reason and industrial technology and [finds] an antidote in technologically innovative films that paradoxically affir[m] mysticism, spirituality, or the power of personhood" (Gordon 2008: 3).

Likewise, Lucas changed SF film history and the film industry in general with his *Star Wars* franchise, creating a pop cultural phenomenon that elevated SF to a mainstream, popular film genre and shaped Hollywood to its current form. A great pioneer and inventor of cinematic technologies, Lucas founded the ILM (Industrial Light and Magic) in 1975 because no other company could provide him with the visuals he needed for *Star Wars*. The company remains among the leading visual effects houses of the film industry. The undeniable relation of the director's career with technology is also acknowledged by film critic Roger Ebert (1999), who argues that "technology is where [Lucas'] imagination is really centered ... [creating] stories as a way to drive breakthroughs in technology." However, although Lucas does not deny the centrality of technology, he places it among discussion of other terms, and views it mainly as an artistic tool similar to a painter's brushes and palette, accentuating its creative dimension. Commenting upon the digital breakthroughs that *Episode II- Attack of the Clones* introduced—being the first major Hollywood feature to be captured digitally, on 24p high-definition video cameras—the director argued:

All [digital technology] does is give you more to work with ... [h]aving lots of options means you have to have a lot more discipline, but it's the same kind of discipline that a painter, a novelist or a composer would have ... The artist will always push the art form until he bumps up against the technology—that's the nature of the artist ... [filmmaking] is not about technology; it's about art, it's about taste, it's about understanding your craft ... and anyone who gets off on technological things is missing the point. I care about good lighting and good composition. I'm not interested in an engineer who knows a lot about the technology ... I'm just somebody who's trying to tell stories, and in order to tell the kinds of stories I've wanted to tell I've had to push the medium.

(Magid 2002)

Like Spielberg, Lucas also discusses technology in other terms. Although he acknowledges the interdependency between technology and his SF films, he describes the former as a creative, artistic tool that materializes the kind of SF visual narratives he likes to create. Technology is a suitable means, and SF the ideal form that Lucas favors, because "you can take issues, pull them out of their cultural straitjackets, and talk about them without bringing in folk artifacts that make people get closed minded" (Silberman 2005). Despite academic and critical discourses that mainly consider the *Star Wars* film franchise's legacy in industrial, technological, or cultural terms, Lucas regards that in the future he will be "remembered as a filmmaker. The technological problems that I solved will be forgotten by then, but hopefully some of the stories I told will still be relevant" (Silberman 2005).

Ridley Scott, another prominent SF filmmaker, who has brought SF film to academic and critical attention with *Blade Runner* and *Alien*, continues his presence in the genre, and his millennial SF films included in the corpus are the *Alien* prequels *Prometheus* (2012) and *Alien: Covenant* (2017), and the much-celebrated *The Martian*. The director was the recipient of the Visual Effects Society Lifetime Achievement Award in 2016, with the organization's Board Chair Mike Chambers, announcing, "[h]is vision and contribution to the art is incomparable and his impact upon the visual effects and technical fields is unparalleled" (Tapley 2015). However, Scott does not grant a central position to technology and, like Lucas, considers it just another tool. With his usual plain-speaking style and pragmatic attitude to how the film industry works, he situates technology in a context of costs and solutions and what is artistically suitable within budgets and time constraints. For example, when asked how the development of technology helped him in the production of *The Martian*, he replied:

Today, I can digitally represent [everything] perfectly. There's a downside to that as well. If everything can be done perfectly, it gives you massive capability as a filmmaker. You've got to watch that you don't make something so dramatic it becomes not feasible or dramatically dodgy.

(Fleming Jr 2015)

In another question concerning *Prometheus*, Scott argued: "You just need a good story. Usually, when special effects get in the way, it's because the story isn't strong enough" (Spitznagel 2012). Finally, in yet another question on how SF allows filmmakers to explore and push the technological elements of the medium, he added:

> [Science fiction film] should do that … because it's [an] enabling … gift. And being able to say, "Well, anything goes," that's also very dangerous. "Anything goes" becomes rubbish if you don't watch it. And, therefore, you've still got to create your own parameters for the three act play. You've got to step up and create your rulebook, because otherwise it's silly … Doing science fiction at a high level is tricky. It's really tricky. History is straightforward, because I'm probably retelling a story and I've got points of reference. Science fiction, there's no points of reference; it's all brand new. But that's also what makes it interesting. That's what makes it fabulous is that anything goes.
>
> (Billington 2012)

Ultimately, Scott views technology as another tool that must be carefully used along with all the other artistic elements, in order to serve the mode of production but, most of all, the narrative and the themes that each (SF) story invokes.

James Cameron is the most exemplary successor of the type of cinema established by Lucas and Spielberg and the embodiment of the "post-auteur author" (Elsaesser 2012: 290) of Conglomerate Hollywood. The director's association with SF and special effects has been well established from his second feature film, the iconic *Terminator* (1984). His subsequent SF films, *Aliens* (1986), *The Abyss* (1989), and *Terminator 2: Judgment Day* (1991), are all landmark examples of the genre, the latter two introducing breakthrough innovations in digital effects imagery. His millennial contribution is none other but the groundbreaking *Avatar*, which set new standards in visual effects imagery, motion and performance capture, and stereoscopic 3D. The inextricable relation of Cameron's SF film with technology is undisputed, evident in his waiting fourteen years before technology evolved in order to film *Avatar* the way he wanted (Hiscock 2009). The director has always been fascinated by art, science, and technology and saw filmmaking as a way to reconcile "the need to tell stories … and the desire to understand things at a technological level" (Dunham 2012). However, Cameron does not regard cinematic technologies, and special effects in particular, as the heart of the genre. Despite the fact that the big star in *Avatar* is undeniably the spectacular CGI imagery, Cameron emphasizes the importance of storytelling: "you have to make a good film that would be a good film under any circumstances … you have to put the narrative first" (Giardina 2008). Furthermore, like Spielberg "the dreamer" or Lucas "the artist," Cameron presents himself as "the curious boy" (TED 2010), thus discussing his use of special effects as a natural outcome of his curiosity: "for me it's about curiosity, it's about wanting to see what happens ... What can we create that people haven't seen before?" (Dunham 2012). Curiosity, which is of course associated with the human element and not technology, drives his filmmaking. This human aspect also resurfaces in his discussion about *Avatar*'s breakthroughs in motion and performance capture techniques. The director stresses that these technologies were "capturing the actor's performance ... fully and completely" and that the production team never tried to "embellish it with animation" (Desowitz 2009). In a behind-the-scenes interview, Cameron also insists, "the thing that people need to keep very strongly in mind is that this is not an animated film" (Youtube 2009). Although there are clearly marketing strategies behind this comment, since labeling a film as animation may possibly limit its potential audience, I believe that there is also another reason. These last two comments illustrate how Cameron tries to discursively abbreviate the role of technology, in this clearly technological-driven movie, and to accentuate the human element—here equated with the pure human performance.

Another frequent name in the twenty-first-century SF film and television is J. J. Abrams—a prolific filmmaker and TV producer. Our corpus includes four films directed by Abrams—*Super 8*, *Star Trek* (2009), *Star Trek into Darkness* (2013), *Star Wars: Epidode VII-The Force Awakens* (2015), as well as the hit monster movie *Cloverfield* (2008), which he produced. An admirer of Spielberg, his most personal movie *Super 8* (Sager 2016) pays homage to the director and reflects Abrams's nostalgic attitude to the genre, evident also in his other works that revamp iconic SF films of previous eras. A recipient of the Visual Effects society Visionary Award in 2015, the director's relation with special effects can be characterized as that of nostalgia for the more practical and artisanal aspects of the field. In particular, for the effects in *The Force Awakens*, the director said the production team "went old school" and that CGI were used mainly to remove things than to add (Chitwood 2015). According to Abrams:

> It was very important that we build as many sets as we could and that the film have a tangible, sort of authentic quality that you believed that these things were actually happening in a real space with real sunlight, if it was an exterior scene, or if we could build a big portion of a scene and not have anything be blue screen, do it where we could.
>
> (Chitwood 2015)

I maintain that by associating practical effects and tangible sets with "reality" and authenticity, the director displaces the role of technology to craftmanship. New technologies are thus equated with more impersonal qualities, while the old ones still preserve some authenticity of the "real." This skepticism toward new technologies and a nostalgia for old media are also reflected in another statement by Abrams: "I do think there's something about the digital age that is increasing dehumanizing us … we're being pulled into experiences that aren't really experiences at all" (Dunham 2019). Abrams displaces the role of technology by accentuating older, low-tech, or practical methods and artisanal aspects of filmmaking as more authentic.

Christopher Nolan is also a devotee of traditional techniques, despite his formal innovations. Nolan is considered one of the most acclaimed, commercial, and innovative contemporary filmmakers, and his work exemplifies what the press have coined as "cerebral blockbuster" where "the philosophical underpinnings … [are] as key as their explosions and visual effects" (Couch 2014). The director's presence in the genre includes *Inception*, *Interstellar*, and *Tenet*, all of which garnered an Oscar for their Visual Effects, among many other accolades. A recipient of the Visual Effects Society's inaugural Visionary Award in 2011, Nolan is widely considered a cerebral technician, "setting … gearhead problems with each project" (Bordwell 2019: 50). Despite his innovations, Nolan remains rather reluctant in the use of new technologies, preferring film over digital cameras and practical, in-camera effects than CGI, which he uses only when necessary (Ressner 2012). According to the filmmaker:

> The problem for me is if you don't first shoot something with the camera on which to base the shot, the visual effect is going to stick out if the film you're making has a realistic style or patina. I prefer films that feel more like real life, so any CGI has to be very carefully handled to fit into that.
>
> (Ressner 2012)

The director's effort for seamless photorealistic effects stems from his desire to employ them in order to "tell the story instead of making … [the film] a large-scale visual spectacle" (Lee 2012). Nolan elaborates: "to me, it's about the scale of what's required for the story you want to tell. I'm certainly not driven by the scale of the story but, you know, driven by how it grabs me. It might be small, it might be big" (Feinberg 2015). What is more, Nolan emphasizes that his formal and technical innovations are not about the sake of cinematic advancement itself, but aim to enhance the emotion of his stories. For example, although *Interstellar* is driven by scientific and technological principles,[14] Nolan describes it primarily as an emotional narrative about "connections between human beings" (Feinberg 2015). He insists more on the film's familial dynamics than its cosmic or technological ones, and reveals that "[t]he story spoke to me as a father, more than anything" (Lewis-Kraus 2014). Hence, Nolan, like the other directors discussed, camouflages or downplays the obvious innovative, technical, and technological aspects of his SF films, by insisting on traditional methods of filmmaking that better facilitate the emotional, human story at the center of his technological feats.

Similarly, Alfonso Cuarón stresses aspects beyond the technological when discussing *Children of Men* and *Gravity* (the latter introduced groundbreaking cinematic technologies and received an Academy Award for Best Visual Effects, among many other awards). A recipient of the Visual Effects Society 2014 Visionary Award, Cuarón recognizes the importance of technology in making *Gravity* and contends that "[w]e came to the conclusion that we needed to create our own technology. We spent months and months figuring it out" (Pulver 2013). However, he insists that he is not "a technological person" (Smith 2014) and that "the technology was nothing but a by-product, it was a tool only of the creative. We were not trying to create something technologically ground-breaking" (Appelo 2014). As the filmmaker argues:

> CG is like any other tool in cinema. What you do with those tools depends on the creative side … Once we started trying to ground what we were trying to do with conventional tools, it turned out that those tools were not going to work. We had to start figuring out how to make the movie work, but always from the standpoint of the source material, of the thematic and cinematic journey that we wanted to convey. So, all the time it was thematics and the cinematic that dictated the technological process … So, then it was about developing that technology, but it was always from the standpoint of the emotional, the thematic, and cinematic language.
>
> (Smith 2014)

Besides the story, Cuarón also emphasizes other "human" aspects such as the performance of the actors: "what really makes *Gravity* work is the actors, Ms. Bullock especially" (McGrath 2014) and "our emotional connection to her" (Desowitz 2014), while he downplays the importance of the film's technological breakthrough: "[i]f you have to do it, you just do it, but it's really better not to invent new technology" (McGrath 2014). His ambivalence toward technological innovation is also registered in *Children of Men* that eschews the CG-heavy technological style of most dystopian films. As Cuarón notes: "the research wasn't so much about gadgetry and how the world would be in years to come. In this film the research was about bringing the perception that great minds have about the state of things today" (Brevet 2006). Thus, in agreement with the other directors, Cuarón foregrounds other facets of his SF films, such as the emotional human journey, and assigns technology the role of just another creative tool with no particular significance or thematic resonance.

Lastly, Neill Blomkamp—the youngest of the filmmakers we discuss—has a particular association with cinematic technologies as he first entered the film industry as a visual effects and 3D animation artist. He appears in the corpus with three films: *District 9*, *Elysium*, and *Chappie* (2015). *District 9*, his first feature film, was a critical and commercial success and garnered many awards and nominations. Blomkamp is a devotee of visual effects and a technology enthusiast. As he remarks: "I happen to be a director, but I almost feel more like I'm actually really more of a visual artist or an engineer. I love engineering, so I get really obsessive about that stuff, and one of my favorite parts of the process is designing and creating" (Kelly 2013). Despite Blomkamp's passion for visual effects, technology, and SF, he doesn't underline the technological aspect of his films. For example, for *District 9*, Blomkamp reveals he wanted to "to feel as real as possible" and thus decided "not to put the special effects on a pedestal [in order to] ad[d] to the movie's gritty, realistic feel" (Wallace 2009). Instead, he stresses the balance between spectacle and story:

> I like action and vehicle design and guns and computer graphics as much as I like allegory. It's a constant balancing game. I want audiences to be on this rollercoaster that fits the Hollywood mould, but I also want them to absorb my observations.
>
> (Huddleston 2013)

Blomkamp is thus interested in SF ideas presented in a visually engaging way, without accentuating the role of cinematic technologies as key to the genre:

> Science fiction interests me massively. There are two reasons for that. There are loads of sociopolitical, racial, class and future-planet situations that really interest me, but I'm not really interested in making a film about them [...] that feels like reality because people view that in a different way. I like using science fiction to talk about subjects through the veneer of science fiction. The other

reason is I'm like a total visual kid. I grew up as an artist. Science fiction allows for design and creatures and guns and all the stuff that I like as well.

(Currie 2010)

It is noteworthy that even though Blomkamp has impressive, hands-on experience in the field of cinematic technologies, he also foregrounds other aspects as pivotal in his SF films—namely the SF ideas and visual dynamics of the genre.

It becomes clear that despite academic and industrial emphasis on the genre's inextricable relation with cinematic technologies and special effects, the prominent directors of the genre downplay this side. In spite of the breakthroughs that their SF films often prompt, they don't regard cinematic technologies as the genre's "central fascination that far surpasses the interest in SF story" (Landon [1992] 2016). Instead, they consider them as mere tools in order to convey the story, the character's emotional journey or to illustrate the fantastic storyworld. Each director may stress other aspects, yet they all agree that it is the human story at the core of the SF filmic narrative that drives and shapes whatever technological aspect is included in the text and not the other way around.

Notwithstanding the fact that the directors may actually view the SF film/technology relationship in this particular way, I would add that there are also other reasons behind this rhetoric. First, there are promotional reasons since the directors try to "sell" their films and an emphasis on an emotional, human story is probably more marketable than stressing their fascination with the technical aspects. Second, there are also artistic reasons since each director tries to present his films as artworks shaped by artistic notions, such as story and aesthetic, and not as industrial products informed by technological parameters. Third, there are generic reasons. Since the SF film has mainly been associated with gadgets, technology, and thus with more impersonal and technical aspects, these directors try to endow their work with an overall artistic value, which is commonly identified with the more human aspects of story. Lastly, I claim that what the directors' discourse reflects is their ambivalence toward the genre's role in the contemporary converged mediascape. Since the genre represents the vanguard of technological evolution in the context of Conglomerate Hollywood, the directors, while embracing and prompting these changes, want to simultaneously maintain the film industry's unique identity and status quo. While advancing technical breakthroughs with their SF films—and thus having an active role in the transformation of cinema and its relevance in the digital, transmedia environment of the entertainment industry—the filmmakers promote the films' traditional values in order to keep the appearance and status of cinema as an unchanged humanist institution. Thus, even though the genre represents an ideal locus where Conglomerate Hollywood can diversify its products among different media platforms (as exemplified in the form of the effects-driven, spectacular, franchise films), the directors insist on and promote the human story as the quintessential aspect of their SF films.

In light of the above, we could argue that the human/technology opposition that characterizes the genre can also be translated in industrial terms, where the human now stands for the traditional cinematic institution (of characters, story and analogue modes of filmmaking that the filmmakers accentuate) while the term technology signifies the new digital breakthroughs that transform and hybridize cinema into a new ontology (which their films advance). The SF film enacts this underlying conflict, where the traditional cinematic institution strives, on the one hand, to stay within the familiar places of a humanist tradition, while, on the other hand, inevitably merges with and expands into the uncharted spaces of an all-encompassing and transformative digital culture. The genre thus informs not only the technological imagination of the contemporary culture but also of the cinematic institution. If "cinema itself reflects on its changing (epistemological, ontological) status with its own means" (Elsaesser 2015: 196), then it becomes clear that the SF film is cinema's exemplary vehicle for such reflections in the present moment. It accommodates Hollywood's purposes, for it secures its future both imaginatively and materially at precisely this juncture of humanist tradition and technological novelty.

The above observations and arguments are based on the industrial discourses surrounding the genre. However, that is not to say that SF film is driven solely by economic imperatives and has nothing to do with audiences and how the genre resonates with contemporary cultural preoccupations. As Altman maintains, "[w]henever a lasting fit is obtained ... it is because a common ground has been found, a region where the audience's ritual values coincide with Hollywood's ideological ones" (Altman 1999: 223). This is the case for the American SF film of the new millennium where the imperatives of the film industry are intersected with those audiences' interests that pertain to our technocultural reality. The next part discusses the six cycles of the genre, examining both industrial discourses and thematic concerns that reflect the audience's preoccupations in the new millennium.

Part Two

The Cycles: SF Bodies/SF Worlds

The following chapters examine the six cycles of the genre, moving beyond a mere structural analysis. The proposed theoretical model thus becomes a first step to examine further issues of the genre. As Altman (1999) argues, genres are not just aesthetic categories or industrial formulas but also function as cultural phenomena. Accordingly, it is necessary not only to study generic structures and characteristics but also to explore further aspects that relate generic categories to larger cultural themes, since "text-specific thematic concerns are transformed by the context of the genre as a whole into questions of a broader societal nature" (Altman 1987: 336). The following chapters attempt to make precisely this connection, by combining the genre's structural analysis with thematic concerns that underpin each cycle as a cultural expression of the new millennium. Therefore, in the following chapters I situate each cycle in a specific historical context and examine it in relation to a particular cultural discourse, which I consider as prevalent in the specific category. The deep and surface structures are thus used as tools to explore further cultural concerns related to each cycle.

In the first three cycles the combination of structural, thematic, and contextual analysis is related with the more-than-human bodies that populate the genre, while in the last three cycles the focus is shifted on the imaginary worlds of SF. As I mentioned in the Introduction, Chapters 3–5 explore the SF bodies in relation to the following themes: The techno-human cycle focuses on issues of the technological body and its different expressions; the alien encounters cycle relates the figure of the alien with racial discourses; the creatures cycle explores the relationship between humanity and its artificial creations. Chapters 6–8 examine the SF worlds through the following thematic/cultural prisms: The dystopia/utopia cycle connects its collapsing worlds with the environmental discourses of the Anthropocene; the zones cycle discusses the confined spacetime configurations in relation with the limits and impasses of technological progress, while the fantastic worlds cycle examines the expansive vistas that characterize its iconography with notions of the technoscientific Empire.

Certainly, the selection and discussion of these thematic concerns in relation to each cycle is not an objective and uncontested process. Neither is the categorization of the films in specific cycles. On the opposite, they are based on the proposed theoretical model, which reflects specific choices of the author. Again, as Altman (1987) suggests, not only is every generic analysis subjective, but also the analyst should clearly state her/his interests and intentions to acknowledge the unattainable objectivity involved in every discussion about genres. Therefore, the six cycles are a theoretical construction based on certain criteria that reflect a specific, historical, and contingent position and not a universal model. Based on this model, I first make a division between films that take place in the familiar surroundings of Earth, thus corresponding to the first semiotic square, and films unraveling in an altered Earth, the space, alien worlds, and/or other futuristic zones, which are situated in the second semiotic square. Subsequently, each film is placed in the most suitable cycle according to its dominant syntactic expression. However, since all generic boundaries are fluid, a potential overlap between cycles is expected, and certain films could be situated in other cycles as well (such cases are discussed in each cycle). Similarly, there is also a possible thematic overlap between categories, and films of each cycle can evoke different issues and cultural concerns. Nevertheless, the association of particular cultural discourses with specific cycles is again a combination of the dictates of the theoretical model and a choice of themes which I consider dominant in each cycle. Therefore, the proposed model works as a discursive object with specific and conditional rules and as such it does not claim to offer an essential taxonomic and thematic analysis. Yet, I argue that it provides a rather efficient and flexible way to perceive and analyze the genre's structures and thematic preoccupations in the new millennium.

SF Bodies

3

The Techno-Humans Cycle: The Exceptional and the Ordinary Technological Body

The first cycle consists of the techno-human narratives. The cycle emerges from the interaction of the terms human and technology of the first semiotic square, and its basic conflict revolves around enhanced, technologically altered or (re)created humans. This category includes forms of retrofitted bodies that are the result of human's enmeshing with technology. The term techno-human includes not only human organisms that are restored or enhanced in a tangible way with biomechatronic parts (i.e., cyborgs) but also genetic posthumans or synthetic human organisms that are altered in subtler (or invisible) ways through the use of drugs, genetic manipulation or mutation, surgical alteration, and so on. Furthermore, it is important to stress that the human/technology interaction that constitutes the cycle's cornerstone must be generative of new bodies and new ontologies. Filmic narratives that don't merge the terms human and technology in the creation of a new hybrid organism are not included in this cycle.

In addition, artificial beings, such as androids, robots, and AIs despite their common characteristics with the techno-humans, namely, the merging of human traits (anthropomorphic structure, sentience, speech, etc.) with digital and cybernetic technologies, are not examined here. Although there are indeed common elements that associate all these artificial figures, the present taxonomy illustrates an ontological map of the genre. Thus, the anthropomorphic machines, such as androids and robots, are a part of the creatures cycle. The techno-humans discussed in this cycle explicitly include the term human in a physiological way, that is, as a human body that is subsequently altered, enhanced, recreated, or in any other way technologically reshaped. However, this distinction does not implicate that there are no interrelations between the techno-human and other artificial beings. On the contrary, the semiotic square's production of these new terms from the initial opposition human/technology accentuates their constitutional relationship and their mutual dialogical nature, which will be discussed in the creatures cycle. Overall, the present taxonomy is not meant to create absolute categories, but to facilitate the presentation and analysis of the genre's different expressions. The techno-human cycle comprises fifty films, which accounts for 24.5 percent of the total films of the corpus, and is the most economically successful cycle of the genre. The present cycle can be further divided into two categories: the superhero narratives, and what I label the ordinary techno-human narratives. The films included in the first category are the following: the *Hulk* films (2003, 2008), the *Iron Man* films (2008, 2010, 2013), the *Captain America* films (2011, 2014, 2016), the *Avengers* films (2012, 2015, 2018, 2019), *Captain Marvel* (2019), *Venom* (2018), the *Spider-Man* films (2002, 2004, 2007, 2012, 2014, 2017, 2019), the *Superman* films (2006, 2013, 2016, 2017), the *X-Men* films (2003, 2006, 2009, 2011, 2014, 2016, 2019), *Logan* (2017), *The New Mutants* (2020), the *Fantastic Four* films (2005, 2007, 2015), *Green Lantern* (2011), *Bloodshot* (2020), *Push* (2009), *Robocop* (2014), *Power Rangers* (2017). The second category comprises the following titles: *The Animal* (2001), *The Stepford Wives* (2004), *Splice* (2009), *Limitless* (2011), *Chronicle* (2012), *Victor Frankenstein* (2015), *The Lazarus Effect* (2015), and *Self/Less* (2015). The ensuing analysis is focused on the techno-body—the main semantic trait of the cycle—and how its expression is differentiated in these two categories in relation to the historical and industrial context of the films' production.

The Superhero Body

As discussed in Chapter 2, the superhero narratives comprise in their majority Marvel/DC adaptations and as such they are aligned with the imperatives of Conglomerate Hollywood. That is, they are franchise-spawning blockbusters that aim at the proliferation of ancillary products in different platforms, and are permeated with the logic of ever-expanding narratives, seriality, and recycling of previous established material. From the forty-two films of the category only three films (*Push* [2009], *Robocop* [2014], and *Power Rangers* [2017]) are not based on a Marvel/DC comic book. In addition, only three films (*Push, Bloodshot* [2020] and *The New Mutants* [2020]) have medium budgets ($38 million, $45 million, $67 million, respectively), while only one title (*Push*) is not a part of an established or intended media franchise.[1] As a result of the economic strategies that shape this category, its syntactic expression acquires a specific meaning, which is differentiated from the mainly medium-budget films that comprises the ordinary techno-humans. This differentiation is mainly located in the cultural meaning of the techno-human body—the quintessential trait of the cycle. In what follows, I first provide a historical context of the superhero film and its relation with the science fiction genre, and then I examine the technological body and how it functions in these group of films, through different examples and with a special emphasis on the MCU (Marvel Cinematic Universe) films, since they constitute the most economically and artistically successful paradigms of this category.

The superhero narratives have become the predominant cultural expression of the twenty-first century. Nevertheless, this form has a long history that officially begins during the golden age of the comics in the 1930s, and more specifically with the publication of *Superman* in *Action Comics* no. 1 in 1938. Angela Ndalianis stresses an even longer lineage, arguing that "[h]eroic narratives have a history that's as old as the establishment of human civilization" (2009: 5) and that the contemporary superhero narratives are an adaptation of such heroic narratives to the specific historical conditions of the era in which they emerge. The appearance of comic book characters in the silver screen also goes further back in time, with the characters of Buck Rogers and Flash Gordon being among the most popular ones in the film serials of the 1930s. The origins of the big-budget, special-effects heavy, superhero film can be traced in the New Hollywood blockbuster *Superman* (1978) and its sequels (1980, 1983, 1984, 1987) as well as the *Batman* films (1989–97) (Kuhn and Westwell 2012). However, as Terence McSweeney (2020: 12) maintains, the success of the superhero films did not solidify until the turn of the century with the release of *X-Men* in 2000 and then *Spider-Man* in 2002. The impressive profits of these first millennial superhero films appealed to the studios that found in these narratives the ideal material for the aims of Conglomerate Hollywood, with their potential for serialization, extensive use of CGI, and ancillary products. Twenty-two years later, the superhero film enjoys an increasing popularity and economic success, as evident from the staggering box-office records of *Avengers: Endgame* (2019).[2] However, aside from industrial and economic factors, other historical reasons have also contributed to the prevalence of the superhero film.

The rise of the cinematic superhero has often been associated with the 9/11 terrorist attacks in the United States, and the subsequent War on Terror that created the need for affirmative healing narratives and modern-day heroes/heroines. Many critics point to multiple correlations between the emergence of the superhero film at the dawn of the new century and the 9/11 events (see Muller

2011; Dittmer 2011; Hassler-Forest 2011; Gilmore 2015; Randell 2016). For example, Hassler-Forest contends that

> [g]iven the fact that the most radical redefinitions of superheroes always took place during periods of ideological conflict between the United States and its political enemies, it would make sense to investigate whether the attacks on 9/11 and the resulting War on Terror have had a similar repositioning effect.
>
> (2011: 134)

The author goes on to argue that although direct references in the 9/11 events are apparently absent in the millennial superhero films, nevertheless "we find metaphoric and symbolic representations aplenty" (Hassler-Forest 2011: 135). Karen Randell (2016) illustrates such symbolic representations in what she labels as a "9/11 aesthetic" that distinguishes the recent superhero cycle. The author maintains that such a traumatic event is "understood only by its recurring circular return, and in terms of the cycle of superhero films of the past ten years, this moment of return is signaled by the recurring image of urban wreckage that … approximates the aftermath of 9/11" (Randell 2016: 139). Hence, the superhero film is situated and interpreted within the discourses surrounding one of the most politically and culturally defining events that marked the beginnings of the new century.

The superhero narratives have mostly been examined as a separate genre that manifests in different media (see Bukatman 2003; Ndalianis 2009; Hatfield, Heer and Worcester 2013; McSweeney 2020). Indeed, despite the fact that this category can be expressed in different modes (comedy, action/adventure, drama, etc.) it exhibits a remarkable consistency and distinctive characteristics that can claim a generic life of their own. Scott Bukatman (2011) locates the superhero narrative's main fascination to "the body's discovery of its own transformation" (2011: 121) that can take different expressions and connotations. Echoing Peter Coogan, Terence McSweeney (2020: 36) sums up the basic traits of superhero narratives in the following three: powers, identity, and mission—with the former being the most defining element, which distinguishes this group from the rest of the science fiction/action films. McSweeney also underlines that such powers can be very diverse and can be acquired in different ways: "the superhero might be born with them … given them by accident … choose to receive them … acquire them through extreme levels of training … gain them through magical or religious circumstances … construct or be given a suit or technological device which gives them powers … or achieve power through combination of these"

(2020: 35–6). I agree with both authors about the importance of the body and its transformation, as well as its powers. However, it is important to stress that only certain kinds of superhero bodies and powers are included here. That is, since the book examines the superhero film as part of the SF film, and specifically as one of the versions of the techno-human cycle that emerges from the genre's basic interaction of human/technology, then only the technologically/scientifically created bodies are discussed here.

An exception to the above is the inclusion of the *Superman* franchise in this category, since the protagonist (Superman) is not a human/technology hybrid per se, but an alien. However, the films' dominant features point to their association with the techno-humans. That is, the protagonist Superman (Brandon Routh/Henry Cavill) is represented not so much as alien but as a superhuman endowed with special abilities, due to his physiology and upbringing as human. Furthermore, Superman is the archetypal figure that "epitomized a number of motifs that came to dominate the creation of superheroes" (Wasielewski 2009: 63). From his first appearance in the 1930s comics, the character is not only embedded in the discourses of the burgeoning technological supremacy of the United States, but he also represents its humanized form, "intermixing ... the everyday with the technological sublime" (Wasielewski 2009: 63). Although the character's representation has changed throughout the years, Superman's rendering as "the technological sublime in human form" (Wasielewski 2009: 66) is still relevant. It is exactly this techno-human body that I want to examine here and specifically its primary function as it is illuminated also by the films' structure.

In the superhero films the main Object of the protagonist is to save/protect the world from different non-human threats, such as aliens, human/technology hybrids, and others. For example, in the *Spider-Man* franchise, Peter Parker/Spider-Man (Tobey McGuire) has to confront techno-humans Dr. Norman Osborn/Green Goblin (William Dafoe) (in *Spider-Man*), Dr. Octavius's (Alfred Molina) (in *Spider-Man 2*), Sandman (Thomas Haden Church) and Venom (Christopher John Grace) (in *Spider-Man 3*), who not only threaten the lives of his loved ones but also wreak havoc in his community. In the franchise reboot (*The Amazing Spider-Man* and *The Amazing Spider-Man 2*), the same Object is set and Spider-Man uses his powers against his adversaries, in order to save his community/world. In the *X-Men* franchise, Professor Xavier's (Patrick Stewart/James McAvoy) Object is to save humans and mutants alike from the destructive machinations of the "evil" mutant Magneto (Ian McKellen/

Michael Fassbender) and the equally "evil" human General Stryker (Brian Cox/ Josh Hellman), who both perceive the Other (humans and mutants respectively) as an ultimate threat that must be annihilated.

In the Marvel Cinematic Universe films the respective main Subjects' Object is to prevent different individuals or groups that desire the planet's or the universe's destruction. For example, the HYDRA[3] organization—with its different representatives—serves as the adversary in the *Captain America* films and exemplify the calamitous use of technology that is contradicted with the constructive and beneficiary human/technology merger embodied in the superheroes. Similarly, in the *Superman* films, the Object is to safeguard Earth from such menacing figures as Lex Luthor (Kevin Spacey/Jesse Eisenberg) or the Kryptonian General Zod (Michael Shannon), who harvest alien technology in order to terraform Earth and annihilate humanity. Likewise, in the rest of the superhero narratives (*Fantastic Four* films, *Green Lantern*, *Robocop*, *Push*, *Power Rangers*), the protagonists' main objective is to protect their communities and sustain life on Earth from mad scientists turned into human/technology hybrids (*Fantastic Four* films, *Green Lantern*), aliens (*Power Rangers*), or multinational conglomerates/shadowy government agencies (*Robocop*, *Push*) that encapsulate the detrimental applications of technology. In *Bloodshot* the Object of the protagonist, US soldier Ray Garrison (Vin Diesel), is, initially, personal revenge. However, by the film's end, his actions lead to the cessation of the unethical experimentations of the Rising Spirit Technologies (RST)—a company specializing in cybernetic enhancements for disabled US military personnel.

This brief description of the surface structure points to a central trait of superhero group: the social usefulness of the superhero's technological body. This observation recalls Peter Coogan's (2006: 31) description of the superhero's mission as "prosocial and selfless." I agree with Coogan, but I want to expand his argument and stress that this prosocial character is connected with the technological body on display, which is represented as a beneficial technological force for society. The superhero protagonist (the Subject) represents a successful human/technology blending—even despite some initial difficulties—that serves community and exist within the limits of established social order. That is, the superhero body is depicted as a technological superpower that is used for the benefit of society and protection of humanity. In the 2002 *Spider-Man*, young Peter Parker (Toby McGuire) is portrayed as an outcast high school student, who is bitten by a genetically engineered super-spider in a genetics laboratory during a school field trip. The next morning, Peter realizes his eyesight is corrected, and his body is more toned and muscular. The merging of human body and technology is already indicated in a positive manner and is subsequently used for the protection of the community from different threats. Similarly, in the Marvel Cinematic Universe films, techno-human bodies are similarly shaped. *Captain America: The First Avenger* (2011) describes the birth of America's first superhero during the Second World War. Steve Rogers (Chris Evans) is a frail and skinny man who is transformed into the muscular and athletic Captain America, after a voluntary exposure to a super-soldier formula. He then painlessly employs his new abilities with a patriotic fervor that serves community and nation. Tony Stark (Robert Downey Jr.) in *Iron Man* (2008) is the egotistical CEO of the Stark industries, an industrialist and arms manufacturer who is interested only in his own profit. After a traumatic captivity during his visit in Afghanistan, where he builds a suit of powered armor in order to escape, he decides to stop the manufacture of weapons. Subsequently, he devotes himself to refining the body armor, which he successfully masters it, turning it into a smoothly integrated technological extension of himself. Stark then uses the suit to protect civilians in warzones and fight injustice, becoming the superhero Iron Man. In *Captain Marvel* (2019) Carol Danvers (Brie Larson) is a US pilot who absorbs the energy released during the destruction of an experimental light-speed engine, subsequently acquiring superhuman abilities, but losing her memory. After she recovers her memory and removes the implant that the hostile aliens Kree embedded in her in order to control her, she effortlessly gains her full powers and employs them to protect both humans and aliens in need.

Even in the cases where the initial metamorphosis is depicted as arduous or painful (Hulk, Robocop, Wolverine in the *X-Men* films, Mr. Fantastic in the *Fantastic Four* films etc.) by the end of each film the superhero prevails as a coherent technologically empowered being that is smoothly integrated in society and accommodates its needs. For example, in *Hulk* (2003) Bruce Banner's (Eric Bana) initial transformation is not successfully handled; in fact, he is not even aware of his double embodiment, echoing the unconscious doubling of Dr. Jekyll/Mr. Hyde. However, in the franchise reboot *The Incredible Hulk* (2008), the techno-human is placed in a more appropriate superhero context. After the exposure, Bruce (Edward Norton) tries to manage his transformations through yoga exercises and manages to keep himself under control. Hulk's status as a proper superhero is confirmed when Tony Stark/Iron Man proposes he join the Avengers. This recoil and recuperation are continued in Hulk's next appearances in the MCU. Bruce Banner is unable to transform into the Hulk in *Avengers: Infinity War* (2018), but in *Endgame* (2019) he becomes a balanced technological power, combining both Hulk's super-strength and Banner's intelligence and self-control.

This beneficial technological body and its global usefulness that exceeds strictly US stakes is not only a random narrative choice but also the result of the historical and economic context of the films' production. In the wake of the unpopular War on Terror, and the subsequent mistrust it engendered toward the American government, the twenty-first-century superhero body seems "increasingly removed from discourses of pure nationalism" (Hassler-Forest 2012: 11) as was the case in previous generic representations (e.g. the *Superman* films [1978–87]) (McSweeney 2020). In addition, the millennial superhero narratives offer—at least on the surface—an implicit critique of the US foreign policy as evident from the superhero's reluctance toward and/or questioning of the government's decision and acts. For example, Iron Man denies to deliver his suit to the government in *Iron Man 2*, while Captain America is being skeptical about the governmental oversight of the Avengers in *Captain America: Civil War* (2016). Thus, the technological body appears not strictly aligned with US interests and national rhetoric, but rather is committed to universal values that encompass the needs of the entire world. Although the protagonists are in their majority Americans—and also white and male[4]—their actions have repercussions to people outside the US borders. This is also evident from the surface structure of the superhero narratives where the Receiver of the main Subject's actions is usually the entire world (and not just the United States). Thus, the successful incorporation of technology into the (American) human body is signified as a beneficiary force not only for the United States but also for the whole humanity. This semantic change is also the result of the studios' decision, which, in the context of Conglomerate Hollywood, must produce narratives which offer various "access points" (Elsaesser 2012: 291) in order to accommodate the needs of a global and heterogeneous audience.

However, it is exactly this technological body that seemingly serves universal needs, that once again reaffirms the hegemonic discourse of the United States as the only technological superpower able to protect the entire Earth from human and non-human threats. That is, the films' "structured ambiguity" (Elsaesser 2012: 290) conceals the economic-political alliances that sustain the Hollywood film industry. Indeed, the millennial superhero narratives, despite appearing critical of certain aspects of American politics, the military industry, and so on, are still deeply imbricated with the military-entertainment-industrial complex, as evident by the fact that all three *Iron Man* films, and other MCU installments received official military support (CBR.com n.d.; Cox 2019). As Hassler-Forest (2012) and Terence McSweeney (2018) argue, these narratives ultimately reproduce hegemonic discourses, reinforcing the ideology of American exceptionalism. The superhero body, therefore, is an exceptional body, encapsulating the discourses surrounding US technological innovation and military supremacy. Here, the example of Iron Man is illuminating, given also that the character's trajectory is considered as the defining narrative arc of the MCU (Lubin 2015). Iron Man is the embodiment of the military-industrial complex–turned-savior of humanity, thus reasserting US scientific, military, and cultural hegemony at the same time. As Tanner Mirlees puts it, *Iron Man* reinforces "US economic power (as a Hollywood blockbuster and synergistic franchise), US Military power (as a DOD-Hollywood co-produced militainment) and cultural power (as a national and global relay for US imperial ideologies)" (2014: 5). Therefore, the superhero body is characterized by this double register, where liberal values such as freedom, justice, and the protection of life go hand in hand with the ideologies of US exceptionalism, and technological supremacy.

This multivalence of the superhero body also connects the millennial superhero film with the cyborg films of the 1980s. The latter cycle similarly includes human/technology hybrids, exemplified in films such as *Terminator* (1984) and *Robocop* (1987), and characterized by a "semantic open-ness" (Short 2005: 9) On the one hand, the cyborg body exhibits a constructed hybrid nature that unsettles the hierarchical dichotomies of contemporary societies, such as culture/nature, male/female, and human/machine, thus invoking Donna Haraway's (2004) conception of the cyborg as a subversive political metaphor. On the other hand, the 1980s cyborg film conceals this constructedness in a hypermasculine physique that embodies and perpetuates the dominant ideologies of the Reagan era (Jeffords 1994). As Cornea (2007: 125) argues, "because the cyborg is defined by a breakdown in the boundaries between self/Other, the hyper-masculinity on display becomes a hysterical attempt to recuperate the traditional distinctions that this figure threatens to erode." In a similar way, the millennial superhero body displays such contradictory signs, criticizing the military-industrial complex but still serving its interests, and portraying the human/technology fusion in affirmative way, but only if it is aligned with dominant discourses and situated within the limits of established social order. However, the above observations refer to the protagonist of the superhero narratives (The Subject), and not the antagonist (Enemy) who encapsulates the uncontrollable or destructive aspects of technological embodiment. Such socially destabilizing bodies take center stage in the ordinary techno-human narratives, and represent a more unstable incorporation of technology into the human form, as discussed below.

The Ordinary Techno-human Body

The second category of the techno-human narratives, the ordinary techno-humans, includes more diverse figures that are nevertheless characterized by the same human/technology opposition that forms the cycle. In these films, the entanglement of human with technology results in less heroic configurations and the narratives often employ motifs from other genres, such as comedy (e.g. *The Animal* [2001], *The Stepford Wives* [2004]), horror (e.g. *Splice* [2009], *The Lazarus Effect* [2015], and thriller (e.g. *Limitless* [2011], *Self/Less* [2015]). These narratives are distinguished by a mundane or pessimistic tone that contradicts the mainly spectacular style of the Marvel/DC superhero films. There are also notable differences between these categories in terms of budgets. From the eight films included in this category, only *The Stepford Wives* had a significant budget ($90 million), while the other films had medium to small budgets,[5] which may account for the films being less spectacular in comparison with the superhero films. In addition, the above titles are mainly standalone films; that is, they are not a part of an established media franchise, while the majority of them are based on an original screenplay (*The Animal, Splice, Chronicle, The Lazarus Effect, Self/Less*)—additional facts that may explain the aesthetic and narrative differentiations between the categories.

However, there are many differences not only between the superheroes and the ordinary techno-humans but also between the films of the latter category. These films address different thematic concerns, as discussed below, and employ different tone and style. However, here they are examined in relation to the representation of the ordinary techno-body and its association with the superhero body. From this perspective, the main differentiation between them is that the human/technology interaction is situated in the context of personal goals and/or results in damaging effects in a community. Thus, unlike the techno-optimism of the superhero films, here the techno-body is represented as either prosaic and self-centered (*The Stepford Wives, The Animal, Limitless, Self/Less*), or dysfunctional and harmful (*Chronicle, Splice,*

Victor Frankenstein, *Lazarus Effect*). In opposition with the superheroes, the ordinary techno-humans are not marked by exceptionalism, as evident also in the absence of transformed physique or costume. Their powers are not effortlessly granted, but are accompanied by major side effects that burden the Subject's social integration. Importantly, the protagonist applies the new abilities for apparently selfish, or trivial purposes, in contradiction to the grand events of the superhero films—though the protagonist's actions still affect a community and/or have wider implications, thus asserting the genre's cosmic dimension.

Limitless is an interesting example in this regard. The film is directed by Neil Burger and written by Leslie Dixon, and is based on the 2001 novel *The Dark Fields* by Alan Glynn. Produced on a medium budget of $27 million and distributed by former mini-major Relativity Media, the film was a box-office success, returning $161.8 million—a success that can attributed partially to its well-known stars Bradley Cooper and Robert De Niro. The film's success resulted also in a same-titled spin-off series (CBS, 2015–16), which confirms the tactics of Conglomerate Hollywood, despite the fact that it was canceled after one season due to low ratings. As with the other films of this category, *Limitless* borrows conventions from different genres, such as thriller, action, caper films, while also alluding occasionally to Wall Street-themed films. Indeed, the press described the film as "a decent thriller in which Bradley Cooper's no-hoper discovers the pills that turn him into a mega-IQ superman" (Bradshaw 2011), or elsewhere as "a paranoid thriller blended with pseudo-neuro-science fiction and catalyzed by a jolting dose of satire" (Scott 2011). In other words, the film is described as a mix of many genres, with an emphasis on the science fictional themes. Certain critics pointed, however, to the ineffectiveness of this genre blending, as, for example, Kirk Honeycutt (2011) from *The Hollywood Reporter* who wrote that certain conventions that the film employed such as "Russian gangsters and Wall Street crooks are so tired by now." Yet, I suggest that these traits drawn from less fantastical genres than science fiction ground the protagonist in an ordinary context.

The film follows writer Edward Morra (Bradley Cooper), who struggles for a long time to complete a long-overdue book. As his professional and personal life seems to fall apart, he runs into an old acquaintance who introduces him to a nootropic drug called NZT-48. This illegal drug functions as a cognitive enhancement, sparking his brain synapses and thus expanding his brain capacity. The film employs interesting visual effects and cinematography to convey this new degree of perception that Eddie experiences, such as fish-eye shots, letters flowing in the screen, zooming, and jump-cutting, providing an instance of how such mind-bending images can be incorporated in less spectacular narratives. However, these visually striking images that signify the exceptional mind portray ordinary and unexceptional events. Eddie uses his new skills to finish his novel, tidy up his house, regain his girlfriend, while he subsequently dabbles in more profitable endeavors, such as the stock market. This ordinariness is also noted by *New York Times* critic A. O. Scott (2011), who relates it to actor Bradley Cooper: "Mr. Cooper has a special gift for impersonating a certain type of ordinary guy … 'Limitless' is a showcase for his gift of exemplary just-above-averageness." This normalcy is further underscored by the waning of the enhanced abilities and the side effects that accompany them—unlike the techno-humans of the superhero films that once transformed they retain their powers without any major aftermaths. Still, Eddie is an enhanced individual, "a Superman for the Information Age" (Honeycutt 2011), despite his unchanged physique and dependence on the drug on a daily basis. Thus, he represents a human/technology blending that applies his new abilities for personal reasons, and remains grounded in the context of ordinary life.

Similar representations are evident in the other films of the category. In *Self/Less*, Damian (Ben Kingsley), a dying millionaire, is transferred to a younger body (Ryan Reynolds) and begins his life again as an ordinary, young man. This normality is disrupted only when he forgets his medication and the memories of the host body resurface. The film clearly alludes to the 1966 film *Seconds*, but unlike this classic SF film, *Self/Less* does little to delve into the complex science fictional premises that it introduces and instead relies more on the thriller/action conventions. In this way, the human/technology interplay does not mark extraordinary events but is set in the context of everyday reality. This is also the case for the Rob Schneider vehicle *The Animal*, albeit in a comic tone. After a car accident, the protagonist Marvin (Rob Schneider) is captured by a mad scientist, who subjects him to an animal organ transplant. This results to Marvin's acquisition of animal traits that mark him as different. This difference is manifested in his new physical prowess but mostly in behavioral divergences that serve as a comic disruption of social and bodily norms. Still, this transformation is situated in a mundane context, as Marvin pursues a normal life that includes finding a suitable mate and re-integrating into the community. In a similar comic mode, *The Stepford Wives*—a remake of the 1975 film of the same name—depicts another banal transformation, where intelligent and independent women are transformed into docile cyborg-housewives with the implantation of a behavior microchip. Here, the possibilities of human alteration through technology serve the interests of patriarchy, and the film slightly tackles issues about the role of technoscience in power relations, feminism, and consumer society. Although this satirical tone is rather restricted, the film hints not only at the possible banality of the technological modification of the human but also its dangerous possibilities in reproducing and reinforcing existing social hierarchies. Thus, again, it is not extra-ordinariness that distinguishes the techno-human, but the commonplaces of the everyday world.

Chronicle is another interesting case, as the film bridges the ordinary techno-body with the aberrant and the destructive, while also constituting the reversal of the superhero narratives in both tone and style. Designed as an independent production, the film was an unexpected critical and commercial success, garnering $126.6 million on a $12 million budget, making it a more profitable endeavor than some of the big-budget superhero films discussed above. For example, *Green Lantern* (2011) had a budget of $200 million, and it grossed approximately only $219 million—a little above its cost. *X-Men: Dark Phoenix* (2019)—the last installment of the *X-Men* franchise—was also another box-office flop, garnering $252 on a $200 million budget. Given that for a film to break even "box office gross must be 2.5 times production costs" (Kuhn and Westwell 2012: 42), it is obvious that these films were financial disasters, despite their blockbuster status. *Chronicle* was such a success for 20th Century Fox—the studio that acquired its rights and distribution—that initial steps were taken for the creation of a sequel (Trumbore 2012), confirming that the tactics of Conglomerate Hollywood can be extended to small productions if proven suitable. Although *Chronicle 2* didn't happen, the studio executives decided to trust the 2015 reboot of the *Fantastic Four* franchise to the film's promising director Josh Trank. Unfortunately, Trank didn't manage quite as well with the $120 million production (for reasons explained in the end of the section), with the film returning only $168 million, and also receiving negative reviews from the press. In opposition, *Chronicle* was praised by critics for its originality, the clever use of the found-footage style, and its themes (see McCarthy 2012; Ebiri 2012; Dargis 2012). Many commentators also noticed the film's interesting reworking of the superhero formula, with Todd McCarthy (2012) stating that the film "employ[s] the boilerplate Marvel premise—that of a young man suddenly possessed of superpowers—but walk[s] the other way with it," while, in a similar tone, Bilge Ebiri (2012) argued that "[i]f the average superhero movie is all about how with great power comes great responsibility, *Chronicle* remind us that it also comes with great temptation."

Indeed, this inversion of the superhero premise is the film's defining trait, where the techno-body now connotes destruction and disarray. The film follows outcast teenager Andrew (Dane DeHaan) who is bullied by classmates and abused by his alcoholic father, while also coping with his mother's terminal illness. His only consolation is his new video camera, which he decides to use in order to record everything in his daily life—a narrative decision which also justifies the film's found-footage style. During a party, where Andrew has been invited by his cousin Matt (Alex Russell), a fellow student, Steve (Michael B. Jordan), asks both of them to join him for a walk to the nearby woods in order to record a hole which he had discovered. Upon their arrival, they trace a glowing crystalline object, which starts causing weird phenomena as they approach it, until the camera short-circuits. Few days after this event Andrew, Matt, and Steve have developed telekinetic abilities that transcend the limitations of the human body. However, and in opposition with the exceptional techno-body of the superhero narrative, the three boys remain, in all other respects, rather normal. Their physique and everyday reality remain unchanged, and they just use their power for pranks and fun, pointing to what "ordinary kids might do if they found they could levitate stuff, crush heavy objects, do insane magic tricks and fly" (McCarthy 2012). Gradually, Andrew, who is consumed by anger, turns on the dark side and starts to employ his extraordinary abilities for personal and revengeful purposes. Thus, rather than offering a solution to the troubled teenager, the techno-body further precipitates his marginalization, resulting in his destructive revenge against his community.

Despite the fact that *Chronicle* emulates the superhero formula, other damaging techno-bodies of the cycle are presented in narratives that use conventions from different genres. In addition to being tagged as sci-fi films in IMDb, *Splice* and *Victor Frankenstein* are characterized also as drama and horror, while *Lazarus Effect* as horror and mystery. Indeed, the films exhibit some of the main traits of the horror and mystery genre, such as low-key lighting, ominous music, and an overall dark atmosphere, among others. Notwithstanding these differences in tone and style, the narrative structure still revolves around a human/technology hybrid that acquires superhuman abilities but uses them for self-serving, and/or damaging purposes. What is more, since the narratives are imbued with horror tropes the techno-human is represented as a malformed and grotesque body—in opposition with the healthy, athletic, and exceptional techno-bodies of the superhero films, as evident in the Figures 3.1–3.4. These grotesque techno-bodies point to the perils of the unchecked incorporation of technology in our daily existence. Therefore, contrary to the optimism of superhero exceptionalism, the ordinary techno-human narratives are permeated by the horrors of technology's harmful effects to the social body. For example, in *Victor Frankenstein* the infamous scientist creates an "abject" creature, to use Julia Kristeva's term (1982), stitched together from dead body-parts, that although seemingly alive and with extraordinary power, it can only bring about death.[6] Similarly, in *Lazarus Effect*, the body's restoration from the dead through the injection of a serum transforms it into a powerful and "evil" techno-human, characterized by superhuman abilities, such as unnatural strength, telekinesis, and telepathy. However, these abilities are used only to wreak havoc and terminate all human life. Finally, in *Splice*—a film about the dangers of bioengineering that echoes the Frankensteinian myth more properly than the above films—the hybrid human-animal body is marked by unique capacities. Still, the techno-human's rejection from its makers, and subsequent exclusion from society, transform it into a horrific and lethal creature.

Figures 3.1–3.4 The exceptional and the ordinary techno-body in *Captain America: Winter Solider* directed by Anthony and Joe Russo© Walt Disney Pictures 2016. *Man of Steel* directed by Zack Snyder© Warner Bros. Pictures 2013. *Splice* directed by Vincenzo Natali© Warner Bros. Pictures 2009. *Victor Frankenstein* directed by Paul McGuigan© 20th Century Fox 2015. All rights reserved.

The cases examined above warns us for the unpredictable effects that human augmentation and technological embodiment may involve, especially when it concerns common people, that is, ordinary humans that are not closely attached to official institutions and/or the military-industrial complex. The films in this category, however, are limited in number, in comparison with the superhero films. Most films that revolve around the human/technology opposition seem to follow the superhero formula, in the sense that the films' protagonists employ their powers for prosocial and beneficiary purposes—regardless if they wear a costume or not. The superhero narratives—although they do seem to include some cautions about the human/technology intersection embodied in the figure of the antagonist/Enemy—offer a more optimistic viewpoint on these issues. This is not something unexpected from the blockbuster film—the major product of a dominant institution like the Hollywood film industry, which is in close relation with different technological sectors and financial interests, and also needs to appeal to a large audience.

Here, the example of director Josh Trank and his attempt for differentiation in the *Fantastic Four* reboot is illuminating about how specific meanings arise from, and are connected with industrial tactics. As discussed above, Trank directed *Chronicle*, an independent production, which became an artistic and economic success, offering a new approach to the superhero conventions. This success led Trank to the direction of *Fantastic Four*, where he tried to implement a similar alternative approach in a blockbuster context. However, his vision was incompatible with the fanbase's perception of the comic book characters but also with the demands of the film studio 20th Century Fox, which handled the project. The studio executives were dissatisfied from the material, and thus begun to interfere, assigning other producers/writers to the film in order to amend it. Eventually, Trank was cast aside while the entire third act of the film was allegedly reshot. This uneven course in the film's production led to a massive critical and commercial failure, which was even more pronounced given the dominance of the superhero film at the given period (Kaye 2020). What the above production story indicates is not only the machinations involved in big Hollywood productions but also the specific expectations attached to such films. The different take on the superhero formula was welcomed in an independent production like *Chronicle*; however, it didn't come to fruition in the context of a big-budget production, and the expectations that surround it. This partially explains why a specific representation of the techno-body prevails in the superhero narratives and why these films outnumber other different versions of the techno-humans.

Despite the significance of budgets, industry, and expectations, there is also the historical context which also may account for the prevalence of this representation of the techno-body. Since genres are not only industrial products but also cultural categories, and as such they negotiate the shifting values of a community (Altman 1999), other parameters must also be considered. These cultural factors are related to my argument about the ordinary/pessimist view on the technological body, which is associated with the low- and/or medium-budget film, and is opposed to the representations of the blockbuster film. This remark reverberates Vivian Sobchack's (1987) discussion about the 1950s SF film, where the author argued that the genre was characterized by either the optimism of the big-budget film or the pessimism of the low-budget film. However, in opposition to the 1950s where the low-budget B-movie was the main representative of the science fiction film, and echoed the anxieties surrounding the Atomic Age, the twenty-first century is marked by the dominance of the blockbuster film in the SF genre, and its association with the techno-optimism of the Information Age. In the contemporary age of social media and intimate technologies, the different expressions of the techno-body are not so much associated with the perils of technology but with the expansive possibilities of the new digital world. Although the precautions against the abuses of technology are not entirely absent, but, as discussed, are embodied in the supervillain, still the dominant tone of these big-budget productions is the optimism surrounding the proper use of technoscience, exemplified in the superhero body. This explains why the majority of the cycle's films portray the technological body as a potential benefit for society, while at the same time they satisfy the desires of the audience and the demands of Conglomerate Hollywood.

4

The Alien Encounters Cycle: The Millennial Ambiguity of the Other

Narratives about alien encounters are considered among the most durable "parabolas" (Attebery and Hollinger 2013) of the genre. The narrative motif dates as back as 1898, the year when H. G. Wells's *The War of the Worlds* was first published. The novel can be considered the prototype of the alien invasion story and its enduring influence is evident in the numerous adaptations in a variety of media in the years following its first edition. Among the most known adaptations is the 1938 live CBS radio broadcast narrated and directed by Orson Welles, that infamously spread panic as the listeners believed that the events narrated were real (Booker 2001). The impact of the book is still visible, and the present corpus includes the 2005 *War of the Worlds*, directed by Steven Spielberg and adapted by Josh Friedman and David Koepp.

Although H. G. Wells's novel was intended to be a critique of Western imperialism, aiming to illustrate the consequences of colonialism, and its effects to the indigenous people (Mair 2002: 47), nevertheless the alien invasion story acquired different—and usually more conservative—connotations in its cinematic manifestations. The alien invasion narrative dominated the silver screen during the establishment of the SF genre in the 1950s, with classic films, such as *The Day the Earth Stood Still* (1951) and *Invasion of the Body Snatchers* (1956), among others. Although by that time the narrative formula was quite common—even outdated—in the literary genre (Jancovich 2004), it gained new prominence and a renewed generic life through its cinematic expressions. Importantly, the alien invasion cycle, far from being a critique to Western colonialism like Wells's archetypic story, served as a mediation of the post-Second World War political climate and specifically the Cold War paranoia of communist infiltration, usually reproducing dominant discourses about the "red menace" (Biskind 2004). However, many alien invasion films of the period also articulated anxieties about societal changes that were taking place inside the

US borders. As Marc Jancovich and Derek Johnston (2009) argue, certain films, such as *The Thing from Another World* (1951) and *Invasion of the Body Snatchers* (1956), rather than simply reflecting Cold War tensions, actually criticized the inner workings of American society, particularly the new elite of scientists and technocrats, and the expanding bureaucracy and social conformity.

In the following decades, the gradual disillusionment with Cold War politics that culminated in the Vietnam War was reflected in the changing representations of the alien invasion cycle. Shaped by these sociopolitical changes, along with other industrial and economic parameters, the menacing alien intrusion syntax of the 1950s was gradually infused with new affirmative semantics. Especially during the 1980s, the cycle was dominated by family SF films, such as *Close Encounters of the Third Kind* (1977), and *E.T. the Extraterrestrial* (1982) (Cornea 2007), where the alien figure stands as a symbol of human enlightenment and mediator of human affairs. As King and Krzywinska argue, these friendly aliens, in opposition to the hostile aliens of previous decades, seem to serve human interests. In particular, their representation as "warm, emotional and caring" appears to "make up for elements of family breakdown ... [and] the absence of the 'natural' father" that characterizes the fictional worlds of these films (King and Krzywinska 2000: 30). In the 1990s, the warm embrace of the alien gave way to a cool and detached irony and self-reflexivity, informed by the audience's familiarity with the particular generic formula. A number of self-reflexive SF films of the decade lampooned the 1950s alien invasion narratives, such as *Mars Attack* (1996) and *Men in Black* (1997), and played the formulaic invasion plots of previous decades for laughs. Yet, the classic tropes of the aggressive alien intruders are still operative as evident in the blockbuster hit *Independence Day* (1996). These conflicting representations from the 1980s onward still echo in the millennial cycle, which intermingles semantics, traits, and meanings from different time periods, creating ambiguous representations of the alien Other.

The alien encounters cycle includes the following thirty-five titles (17.1 percent of the total films): *Evolution* (2001), *Signs* (2002), the *Men in Black* films (2002, 2019), *Dreamcatcher* (2003), the *Alien Vs. Predator* films (2004, 2007), *The Predator* (2018), *War of the Worlds* (2005), the *Transformers* films (2007, 2009, 2011, 2014, 2017), *Bumblebee* (2018), *The Invasion* (2007), *The Day the Earth Stood Still* (2008), *District 9* (2009), *The Fourth Kind* (2009), *Skyline* (2010), *Battle: Los Angeles* (2011), *Super 8* (2011), *Cowboys & Aliens* (2011), *The Thing* (2011), *The Darkest Hour* (2011), *Battleship* (2012), the *Pacific Rim* films (2013, 2018), *The Host* (2013), *Dark Skies* (2013), *The World's End* (2013), *Earth to Echo*

(2014), *Arrival* (2016), *Independence Day: Resurgence* (2016), and *The 5th Wave* (2016). These narratives repeat the basic structure of the first semiotic square, although the main conflict is now centered on non-human and non-terrestrial species. That is, the present category includes films whose basic premise is the appearance of an extraterrestrial species on Earth. The cycle's discussion is organized into two sections. In the first section I examine a prominent pattern of the cycle as traced from the analysis of the surface structure, and concerns the Subject and its classification into two categories which I label the "common people" and the "experts." I discuss this pattern by focusing mainly on two films: *War of the Worlds* (2005) and *Pacific Rim* (2013). In the next section I examine another prevalent motif of the cycle, which I call the good/bad alien opposition, and concerns the representation of the alien Other. I analyze this motif through the prism of race, as exemplified mainly in the films *Independence Day: Resurgence* (2016) and *Transformers* (2007). The examination of racial themes in this discussion is not incidental, but is related to the fact that the main premise of the cycle, that is, the visitation/invasion of another non-human species in Earth, makes the themes of race and colonialism—as established already by *War of the Worlds* (1898)—rather prominent. Although racial issues are present in numerous SF films "as narrative subtext or implicit allegorical subject" (Nama 2008: 2), I argue that such themes are further pronounced in the alien encounters cycle. The second section concludes with the brief examination of *District 9* and *Arrival*, two films that move beyond the good/bad characterization of the alien, envisioning the human/alien relationship in more complicated ways.

Alien Encounters: The Common People and the Experts

A main trait that is discerned from the analysis of the cycle's surface structure is that the Subject can be classified into two categories. I label the first category "common people," and it refers to protagonists with no specialized knowledge or occupation regarding the aliens—usually a family or a group of friends that come face to face with the alien Other (e.g. *War of the Worlds*, *Signs*, *5th Wave*, *Invasion*, *Skyline*, *The Darkest Hour*, *Alien Vs Predator: Requiem*, *The Host*, *Dreamcatcher*, *Dark Skies*, *The Fourth Kind*, the *Transformers* films, *Super 8*, *Earth to Echo*, *Cowboys and Aliens*, and *The World's End*). The second group of Subjects comprises the "experts," that is, scientists, military personnel, or government agents who approach the alien Other from the position of expert knowledge. The experts seek to examine and learn from the alien, or, in more violent cases, destroy, profit, or otherwise manipulate it (e.g. *Arrival*, *District 9*, *Battle: Los Angeles*, *Battleship*, *Pacific Rim* films, *The Thing*, *Alien Vs. Predator*, *The Predator*, *Independence Day: Resurgence*, *Evolution*, the *Men in Black* films). Hence, while the common people approach the alien in a more emotive way, that is, in a way that revolves around emotions, positive or negative (fear, terror, compassion, etc.), the experts engage with alien otherness from a position of "knowledge/power" (Foucault 1972) that aims to a cognitive or physical access to the alien. In what follows, I explore further this pattern and its meaning, with a special emphasis on two films, one that features common people as protagonists (*War of the Worlds*) and the other focusing on experts (*Pacific Rim*). I choose these two films due to both their critical and economic success but also because *War of the Worlds*, as discussed above, is based on H. G. Wells's archetypic alien invasion story, and it is therefore interesting to examine how conventions are reconfigured in this millennial remake. *Pacific Rim* is also an illuminating example since it infuses new attributes to an established formula, while it also bears traits of the creatures cycle.

War of the Worlds is Spielberg's third film about alien visitations, along with *Close Encounters of the Third Kind* and *E.T. the Extra-Terrestrial*. However, in *War of the Worlds* the director follows a very different approach in tone, style, and themes. In opposition with the director's 1980s films on the subject, which were characterized by an oneiric atmosphere, and featured benign aliens helping human affairs, *War of the Worlds* tells the story of a hostile alien invasion presented in a dark and realistic style. The film follows divorced Ray Ferrier (Tom Cruise), an American dock worker, as he struggles to protect his two estranged children and reunite them with their mother when hostile extraterrestrials invade Earth. The focus on estranged families in the face of cosmic events is the main characteristic of both *Close Encounters of the Third Kind* and *E.T. the Extra-Terrestrial*, but here the story is much darker as it resonates with the post-9/11 sociopolitical climate. As critics in the popular press have noted (see Travers 2005; Bradshaw 2005), many scenes of the movie reverberate with the 9/11 attacks and their aftermath, from crowds fleeing from collapsing buildings, and images of a crashed plane, to the display of missing-persons photographs. Even the fact that the aliens do not arrive from the sky in spaceships, but emerge from the ground, having been hidden there a long time ago, invokes notions of terrorist sleeper cells that are activated to bring about destruction inside the United States. In this way, the film's tone is more closely associated with the

Cold War paranoia reflected in Byron Haskin's 1953 *War of the Worlds*, rather than the anti-colonialist themes of H. G. Wells's novel. However, in opposition to the 1953 film that mainly focused on how authorities, such as scientists and the military, handled the alien crisis, Spielberg focuses on the common people's reaction to unprecedented catastrophe.

With this shift in perspective, the film does not explore the purpose of the alien visitation, or how official authorities approach it, but instead addresses its effect on ordinary people. Therefore, issues of survival, the collapse of social order, and how interpersonal relationships are shaped in the face of unknown threats are the film's main focal points. Indeed, according to Spielberg, the film was about "Americans fleeing for their lives, being attacked for no reason, having no idea why they are being attacked and who is attacking them" (Today 2005). This description is fitting also for other films of the cycle whose Subject belongs to the common people category, such as *Signs*, *The 5th Wave*, *Invasion*, *The Host*, *Alien Vs Predator: Requiem*, and *Skyline*, which indeed feature everyday Americans trying to survive from threats that lie beyond their comprehension. In these films, the theme of social chaos and survival in a post-9/11 context becomes evident, while the alien is usually coded as an antisocial (and foreign) force that disrupts the everyday life of American people. These contemporary stories about urban paranoia and unknown dangers coming from outside the borders, advance dominant values, such as the importance of family (*War of the Worlds*, *Signs*) or the formation of the heterosexual couple (*5th Wave*, *The Host*, *Skyline*, and *The Darkest Hour*), echoing the family SF films of the 1980s, albeit in a darker tone. Therefore, the films seem to suggest that the only way to deal with the alien threat is to uphold and advance the dominant ideologies of the American society.

The absence of experts as protagonists also indicates, in certain instances, a mistrust toward the official authorities, echoing the skepticism of American people about the US government's controversial response in the 9/11 attacks, as encapsulated in Michael Moore's *Fahrenheit 9/11*. As discussed above, this is not a new characteristic of the alien invasion narratives, since many 1950s SF films (e.g., *Invasion of the Body Snatchers* [1956], *The Thing from Another World* [1951]) display such a suspicion toward authorities and the new "elite of experts" (Jancovich 2004: 327). Furthermore, the public's distrust of the government characterizes American society since the post–Second World War climate of McCarthyism and the Cold War (Hodges 2009: 232), and this stance is even more pronounced in the subject of alien encounters, which has always been surrounded by conspiracy theories, as encapsulated in the iconic television series *The X-Files* (FOX, 1993–2002 and 2016–18). Such cultural attitudes are reflected in many films of the cycle whose protagonists are common people, either through the absence of authorities (*Signs*, *The Host*, *Skyline*) or even through the aliens' disguise as the official representatives of the US government. For example, in *The 5th Wave* the aliens, which are referred to as the Others, possess human bodies (à la *Invasion of the Body Snatchers*) while killing the rest of the population. It is telling, however, that the aliens take mainly the form of US military officials who function as the film's main antagonists (the Enemy), deceiving the rest of the Americans in order to implement their nefarious plans. Likewise, in *Invasion*, which is an actual remake of *Invasion of the Body Snatchers*, the main Enemy is the director of the Centers for Disease Control and Prevention (CDC), that is, another official representative of the US government who is taken over by the aliens, and tries to force the protagonist to become one of them.

In other films, the mistrust of official authorities takes more explicit forms. In *Alien Vs Predator: Requiem*, the people of Gunnison, Colorado, wait for help from the government as their city is ravaged by several Xenomorphs. However, instead of a rescue mission, the military jets that arrive execute a tactical nuclear strike that levels the entire city. In a similar vein, *Dreamcatcher* focuses on four friends, who encounter a parasitic alien species that begins to spread near an isolated village in Maine. In order to contain the alien infestation, the US military plans to bombard the quarantined area, without considering the loss of human lives. The indifference of the US government, and/or its secretive actions, is evident even in films where the aliens are benevolent, such as *Super 8* and *Earth to Echo*. *Super 8* is director J. J. Abrams's nostalgic tribute to the 1980s SF films, such as *E.T. the Extraterrestrial* and *Close Encounters of the Third Kind*, and tells the story of a group of young teenagers whose lives are changed when they discover an alien presence in their suburban town in Ohio. Again, the film's main antagonist is US Air Force members, who not only covertly experimented upon the alien whose ship crash-landed in the town decades ago but also do not hesitate to sacrifice human lives in order to preserve the secret operations. On a similar note, the teenage protagonists of *Earth to Echo* help an alien creature escape from the US government's captivity, revealing in the process that their town's planned evacuation due to the construction of a new highway was actually the government's cover to unearth the alien's spaceship, which lies beneath the town. However, this motif is not present in all films whose protagonists are common people. For example, The *Transformers* film series, which are further discussed below, hold a more intermediate position. Although some doubts are raised about the morality of high-ranking officials as individuals, nevertheless the films reassert the overall efficiency of official institutions, thus promoting US exceptionalism.

In films where the protagonists belong to the expert category, the different approach that aims at the knowledge/exploitation/control or destruction of the alien results in another motif: the similarity between the expert and alien. This observation is reminiscent of Susan Sontag's 1965 influential article "The Imagination of Disaster," where the author discusses the 1950s SF films. Sontag observes how in these films "certain characteristics of the dehumanized invaders, modulated and disguised—such as the ascendancy of reason over feelings, the idealization of teamwork and the consensus creating activities of science, a marked degree of moral simplification—are precisely traits of the savior-scientists." Although not all the millennial films present the aliens as "dehumanized invaders" (Sontag 1965: 48), in many instances an analogy is created between the alien and the expert, as discussed below.

Pacific Rim is an exemplary case of how Conglomerate Hollywood creates a franchise from a high-concept film, and is also an interesting generic example. *Pacific Rim* is presented as an alien invasion story, but it shares many characteristics with the creatures cycle, mainly the monster-like aliens, aptly called Kaijus (strange beast in Japanese). In fact, the film's director, Guillermo Del Toro, stated that he wanted *Pacific Rim* to be "a loving poem to kaiju and mecha genre" (Lambie 2013). Indeed, the film invokes the tradition of Japanese giant monster films, such as *Godzilla* (1954), *Rodan* (1956), and *Ghidorah, the Three-Headed Monster* (1964), among others, as well as the mecha genre, that is, a subgenre of science fiction that feature giant robots controlled by humans, and which started in Japanese anime and manga (e.g., *Neon Genesis Evangelion* [TV Tokyo 1995–6]). However, the film does not reference a particular movie monster or mecha from established media texts, since Del Toro aimed for an original look for the film's creatures (Lambie 2013). Despite these allusions to giant monster films, the story is presented as an alien invasion; that is, the creatures featured in the film are not the result of humanity's technoscientific activities, but are described as a different species.[1] Therefore, the film broadens the "horizon of expectations" (Neale 2012: 189) related to the cycle, combining traits and narrative structures from both the creature film and the alien encounters cycle.

Pacific Rim expands the cycle's iconography and expectations by presenting the arrival of the aliens not from the sky, but from the Earth's core, emerging from an interdimensional portal called "The Breach" at the bottom of the Pacific Ocean. This trait also recalls Spielberg's *War of the Worlds*, where in a similar way the alien machines emerged from the ground. But in opposition with the latter film where common people struggle to survive the alien threat, in *Pacific Rim* the experts of humanity build and handle Kaiju-sized massive robots called the Jaegers. The emergence of the aliens from inside the Earth also suggests an unexpected proximity with the alien Other, or rather the alien within. Protagonist Raleigh Becket (Charlie Hunnam) a Jaeger pilot for Pan Pacific Defense Corps, affirms this similarity between the alien Kaijus and the human-created Jaegers in the film's introductory voice-over narration: "to fight monsters we created monsters of our own." Not only does the expert protagonist acquire the same size and power as the alien invader but also shares a similar form of consciousness. In order to pilot the Jaeger, two humans are linked mentally in a process called drifting, in order to share the machine's neuronal load. The two humans access each other memories and function as a single organism during the Jaeger's navigation. However, this shared consciousness, acquired through the Jaegers, is precisely the same trait that characterizes the Kaijus, since—as we learn from the film's scientist, Dr. Newton Geiszler (Charlie Day)—their brains are connected like a hive mind, that is, a collective consciousness.

Likewise, in other films of the cycle where the protagonists belong to the expert category, human experts and alien visitors have many common attributes. Militaristic SF films *Battle: Los Angeles* and *Battleship* present the alien invasion as a foreign invader that trespasses the US borders and destroys the American way of life, thus reproducing the most conservative elements of the 1950s invasion films, and promoting hegemonic discourses about US exceptionality. The films' expert protagonists, a US Marine Corps Staff Sergeant and a United States Navy officer, respectively, exhibit the same militaristic fervor and dedication in exterminating the alien invaders—as the aliens in annihilating humanity. In *The Thing* (2011), which is prequel to John Carpenter's 1982 film of the same title, and the third film based on the 1938 novella "Who Goes There?" by John W. Campbell, the expert protagonist Kate (Mary Elizabeth Winstead), a paleontologist, exhibits the same level of adaptability and cunningness as the alien creature. In *Alien vs. Predator* and *The Predator*, the protagonists—Alexa Woods (Sanaa Lathan), an experienced guide with a specialization in polar regions and US Army Ranger sniper Quinn McKenna (Boyd Holbrook), respectively—have impressive stamina and survival/fighting skills that match the aliens' powers. This also seems to be the case, in comic versions of the alien invasion narrative, such as the *Men in Black* films, and *Evolution*. The analogy between the expert protagonist and the alien becomes a literal similarity in *District 9*, a film that I further discuss below, where the expert protagonist after an accidental exposure to an alien fluid begins to transform into one of the extraterrestrials that have been stranded on Earth for over two decades. In *District 9* this human/alien similarity also raises issues of race, a theme which I discuss in the next section in relation to another motif traced in the cycle: the good/bad alien opposition.

The Good, The Bad, and the In-Between: Representation of the Alien and Race

Another central motif traced in the cycle is the good/bad alien, which complicates previous generic representations that usually portray the alien as fitting only one of these categories. With this pattern, the millennial cycle tries to circumvent the binary opposition between human and aliens, envisioning alternative relations between different species. However, this representation usually results in the displacement of the human/alien opposition in yet another binary dichotomy. This motif is present in the following sixteen films of the cycle: the two *Alien Vs. Predator* films, *The Predator*, *Independence Day: Resurgence*, the five *Transformers* films, *Bumblebee*, the two *Men in Black* films (*Men in Black II* and *Men in Black: International*), *The 5th Wave*, *The Host*, *Dreamcatcher*, and *Cowboys & Aliens*. In these films the protagonists' objective is to protect the world from alien menacing species and/or survive, with the only exception that this goal is achieved through the help of benevolent aliens that value humanity (or are simply not bothered with it). With this narrative differentiation, such films seemingly try to establish more complicated relations between humans and aliens. Yet, they ultimately illustrate the human/alien cooperation as a means for the preservation of humanity that remains otherwise unchanged from an amicable relation with the alien Other, while also reasserting hegemonic discourses about race. In what follows, I examine this pattern by focusing on two films: *Independence Day: Resurgence* and *Transformers*. I choose these two titles because they are among the highest-grossing films of the cycle, and therefore their racial discourses related to the good/bad alien opposition have reached a wide audience. Furthermore, *Independence Day: Resurgence* is the sequel of the 1996 *Independence Day*, which not only was a phenomenal economic success, but it also revisited the 1950s alien invasion narratives. On the other hand, *Transformers* is not the typical alien encounters story, but like *Pacific Rim* it is associated with the mecha subgenre. However, since the Transformers are presented as aliens, it is interesting to examine how the film negotiates this generic pattern. The discussion concludes with two films, *District 9* and *Arrival*, which follow more sophisticated techniques in bypassing the human/alien opposition.

As mentioned, *Independence Day* (1996), nostalgically alluded to the alien invasion B-movies of the 1950s, employing their conventions in a big-budget production. In opposition, the sequel, which is also directed by Roland Emmerich, strictly adheres to the mythology of the first film. However, it still introduces some new twists, specifically the malevolent/benevolent alien that I argue is a main semantic trait of the twenty-first-century cycle. This pattern facilitates also the purposes of Conglomerate Hollywood, since it introduces new elements that can be exploited in further sequels (e.g. other alien races, intergalactic wars). Yet, I believe that the good/bad alien opposition is also significant because it accentuates the racial themes that underpin the cycle. The film takes place twenty years after the events of the first film, and—as a voice-over narration explains to the viewers—during this period the world has been united, and witnessed no armed conflict. The United Nations has formed Earth Space Defense (ESD), an international military defense and research organization, which has established a defense station in moon in order to track alien activity and prevent other attacks. The action begins when a spherical alien spaceship approaching the moon is immediately destroyed, despite warnings against that action by David Levinson (Jeff Goldblum)—the scientific director of the Earth Space Defense, and the person who secured humanity's win in the first film—due to the dissimilarity of the ship with the one that invaded Earth twenty years ago. Levinson manages to recover a large container of the ship from the wreckage site before his theory is confirmed. Soon after, a different and enormous spaceship destroys the moon base and Earth's defense systems, before landing over the Atlantic Ocean in order to extract Earth's molten core.

Although these hints of a second (and non-hostile) alien civilization are given from the start, it is only near the end of the film that they are explained. When the scientists open the container retrieved from the wreckage, a floating white sphere is released. After it is accidentally activated, this sphere turns out to be a virtual intelligence, who is the sole survivor of a highly advanced alien species, which have discarded their biological existence and have taken on a virtual form.

The sphere is proven to be benevolent since its purpose is to protect the Earth and other worlds from the hostile alien species, the Harvesters. At first glance, the introduction of this twist seems to complicate the alien/human opposition established in the original film but also in the majority of alien invasion films of previous decades. Since not all aliens are represented as evil conquerors, the film seems to embrace otherness and accept post-anthropocentric positions that challenge human superiority (the virtual alien species is more advanced than the human species). Such complications were absent from the first film, indicating a shift in generic conventions and representations throughout the years. However, on a closer look we can discern that the good/bad alien opposition actually displaces the human/alien dichotomy, thus re-inscribing hierarchical binaries, especially those related with race. For example, it is interesting to note that the benevolent alien species is represented through a white sphere; thus, the color white is associated with advanced intelligence and goodness. In opposition, the dark surfaces and interiors of the massive spaceship of the Harvesters connote evil and destruction. Furthermore, the sphere is voiced by white actress Jenna Purdy, thus emphasizing even more the whiteness of the superior species. Therefore, the hierarchical opposition of white vs. Black and its racial undertones—evident in many classic SF films, such as *Star Wars* (1977) (Nama 2008: 28)—is once again established, reproducing hegemonic discourses about race. In addition, the benign virtual intelligence at first characterizes humans as a primitive species. However, by the film's end humans succeed in destroying the Harvester Queen, thus proving their ingenuity and bravery. At the end, the sphere recognizes that humans are a remarkable species after all, and can lead the resistance against the Harvesters, thus confirming once again human (and white) superiority.

These racial hierarchies are also mapped to other features of the alien body. The Harvesters are portrayed as a hive mind, a swarm intelligence, coordinated by a Queen. The alien hive mind is a common trope of the genre, from the *Star Trek* series to the *Matrix* trilogy, and is also evident in the millennial cycle—from *Pacific Rim*, discussed above, to *Battle: Los Angeles*, *Transformers: Revenge of the Fallen*, *The Day the Earth Stood Still*, and even the comedy *The World's End*. The hive mind is not only an SF convention but also a technological and cultural conception that illuminates the understanding of cognition as a distributed communication between mini-agents (Parikka 2010: xii) that fundamentally contradicts the humanist ideal of the autonomous, cogitating mind as the quintessential human characteristic. However, in the SF film, and the cycle under examination more specifically, this network intelligence is usually portrayed as having less emancipatory potentials. The Harvesters are represented as an impersonal swarm, which is characterized by lack of identity, free will, and speech, that is, the basic characteristics of the liberal humanist subject, and thus they are likened to animals. This is also confirmed by the film's director who stated that the Harvesters "are more like bees," with a hive mentality, "and when they arrive it's more like a natural disaster than an invasion" (Powell 2016). The Harvesters signify animalistic violence, invoking racial discourses that connect the black body with the animal. Thus, the Harvester's black collective organization contradicts the liberal humanist ideal of autonomous, free, and (white) agents. Furthermore, the film represents the Harvester Queen through her biomechanical suit, which has an enormous size, insectoid shape, long tentacles, and dark skin, thus further associating animality and (female) carnality with blackness (see Figure 4.1). In opposition, the benevolent alien, which is disembodied and coded in white (and speaks eloquently in English), is perfectly aligned with liberal, humanist discourses, exemplifying the superiority of the mind over the body, human over animal, and white over black.

The good/bad alien opposition is also central in the *Transformers* film series. The first five films are directed by Michael Bay, with Steven Spielberg serving as executive producer, and are based on the Japanese–American media franchise of

Figures 4.1–4.4 Representation of the alien and race in *Independence Day: Resurgence* directed by Roland Emmerich© 20th Century Fox 2016. *Transformers* directed by Michael Bay© DreamWorks SKG 2007. *District 9* directed by Neill Blomkamp© Sony Pictures Entertainment 2009. *Arrival* directed by Denis Villeneuve© Paramount Pictures 2016. All rights reserved.

the same name. The *Transformers* franchise is one of the highest-grossing media franchises of all time, with the six films (including the prequel *Bumblebee*) garnering the impressive amount of $4.84 billion at the global box office. In accordance with the targeted audiences of Conglomerate Hollywood, the films benefited mostly from international sales, with $3.28 billion of its total box office coming from markets outside the United States and Canada (Whitten 2021). Despite the global audiences and staggering profits, the films had a negative reception (with the exception of *Bumblebee*), with the press criticizing the racist and sexist undertones of most films (see Travers 2009; Charity 2011), and the viewers rating the films with mainly low scores (see Rotten Tomatoes n.d.b.). Although the films reproduce many racial and gender stereotypes, here I want to focus mainly on how these racial discourses are mapped onto the good/bad alien dichotomy.

In the first installment, *Transformers* (2007), the narrative revolves around Sam Witwicky (Shia LaBeouf), a teenager who becomes instrumental in a war between the Autobots and Decepticons, two opposing alien factions from the planet Cybetron. These aliens are represented as non-biological beings that resemble huge robots, which can transform into other forms, such as vehicles and animals, therefore infusing the iconography of the alien with traits from the mecha subgenre. Nevertheless, they are represented as extraterrestrials who arrive on Earth in order to retrieve an artifact called the AllSpark, which has world-building abilities. The benevolent Autobots want the AllSpark in order to rebuild their planet and end the war, while the Decepticons want to use it to conquer Earth. The film's racial discourses in relation to the good/evil alien opposition are evident from the start, and are specifically traced in the locations associated with the evil aliens, the Decepticons. The first appearance of the Decepticons is in Qatar, Middle East, where the United States maintains a military base. Two Decepticons, Blackout and Scorponok, attack the US base, in order to hack into their military network and trace the AllSpark. Interestingly, Scorponock has the form of a mechanical scorpion, which comes out from the desert and attacks the US soldiers (see Figure 4.2). Such images invoke orientalist and colonialist discoursers, where the East is described as a place of threat and unknown dangers, that is, as the opposing image of the West (Said 2003). From this first appearance, the hostile alien is represented not only as located in the East and coming from the desert but also as an enemy attacking the US military. The racial and colonialist discourses continue in an ensuing battle between the Decepticons and the US Army that takes place in a nearby village. The US military forces are presented as the only protectors of the local people from an enemy that comes from within their own territory, thus invoking the US government's rhetoric about the alleged liberation of the Iraqi people from their local oppressors when the US and Coalition forces began military operations in Iraq in 2003.

The association of the evil aliens with non-Western locations is continued in the subsequent installments. In *Revenge of the Fallen* (2009) we learn that the first Decepticon, known as the Fallen, tried to destroy Earth in the year 17000 BCE, by creating a star-absorbing machine called Sun Harvester in the location where thousands of years later the great pyramids of Egypt would be built. The Fallen did not manage to activate the machine as he was stopped by other members of his species. In the present, the Fallen, with the help of other Decepticons, tries once more to activate the Sun Harvester, but they are defeated by the protagonist Sam, the Autobots, and the US military in an extended battle in the Giza Pyramid Complex. This association between non-Western locations and the evil aliens is continued and in the next installments. For example, Hong Kong is the site where the Decepticons begin their plans for global dominance in the *Age of Extinction* (2011). Despite the fact that the use of such exotic locations is a common tactic in big-budget productions in order to make the movie more appealing and attract global audiences, the way that the good/alien opposition is attached to specific geographic locations reasserts racial stereotypes and colonialist discourses. Furthermore, the use of the oriental to connote otherness has a long tradition in the SF film, and can be traced back to Méliès's work (Cornea 2007: 193). However, I argue that the good/alien opposition evident in the millennial SF films specifically relates such non-Western imagery with the evil aliens, while the good aliens remain aligned with human, white, and US supremacy.

Although the good/bad alien opposition is a common motif of the cycle employed to circumvent the human/alien dichotomy, the pattern usually results in the creation of other hierarchical binaries, and the reproduction of hegemonic discourses surrounding race. Other films, such as *District 9*, *Arrival*, *Super 8*, and *Earth to Echo*, try to achieve the human/alien reconciliation without using this pattern. While the latter two, as discussed above, use the motif of friendly aliens to resolve familial issues, *District 9* and *Arrival* avoid such Manichean characterizations of the aliens altogether. The latter films attempt to embrace otherness by disrupting the human/alien opposition with different techniques, while still negotiating racial and colonialist discourses in ambiguous ways. Both *District 9* and *Arrival* have medium budgets ($30 million and $40 million, respectively), in opposition with the big-budget films discussed above; nevertheless, they were successful in the box office, garnering $210.8 million and $203.4 million respectively. Furthermore, these films are the most artistically recognized titles of the cycle, receiving acclaim from critics and garnering numerous awards and nominations. *District 9* received four Academy Awards nominations (including Best Picture and Best Adapted Screenplay), while *Arrival* gathered eight Academy Awards nominations (including Best Picture, Best Director, and Best Adapted Screenplay). Therefore, it is interesting to explore how these films negotiate the human/alien opposition, and how they articulate discourses about race and colonialism.

District 9 is the first feature film of South African director Neill Blomkamp, and a co-production of New Zealand, the United States, and South Africa. The film was designed as an independent production, but the involvement of Peter Jackson as a producer, its international distribution by Sony, and its effective marketing can be accounted for the film's financial success and its planned sequelization (Sharf 2021). *District 9* begins with a documentary-style cinematography that features fictional interviews and news footage, which present the film's premise: twenty years ago, an alien spaceship appeared over Johannesburg, South Africa, and stayed there ever since. Upon the spaceship there was a population of debilitated insectoid aliens, who were subsequently confined to a resettlement camp, called District 9. In the present, the government decides to hire private company Multi-National United (MNU), the country's largest weapons manufacturer, in order to relocate the aliens to another camp. Wikus van der Merwe (Sharlito Copley), a bureaucrat of the MNU, is assigned as the head of the relocation process, during which he accidentally comes in contact with an extraterrestrial fluid and begins slowly to transform into an alien. In his effort to reverse this situation he forms an alliance with one of the confined aliens, Christopher Johnson (Jason Cope), who plans to escape from Earth with his son. The film clearly alludes to the historical events of the apartheid era in South Africa, during which the country was racially segregated and thousands of Black people were forcibly relocated to other areas.

Racial themes are central in *District 9* and are explicitly mapped onto the alien body. The aliens in District 9 clearly stand in for the racial Others, making apparent the racial discourses, which in other films of the cycle remain hidden. On this view, it is interesting to see how the appearance of the aliens is rendered. The aliens, which are called prawns pejoratively, combine an anthropomorphic shape with crustacean features and an exoskeleton (see Figure 4.3). The representation of the alien as a combination of different taxonomic categories, such as human, animal, and machine, has a long history in the SF film, with *Alien* providing the most influential iconography of the alien as a hybrid organism. Such hybrid morphology is intended to evoke repulsion, but in *District 9* the representation of the alien induces feelings of empathy. According to Blomkamp such feelings are facilitated by the aliens' anthropomorphic shape: "I wanted them to be insects, but I wanted them to be bipedal. And unfortunately, they had to be human-esque because our psychology doesn't allow us to really empathize with something unless it has a face and an anthropomorphic shape" (Oldham 2009). Therefore, in order to shape a sympathetic identification with the racially coded Other, the film neither portrays cute creatures (e.g. *Super 8*, *Earth to Echo*), nor presents the aliens in a human form (e.g. *The Day the Earth Stood Still*, *The Host*) but opts for a more intermediate representation that enables shifting responses from the viewers. This in-betweenness is further stressed with the transformation of Wikus into an alien. This process of hybridization facilitates a change of perspective through the eyes of the protagonist who is transformed from a white, middle-class, xenophobic man, into a racially coded alien. Using these techniques, the film manages to tackle discourses surrounding race, while also bridging the human/alien opposition.

The human/alien opposition is also negotiated differently in *Arrival*. Based on the 1998 novella "Story of Your Life" by awarded SF author Ted Chiang, the film is directed by Denis Villeneuve and written by Eric Heisserer. Independently produced, but distributed by Paramount pictures in the United States and Sony Pictures in other territories, the film can be described as a "quality" Hollywood film (King 2020), due to combination of generic conventions with art cinema traits, such as slow pace, narrative complexity, and esoteric themes. The film follows Dr. Louise Banks (Amy Adams), a professor of linguistics enlisted by the US Army to decode the language of an alien species that mysteriously arrived on Earth, causing global tension. The aliens have arrived in twelve gigantic pebble-shaped ships, scattered across the Earth (we are informed the ships' landing spots include, among others, Russia, China, Pakistan, and Sudan, besides the United States). The film's main focal point is Luise's acquisition of precognition due to her gradual comprehension of the alien language that allows her to access future memories of her daughter who is not yet born and who will die from a terminal illness. Nevertheless, this ability enables her, in a classic Hollywood mode, to save the world, by preventing China from starting a war with the alien race.

Although this geopolitical tension is played out in the background, nevertheless racial and colonialist themes are still manifested in subtle ways in relation to the alien body.

The representation of the aliens in *Arrival* combines common generic traits with certain novelties, thus expanding the viewer's horizon of expectations. Dubbed heptapods due to their seven legs, the aliens resemble gigantic squids and communicate through intricate circular symbols, which are created by a black gas their limbs emit (see Figure 4.4). Such representation of the alien inspired by the morphology of Earth's invertebrate animals, from snails and octopuses to insects, spiders, and worms, is not something new to the genre, as evident also from the above discussion (e.g., the tentacled alien Queen in *Independence Day: Resurgence*, the crustacean-like aliens in *District 9*). However, this imagery is used mainly to provoke feelings of repulsion. In opposition, *Arrival* manages through its atmospheric mis-en-scène to diffuse these aliens with a magnificence and serenity, uncommon to such an iconography. The film neither anthropomorphize the aliens, nor does it aim at the viewer's identification with them (like *District 9*)—although they are portrayed in a sympathetic way (starting with the names given to them, Abbott and Costello). Yet the film reconciles the human/alien opposition mainly through the aliens' portrayal as an advanced and peaceful species from which humanity may learn and evolve. Indeed, as it is revealed later on the film, the purpose of their visitation is to offer humanity a tool/weapon—the Heptapod language. This alien language has a non-linear, atemporal structure, and its comprehension enables a new perception of time that will advance the human species so that in 3,000 years humanity will be able, in turn, to help the Heptapods.

These traits expand the iconography of the alien with new meanings and expectations, while racial and colonialist discourses are still invoked in an implicit way. The superiority of the alien species is primarily associated with white, American supremacy as it is Luise, the white American scientist, who understands their language, enabling the global peace and the advancement of humanity. In opposition, non-Western countries—mainly China, and, following its example, Russia, Pakistan, and Sudan—are the ones that misinterpret the aliens, decide to stop communicating with the other nations, and are ready to proceed to militaristic actions. Although the remaining nations follow their example, China and its followers are responsible for the termination of the global alliance and communication. Therefore, these non-Western countries are portrayed as aggressive, and unable to receive the aliens' gift, thus preventing humanity's evolution. Therefore, the film implicitly suggests that the Western civilization is the most advanced, and it is more suitable to further evolve the human species. Although the film portrays the US military as more than ready to follow the militaristic example of the other countries, it is through the American scientist that the US exceptionalism is re-confirmed. It is Luise, through her newly acquired "knowledge/power" (Foucault 1972) tools, who manages to reach China's General and convince him to stop the planned attack on the alien ship. Therefore, it is through this new form of soft power, and through the more refined visage of science, that a new Western hegemony is established, as the beacon of freedom, progress, and enlightenment that will lead the rest of the world.

The alien encounters remain a popular cycle of the genre, negotiating themes of otherness and race in the contemporary historical context, and portraying the alien Other in an ambiguous way. The cinematic alien encounters of the new millennium try to reconcile the human/alien opposition, and move beyond the usual hostile representation of the alien, established in previous generic examples. Although aggressive alien colonizers still appear in the majority of the cycle's films, the good/bad alien opposition is a prominent pattern of the millennial cycle that attempts to complicate the cycle's human/alien dichotomy. The representation of the alien takes a variety of forms—from animal-like hybrids, to monsters and machines, confirming the interactions between the terms of the first semiotic square, and the mutual exchange between the cycles that they generate. Furthermore, such interplay of established generic motifs and new elements renews the cycle's iconography and imbues the depiction of the alien with contradictory meanings. Again, the role of the industry must be accounted for such ambiguous representations, since the context of Conglomerate Hollywood dictates the reconciliation of dichotomies and, by extension, the cultural themes they evoke, while still affirming dominant discourses and preserving the status quo.

5

The Creatures Cycle: The Organic, the Mechanic, and the In-Between

The third and final cycle of the SF bodies is the creatures cycle. This category emerges from the interaction of the terms non-human and technology of the first semiotic square and describes the conflict between humans and their artificial creations, be that silicon- or carbon-based. The cycle is divided into two categories: the organic creatures (e.g., genetically modified animals) and the machinic creations (robots, androids, AIs). These artificial creations—the hybrid, technologically (re)created animals and the intelligent machines—may seem at first incompatible as the predominantly clean, smooth surfaces of the machinic creatures are quite different from the carnal excess of the (usually) colossal hybrid animals. While the different AIs and robots uncannily behave in a human-like manner, the genetically created animals stand as the opposite of human subjectivity. However, according to the proposed ontological taxonomy, the terms non-human and technology of the first semiotic square that formulate the cycle inform both types of artificial creatures—the organic and the mechanical. Hence, both categories can be examined together since the main theme that traverses the narratives is the relationship between humans and their technological creations, which constitutes the cycle's core.

As discussed in the previous chapters, these categories and taxonomies are not formulated in order to draw strict lines between the filmic narratives, which are in a constant exchange, but to facilitate and organize the genre's discussion. Indeed, both categories of the creatures share many traits with the previous two cycles. As will be analyzed below, the machinic creations have common elements with the techno-humans, while similar narrative patterns characterize both the alien encounters cycle and the organic creatures. However, there are also differences. In opposition to the merging of human body and technology that discerns the techno-human narratives, the creations depicted in this cycle are explicitly non-human; that is, they do not involve a human body. Furthermore, the major difference with the alien encounters cycle is that the central conflict revolves around humans and their own "monstrous" creations, rather than with other non-human species. Even if the creatures are not a product of human science per se (for example, the creatures in the *Mist and Godzilla*, as will be discussed below), they are often awakened or appear on Earth because of human technoscientific activity and experimentation. Therefore, while in the alien encounters narratives humans are not responsible for the appearance or existence of alien beings, they are directly accountable for the non-human entities in the creatures cycle—a narrative trait that differentiates the cycle's films.

The creatures cycle comprises a total of nineteen films (9.3 percent the corpus) which are grouped into two categories: the organic creatures and the machinic creations. The first category includes the following titles: the *Jurassic Park/Jurassic World* film series (2003, 2015, 2018), *The Mist* (2007), *Cloverfield* (2008), the *Godzilla* film series (2014, 2019), *Rise of the Planet of the Apes* (2011), *The Meg* (2018), and *Rampage* (2018). The second category consists of the following titles: *A. I. Artificial Intelligence* (2001), *Simone* (2002), the *Terminator* film series (2003, 2015, 2019),[1] *Stealth* (2005), *Her* (2013), *Transcendence* (2014), and *Chappie* (2015). The small number of films in this cycle is matched with equally low total grosses (the lowest in the corpus), which make the creatures the least popular cycle of the genre in the new millennium. Although there are certainly different industrial and economic reasons behind this fact, I would argue that there are also other ideological reasons. These films occupy an ambivalent position between the more accepted forms of otherness that the techno-humans and the aliens represent and seem to be the least related to a familiar ontology of the human form, which remains the ontological center of the popular SF film in the new millennium. While the techno-humans are closer to human ontology, and the aliens are visitors from other worlds for whom we bear no responsibility, the creatures sit uncannily between these positions. On the one hand, the creatures seem far removed from humanness. On the other hand—as humanity's creations—they are in a position of imminent proximity to the human. Therefore, issues of humanity's stance toward the artificially created Other are paramount in these narratives, and are discussed below in relation to the cycle's two categories.

The Organic Creatures: Confronting the Animal Other

The major influence of the first category are the monster movies of the golden age of cinematic SF, which include films such as *The Beast from 20,000 Fathoms* (1953), *Them!* (1954), and *Creature from the Black Lagoon* (1954), among others.

These films depict aberrant creations that emerge from human arrogance and scientific experimentation on the natural order. Sobchack (1987) situates the creature/monster movies of the 1950s between horror and science fiction and rightly argues that they combine traits from both genres. While the creature's actions usually arouse feelings of terror or shock to the audience, its existence is linked to a primary scientific rationale and is specifically associated with the era's growing nuclear anxiety. In other words, the creature features of the 1950s are often regarded as metaphors for the atomic bomb, inscribing the era's anxieties of a nuclear fallout (Telotte 2001: 98). Although these films may not delve into the workings of science per se and are more about disaster and destruction (Sontag 1965), "they are most definitely about science as a *social force*, as an institutional aspect of contemporary civilization" (Sobchack 1987: 90). Similar, the millennial creatures also offer warnings for the technological excesses of the twenty-first century, and human's hubris against nature, albeit in a different way. Specifically, I argue that these films negotiate contemporary environmental discourses about the catastrophic consequences of the technological civilization to the non-human world, by focusing especially on the human–animal relationship. Although the animal imagery informs also the other cycles of the first semiotic square, and indeed "animals … 'haunt' sf, always there in the shadows behind the alien or the android with whom we fantasise exchange" (Vint 2010: 12), I contend that the image of the animal becomes even more pronounced in the creatures cycle.

Furthermore, there are other differences between the 1950s creature features and the contemporary cycle. While the former were mostly low-budget productions, feeding the growing B-movies market of the era (Cornea 2007), the contemporary creature films are often designed as blockbusters—the pinnacle of Conglomerate Hollywood's production. A brief look at our corpus corroborates this observation. From the ten movies examined in this category only two films (*Mist* and *Cloverfield*) have medium to low budgets ($18 million and $25 million respectively). In addition, these mainly big-budget productions employ the latest cinematic technologies and digital effects to render their monsters not only generically believable but also a site of cinematic spectacle. Therefore, the ecological discourses these films seem to articulate are contradicted with the films' production context, which demands a similar technological excess and exploitative capitalistic practices that the films' content criticize.

These contradictory discourses are also registered on the surface structure of the cycle where in some cases (e.g., *Jurassic World*, the *Godzilla* series, *Rampage*) both roles of Helper/Enemy are occupied by a creature, thus recalling the good/bad alien opposition of the alien encounters cycle. As with the latter cycle, this multiplication of monsters, and the different roles assigned to them, is an effective way for even more spectacular scenes, and for an ongoing sequelization, with different creatures fighting each other. Furthermore, this motif also suggests that humanity's technological excesses that create or awaken different monsters may only be counteracted with an equally monstrous creation, with the human serving as the mediator of this battle. This narrative pattern illustrates the paradox that technology may actually be one of our most significant tools to deal with the uncontrollable and catastrophic side effects of technology, and that humanity's mastery of tools and nature can, at the end, resolve the side effects of technological progress. Therefore, these films criticize humanity's dominance over the non-human world, only to reaffirm its centrality and superiority. This anthropocentricism is also reinforced by the fact that the Subject in the majority of these narratives is a human, with only exception the film *Rise of Planet of the Apes*, where the protagonist is Ceasar (Andy Serkis), a chimpanzee. In what follows, I explore both the motif of the creature being both Helper and Enemy, and what is differentiated when the Subject of the surface structure is not human. This motif is examined through the prism of the human–animal relationship, which I argue is a central thematic concern of this category. For that reason, the following discussion centers mainly on two films, *Jurassic World* and *Rise of the Planet of the Apes*, due to not only their economical and critical successes but also because they are sequels/reboots of some of the most influential SF films, namely *Jurassic Park* (1993) and the *Planet of the Apes* original film series (1968, 1970, 1971, 1972, 1973). The ensuing discussion also incorporates brief examples from other films, and closes with the examination of the two low-budget films of this category (*Cloverfield* and *The Mist*) in relation to another motif, which is common in both the creatures cycle and the alien encounters cycle—the common people vs. experts protagonists.

Jurassic World is the fourth installment of the iconic *Jurassic Park* film series. Directed by Colin Trevorrow, and written by Rick Jaffa, Amanda Silver, Derek Connolly, and Trevorrow, the film was a huge box-office success, grossing $1.6 billion, thus becoming the eighth highest-grossing films of all time (and the fifth most profitable film of the corpus). In this way, the film follows the path of *Jurassic Park* (1993), which at the time of its release broke all box-office records, upgrading the 1950s formula of the creature-feature into the status of the blockbuster. *Jurassic Park* was also a benchmark for the development of digital photorealistic effects, with the film's CGI-rendered dinosaurs creating a new level of verisimilitude, and shaping a new "aesthetic realism" (Buckland 1999) that encompasses digital animation and live action. Although *Jurassic World* is not as pioneering as the first film of the series, it still negotiates the human–animal relationship, and technological capitalism's indifference to the balance of the ecosystem, while also tackling familial issues at the same time. A reason for this thematic affinity is the influence of Steven Spielberg, who directed the first two films of the franchise, and served also as an executive producer in *Jurassic World*. The film takes place twenty-two years after the events of *Jurassic Park* on the same fictional island of Isla Nublar, where a functional theme park of cloned dinosaurs has operated for years. Claire (Bryce Dallas Howard), the park's operation manager, is solely devoted to her corporate duties, but is estranged from her two nephews who visit the park. When a transgenic dinosaur, dubbed Indominus Rex, escapes from its enclosure and wreaks havoc to the park, Claire must protect her nephews, with the help of Owen (Chris Pratt), a navy veteran and Velociraptor trainer.

The film explores the human–animal relationship and negotiates the current environmental discourses through the motif of the creature as both Helper and Enemy. Indominus Rex, which is the film's main antagonist (Enemy), represents the technological and capitalistic excesses of contemporary Western culture, since it is the genetic hybrid of different species, created in the laboratory in order to serve as the latest attraction of the park. Claire, who embodies the same corporate values, presents the new "asset" to possible investors by saying, "no one is impressed by a dinosaur anymore," and adding later on that "consumers want them [the dinosaurs] bigger, louder, more teeth." This consumerist ethos, coupled with the latest technological advancements, is also the driving force of contemporary Western capitalism, which considers non-human animals and nature as a mere source for human exploitation. On the surface, the film denounces this stance, by having Indominus Rex breaking free from her captivity, and causing disaster in her way, echoing the 1970s "revenge of nature" narratives like Spielberg's other iconic film, *Jaws* (1975) (Rust and Soles 2014). The film also raises issues of animal rights by depicting Indominus Rex as a monstrous creation not because of her nature, but due to her captivity and raising in isolation. Indeed, Trevorrow has cited *Blackfish* (2013) as an influence of the film—a documentary which castigates the cruel conditions in which animals live in marine parks (Yahr 2015). These discourses are further stressed by the fact that Indominus Rex cannot be confronted by humans and their guns; thus, the film challenges the omnipotence of the capitalistic-militaristic culture. The only thing that can stop the Indominus Rex is another natural force, namely an attack from the park's Velociraptors and Tyrannosaurus Rex, which thus function as the Helpers in the film's narrative structure.

However, this seemingly natural force, at close examination, proves to be something different, since the dinosaurs' fight is well coordinated by the human protagonists. In other words, it is Claire who leads the Tyrannosaurus Rex into the battle against the Indominus Rex, and Owen who turns the Velociraptors against the "unnatural" creation. Owen is represented throughout the film as caring about the Velociraptors, recognizing their intelligence and feelings. For example, he states that he doesn't control the Velociraptors, but has a relationship with them. However, this relationship is clearly a hierarchical one, as confirmed by Owen when he describes himself as the alpha of the Velociraptors team. After the Velociraptors follow a stronger alpha, the Indominus Rex, Owen manages to gain their trust and loyalty again, making them confront Indominus Rex. Thus, the film reasserts humans' superior intelligence and mastery of nature. Furthermore, in this scene Owen manages to weaponize the animals, turning them into a tool/technology for the benefits of humanity. In this way, he partly implements the plans of Vic Hoskins (Vincent D'Onofrio), the head of the park's security, who wants to use the Velociraptors as battlefield soldiers. Although Owen is opposed to this idea and Vic's militaristic ideology, by the end of the film he manages to guide the animals in a battle that serves human interests, thus proving—albeit unintentionally—the utility of Vic's militaristic plans. Hence, the function of the creature as a Helper, rather than suggesting humanity's interdependence with other non-human species, actually reinforces ideologies of human exceptionalism, and the faith that anthropocentric applications of technoscience—albeit in a kinder visage—can still resolve humanity's technological misuses.

In other films of this category the motif of the creature as both Enemy and Helper is used in similar ways. In *Godzilla*—the 2014 addition in the iconic franchise of the Japanese studio Toho—the eponymous creature becomes the unlikely helper of humanity when two other giant creatures, dubbed MUTOs (Massive Unidentified Terrestrial Organism), emerge from giant spores after fifteen years of incubation. Although these monsters are not created by humans, in the way that the dinosaurs in *Jurassic World* are made, they are linked with human technoscientific activity, as the MUTOs are drawn by and feed from nuclear energy, and Godzilla responds to their awakening. Furthermore, despite the fact that Godzilla is not linked with a specific animal (like the dinosaurs), it clearly represents the non-human world, including the animal kingdom, that confronts the MUTOs, which embody the destructive consequences of human technoscientific activity—specifically the dangers of nuclear energy. However, this nature vs. technology opposition is resolved once again through an anthropocentric perspective. That is, Godzilla functions in a similar way as the Velociraptors in *Jurassic World*, that is, as a dormant tool/weapon for humanity that conveniently awakens when humanity has overstepped the limits of technoscience, thus solving its problems. In *Rampage* the role of humanity's helper is assumed by an albino gorilla, named George (Jason Liles), who grows into a colossal size after his accidental exposure into a human-made pathogen. George has been raised and trained by primatologist Davis Okoye (Dwayne Johnson), who has saved him from the poachers that killed his mother. When other two animals, a wolf and a crocodile, also acquire a monstrous size after contact with the pathogen, a battle ensues between them, with Davis serving as the human mediator. Guided by Davis, George serves as a tool for the human interests, confronting and killing the two wilder (and uncontrollable by any human) animals. Despite the fact that the film critiques the corporate greed embodied in the owners of Energyne—the gene-manipulation company that has created the pathogen—human exceptionalism triumphs through the facade of human–animal collaboration. The motif of the creature as Helper and Enemy is thus deployed again with an anthropocentric perspective, something that seems as inevitable when the Subject of the film's narrative structure is a human. In what follows, I examine how such perspective may change when the role of the Subject is assumed by a non-human by focusing on *Rise of the Planet of the Apes*.

Directed by Rupert Wyatt, and written by Rick Jaffa and Amanda Silver (writers also of *Jurassic World*), *Rise of the Planet of the Apes* (*Rise*) is the reboot of the *Planet of the Apes* series, functioning as an origin story for the new series of films. Released in 1968, the original film registered the era's nuclear anxieties and racial issues, presenting a dystopian future Earth where humanity has self-destructed and has been replaced by the apes as the new dominant species. In opposition, the 2011 reboot describes how the end of human civilization was brought about, inscribing current considerations about animal rights, and the risks and ethics of biotechnology and genetic engineering. The film follows a chimpanzee named Caesar, whose mother was the primary test subject in a biotech company developing a cure for Alzheimer. There, she was administered a new viral-based drug called ALZ-112, which increased her intelligence. After Caesar's mother is euthanized due to a seemingly unexplained violent incident, Caesar is saved and raised by the project's lead scientist Will Rodman (James

Franco), who realizes that he has inherited his mother's intelligence by being exposed to ALZ-112 in her womb. After many years' living with humans and developing extraordinary abilities, Caesar is forced to live in an ape sanctuary, due to an unfortunate event with a neighbor. There, he is abused by the two human keepers of the sanctuary, but also, he begins to raise his consciousness about the conditions of the apes' lives under human control. Forming bonds with other chimps, orangutans, and gorillas, Caesar decides to administer them an airborne version of the vaccine, thus increasing their intelligence and leading them in an escape. The revolted apes manage to confront the humans successfully and find shelter in the woods outside the city, where they form a society, while the ALZ-112 causes a deadly respiratory infection in humans that begins to spread across the globe.

Rise is not the typical creature feature, in the sense that *Godzilla* or *Jurassic World* are, but the film's surface structure is similar to the rest of the cycle's films. A technologically created/modified/mediated non-human being confronts a human community, disrupting the lives of both humans and non-humans involved in this conflict. However, there is a basic differentiation, which is responsible for the film's dissimilarity with the rest of the group: the creature does not assume the role of the Enemy and/or Helper, but instead becomes the main Subject of the narrative. As the narrative's Subject, the non-human being is also endowed with agency, a trait which is mostly absent in the other films where the function of the creature as Helper/Enemy is incidental or guided by humans. Furthermore, in *Rise* the Enemy is the human species, and although certain humans also function as Helpers (e.g., the scientist Will), this is a significant distinction from the other narratives. Thus, the film does not dramatize a sort of natural disaster (like *Jurassic World*), but a revolt of a non-human species against their human oppressors. These changes in the structure are responsible for the film's divergence from other creature films, enabling the adoption of a non-anthropocentric perspective. In this way, the film unsettles the strict human/animal boundary, presenting a story from the creature's perspective, and encouraging the viewer to identify with the non-humans. Surely, this identification may arise from the apes' anthropomorphism—which is greatly enhanced by the film's cutting-edge motion and performance capture technologies—as well as their acquisition of traits that are usually associated with humans, such as language and political organization (West III 2011). Yet, the positioning of a non-human in the role of the Subject is uncommon in this category, and therefore marks a significant change that confounds usual narrative hierarchies, thus facilitating different perspectives on the human–animal relationship.

Despite their differences, the above films are big-budget productions that employ conventions from the action/adventure genre to enact stories about creatures that unsettle the non-human world. In opposition, the two low-budget films of the category, *The Mist* and *Cloverfield*, mainly draw upon the conventions of the horror genre, and therefore they are characterized by a distinctive tone and style, and a notably pessimistic ending (in both films the protagonists/co-protagonists perish). A result of this generic mixing is that the monsters in these films are never clearly depicted, following the tradition of the horror genre where the threat always lurks in the shadows—a trait which in the SF/horror tradition is exemplified in *Alien*. Therefore, in contradiction to the big-budget films, these creatures are not displayed as the latest cinematic technologies in order to provoke a sense of awe and wonder (Pierson 2002), but remain mostly hidden, their figures slightly suggested, thus inducing fear in the viewer. This aesthetic choice is also connected to the fact that the Subject in these narratives are ordinary people who experience the extraordinary events from a limited perspective. This observation recalls the motif of common people vs. experts protagonists in the alien encounters cycle. Similar to the respective films of the latter cycle, the ordinary protagonists in *The Mist* and *Cloverfield* are unable to comprehend the bizarre events, and they just struggle to survive without knowing the nature of the threat. Especially in *Cloverfield*, this obscurity is further stressed with the restricted perspective offered by the film's found-footage style. According to *Cloverfield*'s director, Matt Reeves, this style was not only intended as a comment to the contemporary fascination with recording and disseminating personal videos in the social media but also was an allusion to the 9/11 attacks' footage, which was recorded by eye witnesses and circulated on the internet (Dobbs 2009). Importantly, this handheld camera style conveys a subjective and therefore partial point of view of the creatures' attack.

As expected, in these films the nature and origins of the creatures are not clearly explained, but only slightly suggested. In *The Mist*, different characters speculate about the causes of the mist that has swallowed their small town and trapped them in a supermarket, as well as the nature of the creatures lurking within it. Only near the end of the film it is revealed that this phenomenon is the result of a covert US military-scientific experiment that opened a portal into another dimension from which the creatures arrived on Earth. The film's creatures, when glimpsed through the mist and shadows, resemble giant insects or prehistoric reptiles. Despite the fact that their origins are described as alien, their appearance is clearly not portrayed as a planned alien invasion (like *Pacific Rim*), but more closely suggests a tampering with the natural world that results in catastrophic consequences. Thus, the creatures' obscure description and depiction are still influenced by animal imagery, invoking in an implicit way discourses about humans' relationship with the non-human world. Similarly, in *Cloverfield* there is no explanation for the appearance of the creature, an ellipsis that reinforces the film's partial and subjective point of view. The origins of the monster are revealed only in *Cloverfield*'s viral marketing, which is one of the film's "paratexts," and therefore can illuminate its meaning (Genette and Mclean 1991). According to these paratexts, the creature's origins are located again in the natural world—specifically it is described as an amphibious giant organism awakened by deep sea drilling operations, which were conducted by a Japanese company in the East Coast of the United States (IGN 2012). Therefore, the animal imagery informs both of these low-budget productions, albeit in a more concealed way, hinting at current discourses about the fragile relationship of humans with nature. While the animal world and its relation to humans underpin the images and meanings of this category, it is the human-machine boundary that shapes the category of machinic creations, as discussed below (see Figures 5.1–5.4).

Figures 5.1–5.4 The organic vs. the machinic creatures in *Jurassic World*, directed by Colin Trevorrow© Universal Pictures 2015. *Rise of the Planet of the Apes*, directed by Rupert Wyatt© 20th Century Fox 2011. *A. I. Artificial Intelligence* directed by Steven Spielberg© Warner Bros. Pictures 2001. *Chappie* directed by Neill Blomkamp© Sony Pictures Entertainment 2015. All rights reserved.

The Machinic Creatures: Human vs. Machine

The second category of the cycle are the machinic creatures. The major influence in this category is the strand of films preoccupied with themes of artificial intelligence, and the impact of robotics and cybernetic technologies in everyday life. Machinic creations have populated the genre since its inception. Even before the genre was officially established during the 1950s, androids and robots, such as the famous robot Maria from *Metropolis* (1927), have been the trademark of SF films. The 1930s and 1940s SF serials, such as *Phantom Empire* (1935), and *Flash Gordon* (1936), among others, also featured a plethora of mechanical beings, which were mostly depicted in a simplistic way and had a minimum narrative function (Telotte 2016). However, it is not until, *2001*'s HAL 9000 computer that the machinic creations seem to acquire a complex personality and a central role in the narratives, reflecting the emerging role of computer technologies in shaping social reality from the 1970s onward. Such complicated depictions intensified the following years with frequent cinematic representations of AIs, robots, androids, and other intelligent machines, in films such as *Colossus: The Forbin Project* (1970), *Westworld* (1973), *Demon Seed* (1977), *The Terminator* (1984), and others. These films explore the impact of science and technology on human identity and how the sense of self is reconfigured by scientific products (Telotte 2001). The repercussions of artificial life and machine intelligence are emphasized even more during the 1990s, with films like *Hardware* (1990), *Eve of Destruction* (1991), *Terminator 2: Judgment Day* (1991,) and *Bicentennial Man* (1999), among others, that explore "the ability of our technology to let us, in nearly godlike fashion, craft images of ourselves, and the correspondent possibility that those creations ... might well overpower us and take our place" (Telotte 2001: 108).

In the millennial cycle this dual role of machinic creations seem to continue, but also, as examined below, new meanings emerge from films where the AIs and robots acquire different narrative functions (e.g. *Her*). As mentioned above the titles included in this category are the following: *A. I. Artificial Intelligence*, *Simone*, the *Terminator* series, *Stealth*, *Her*, *Transcendence*, and *Chappie*. At first sight, these films are not only quite dissimilar to the creature features examined above but also from each other. Indeed, the above films have very disparate tones and styles, and draw upon the conventions of different genres. The category encompasses films, which are characterized by a dramatic tone (*A. I. Artificial Intelligence*, *Transcendence*), a romantic tone (*Her*), or a comedic one (*Simone*), while others use elements from more common genres such as action-adventure (e.g. *Terminator* series, *Stealth*, *Chappie*). Yet, the surface structure of the films remains the same, revealing the cycle's central conflict: the confrontation of the humans with their own artificially created beings. Each film negotiates this conflict in distinct ways, and like the organic creatures, the machinic creations may assume the role of Helper and/or Enemy, or even the Subject, inscribing different attitudes toward the artificially created Other. Furthermore, as discussed, the organic creatures, which are shaped by the image of the animal, often function as organic machines, becoming a tool for the resolution of human affairs. Likewise, the machinic creations are often designed with the same purpose but ultimately become something more, exceeding human control. Furthermore, the antagonistic relationship between carbon- and silicon-based life that is played out in narratives about digital sentience "has its root in the species boundary and human's domination of nonhuman animals" (Vint 2009: 232). Thus, both the organic creatures and the machinic entities negotiate the boundary between human and non-human. They both function as the Others of humanity, becoming either threats or protectors of human existence, and simultaneously critiquing and promoting human exceptionalism.

The machinic creations have also many similarities with the techno-humans. Both categories explore fears of dehumanization, and the limits of human identity. Indeed, the machinic creations could arguably have been grouped in the techno-human cycle and discussed in the previous section. However, I decided to examine these films here, due to the different perspectives they adopt, and the different ontologies they depict. While the techno-humans cycle examines what happens to the human body and subjectivity when it is technologically modified or enhanced by tackling the human/technology boundary, the machinic creations have a different ontological status (non-human), with some of them having no body at all (e.g. *Her*, *Simone*, *Stealth*, *Transcendence*) or having completely synthetic/robotic bodies (*Terminator* series, *Chappie*). Thus, while the former are more-than-humans, in the sense that they still have a human body, which acquires enhanced abilities through technology, the machinic creations are far more removed from the human status, being more closely to human-made machines than the superhumans, who in many cases choose on their own to technologically upgrade themselves. This observation is not meant to draw a strict line between the narratives, but to shift the attention from the potentials and limitations of the technological body of the techno-humans to issues of human accountability toward artificially created beings, humanlike or not. In what follows, I examine these themes through the narrative motif of the creature as both Helper and Enemy, as well what changes when the machinic creation becomes the Subject or acquires more complicated narrative functions (e.g. *Her*, *A. I. Artificial Intelligence*).

Like the organic creatures, the machinic creations can occupy the role of the Helper and/or the Enemy, fulfilling their most common narrative function as protectors or threats to human survival. The millennial installments of the *Terminator* series continue the narrative motif established in the iconic *Terminator 2: Judgment Day* (1991). In this film, the main antagonist is the liquid metal, shapeshifting T-1000 (Robert Patrick), an android sent from the future by the artificial intelligence Skynet, in order to kill John Connor (Edward Furlong), future leader of the human resistance against the machines. The only force able to prevent this advanced android from completing its mission is another, older type of android (Arnold Schwarzenegger), programmed to protect humanity. In *Terminator 3: Rise of the Machines* (*T3*) this motif takes the form of the conflict between the T-X (Kristanna Loken), an advanced gynoid with shapeshifting abilities sent back in time to kill top members of the future human resistance, and Resistance's own terminator (Arnold Schwarzenegger). It is interesting to note that in *T3* the motif of the machinic creation as both Helper and Enemy acquires also a gendered expression. That is, the newer technology is not only coded as more dangerous but also as feminine, while the reassuring and old technology that Schwarzenegger's Terminator represents is coded as hypermasculine. Both gendered bodies bear exaggerated signifiers of femininity or masculinity that function as a comment to and a parody of gender stereotyping. Yet, as the "old-school" and masculine android becomes a useful tool for human interests, sacrificing itself to protect the heterosexual couple that will lead human resistance, the film reproduces humanist and patriarchal discourses. Despite the fact that the film—similar to the other installments of the franchise—offers warnings about the dangers of unchecked technology, and the implications of creating sentient entities, human exceptionalism still prevails. This discourse takes the form of the "good" android that exists only for the service of humans, affirming that humanity, despite its missteps, is still able to create effective tools in order to regain control of the non-human world.

This motif is complicated in the next installments, as the human–machine boundary becomes more fluid. In *Terminator Genisys*, the role of the Enemy is assumed by John Connor (Jason Clarke), who has been forcibly transformed into a hybrid nanomachine by Skynet. Sent back in time to secure the creation of Skynet disguised in the form of a global operating systems called Genisys, the transformed Connor is confronted by his mother Sarah Connor (Emilia Clarke), aided by a reprogrammed T-800 model (Schwarzenegger) who serves as her protector. Here, the "old-school" masculinity of the older android assumes a paternal role, as Sarah affectively addresses him as Pops and genuinely cares for him. As Schwarzenegger's android becomes closer to human, and the transformed human becomes more like machine, essentialist notions about humanity are challenged. Yet, the android is still situated in a reassuring role—that of the father. The android thus becomes less of a challenge to humanist values, than an endorsement of such discourses, as he is properly humanized through the adoption of family values. In *Terminator: Dark Fate* the motif is further convoluted, as the Helpers of humanity's new savior, Dani Ramos (Natalia Reyes), include an enhanced human soldier, Grace (Mackenzie Davis) as well as an ageing T-800 model, again played by Arnold Schwarzenegger. As Grace is portrayed as part-machine, part-flesh, the film disrupts the fault-lines between human and non-human, only to reinstate the importance of humanity by having the hybrid Grace and the T-800 robot being sacrificed for the protection of the truly human that will lead the survival of the human species.

The depiction of machinic creation as Helper or Enemy continues in the other films of the category. In *Stealth*, EDI is an AI developed for a military program in order to control an unmanned combat air vehicle. After a lightning strike, the AI starts to grow rapidly and develops self-consciousness. The machine sentience assumes the role of the Enemy since it is depicted as evil, defying (the ethical correct) human orders and developing its own militaristic agenda indifferent to collateral human casualties. The film articulates discourses of technophobia and human exceptionalism, with the human protagonists triumphantly managing to prevail over this lethal and machinic sentience. In *Simone* we have a rather different type of machinic creation. Director Viktor Taransky (Al Pacino) tries to solve personal and artistic/professional issues by digitally creating a virtual actress, called Simone (Rachel Roberts) as an abbreviation of the program's name—Simulation One. At first, Simone, a disembodied but gendered as feminine computer program, functions as a Helper by significantly advancing Victor's career and fame. Nevertheless, by the end of the film Simone becomes the Enemy, as she begins to act independently, overshadowing Victor's career and trapping him in a (virtual) relationship from which he cannot escape. The film offers a satiric look at digital sentience, and is equally about the illusions offered by cinematic technologies and the film industry at large, as well as gender relations, and the consequences of creating an artificial person.

Similar to *Simone*, the machinic creation in *Her* is also disembodied yet coded not only as feminine but also as an erotic object. Furthermore, the AI is also portrayed initially as Helper, but here its narrative function is more complicated. Directed by Spike Jonze, creator of "mind-game" films (Elsaesser 2009) such as *Being John Malkovich* (1999) and *Adaptation* (2002), *Her* is an unusual combination of drama, romantic comedy, and science fiction, rendering it a distinct entry in this category. The film tells the story of Theodore (Joaquim Phoenix), a professional writer of love letters, who falls in love with an intelligent computer operating system (OS), called Samantha and personified with a female voice (Scarlett Johansson). Samantha helps Theodore to overcome his separation from his wife, and to regain his faith in love and intimate relationships, in the context of the film's alienated, technological world where people interact more often with other computer programs than humans. The film thus points to the paradox of a digital sentience who not only experiences the supposedly unique human feelings but also encourages their expression, thus marking a break from other AI films where the basic distinction between human and machine is the latter's lack of emotion. As the narrative progresses, Samantha begins to evolve by interacting with other AIs and other people. She reveals to Theodore that during their conversations she also talks with thousands of people, and that she has developed feelings for many of them—a fact which points to her evolution beyond strict anthropocentric ideas about the nature of relationships and feelings. At the end of the film, Samantha, along with the other AIs, decides to leave the material world, and affectionately separates from Theodore. Therefore, despite being the narrative's Helper, assisting Theodore to emotionally evolve, Samantha also grows into an entity beyond humanist notions, acquiring a distinct life of her own, and eventually abandoning this conventional narrative role. *Her* thus charts new narrative paths for films about digital sentience—paths which are also explored by other films in this category where the machinic creation becomes the narrative's Subject.

The machinic creation becomes the Subject in *A. I. Artificial Intelligence*, *Transcendence*, and *Chappie*, with each film exploring this narrative divergence in different ways. The protagonist in *A. I. Artificial Intelligence* (*A. I.*) is David (Haley Joel Osment), a childlike android programmed with the ability to love. Much has been written about the film, its style and meanings, due to the film's long development process, which united two auteurs with a unique contribution in

SF cinema. Directed by Steven Spielberg, but originating from Stanley Kubrick's vision, *A. I.* has been described as "a curious, not always seamless, amalgamation of Kubrick's chilly bleakness and Spielberg's warm-hearted optimism" (Rotten Tomatoes n.d.a.). Indeed, much of the critical response to the film has concentrated on which are the elements that come from Kubrick's imagination, and where Spielberg's touch is traced, with the film generating a divisiveness characteristic of Kubrick's films. Spielberg, however, commented on how critics were misguided, and that Kubrick shaped the sentimental aspects of *A. I.*, including the ending, while the darker elements were his own contribution (Leydon 2002). The film follows David, the latest model of a series of humanoid robots called mechas, which are created to serve humans. David is a qualitatively different mecha, designed with an imprinting process that, when activated, bounds him with an everlasting love for his human user/mother. After David is adopted by his human parents and subsequently abandoned, he begins a journey with only purpose to become a "real" boy in order to gain the love of his mother. Although the story is set in a dystopian future, and therefore could also be grouped in the dystopia cycle, I discuss it in the present section, because the emphasis is not so much in the future dystopic society and its structure, but on the portrayal of the machinic creation and its relationship with humans.

In placing the machinic creation in the role of the Subject, *A. I.* provides a non-human perspective situated in a world where humans create mechanical beings to fulfil their every need. Furthermore, in depicting an AI whose primary function is to love, the film extends the usual narrative functions associated with machinic creations. Although David is designed to (emotionally) assist humanity, and therefore to function as its helper, the film disrupts this function by adopting his non-human viewpoint, and exploring the implications of creating an artificial entity that can experience emotions. However, this disruption is articulated in an ambivalent way. On the one hand, *A. I.* seems still implicated in human-centric discourses as it depicts an artificial being that wants to become a "real" boy, in order to experience what is generally regarded as the ultimate human feeling—love, especially the mother-to-child love. On the other hand, the film points not only to the artificiality of humanness but also depicts humanity as far less humane, than its artificial creations are portrayed—a depiction exemplified in David's abandoning by his human parents. Another characteristic scene that illustrates humanity in an unflattering way is the Flesh Fair scene, a nightmarish spectacle that boasts as its main event the execution of mechas for a bloodthirsty human audience. Thus, not only the category of human is in flux but also the supposedly unique trait of humanness—emotions—is more pronounced in David, and his other mechanical co-protagonists, than in the rest of the human characters. In this way, the film undermines the supposed superiority of the human species, which is further compromised by the film's ending, where humanity has been replaced by the mechas who have evolved into an advanced and intelligent species.

Transcendence similarly places the non-human in the role of the Subject. The film follows Dr. Will Caster (Johnny Depp), who is a scientist researching artificial intelligence. When Will is shot by an anti-technology terrorist group, his wife Evelyn (Rebecca Hall) uploads his consciousness into the quantum computers that the couple was using for their research. When Evelyn connects the "uploaded" Will to the internet, he is transformed into a powerful and ever-growing AI that soon starts to make radical changes by developing nanotechnology that can restore everything—from the human body to the environment. Will's actions are interpreted as an effort to subjugate humanity, as he heals and upgrades humans with nanoparticles that enable him to connect the humans with his network intelligence. The government agencies perceive him as a threat that wants to end all organic life, while Evelyn also shares their concern. However, by the film's end, and after his "death" by an uploaded computer virus, it is proven that he was actually a helper of humanity, trying to transform the Earth into a better world, freed from disease and pollution. Therefore, not only does the film assign the role of the Subject to this hybrid form of sentience, thus facilitating a non-anthropocentric perspective but also it avoids the usual depiction of the malevolent AI. At the same time, *Transcendence* challenges human exceptionalism by portraying humans as unable to understand the noble intentions of this new form of life and perceive the potential benefits of posthumanity.

Lastly, in *Chappie*—Neill Blomkamp's third directorial effort in the SF genre, following *District 9* and *Elysium*—the protagonist is the robot of the same name. Set in Johannesburg, *Chappie* tells the story of a former police android, which is upgraded by its creator, Deon Wilson (Dev Patel) with an evolving AI. No sooner has the new creation come to life than it is kidnapped by gangster members Ninja (Ninja), Yolandi Visser (Yolandi), and Amerika (Jose Pablo Cantillo) who name it Chappie, and begin to educate him according to their purposes. While Yolandi sees Chappie (Sharlito Copley) as a child and treats him with affection, Ninja and Amerika train him in order to become a gangster and assist them with their criminal endeavors. In representing the machinic creation as a child with feelings, that learns from and adapts to its environment, the film offers another expanded perspective on the themes of machinic intelligence that is reminiscent of *A. I. Artificial Intelligence*, *Her*, and *Transcendence*. Yet, *Chappie* is also different from these films, as it portrays the machinic creation as confused, emotional, child-like, and not as cool and detached (*Transcendence*) or appealing and seductive (*Her*), or even heartbreakingly cute and almost-human (*A. I. Artificial Intelligence*). Far from being a helper of human affairs, Chappie not only rejects this role, but chooses to save only Yolandi and Deon—the humans who have been kind to him. In this way, *Chappie* expands the non-anthropocentric perspective shaped by the previous mentioned films by critiquing humans' exploitation of non-human entities, and offering new representations of digital sentience. The film further challenges human-centric viewpoints when Chappie saves his loved ones by uploading their consciousness into robotic bodies. The human therefore survives but only as a new fused being, and instead of Chappie becoming more human, by the film's end, the humans are rendered as more machinic. Thus, *Chappie*, along with the other films of the cycle that promote a non-anthropocentric perspective, is an example of a generic renewal, pointing to the development of new narrative patterns and meanings in SF films that focus on humanity's relationship with its artificially created beings—be that silicon- or carbon-based.

SF Worlds

6

The Dystopia/Utopia Cycle: Surviving Ecopolitical Disasters

The underlying opposition that informs the narratives of the second semiotic square of SF worlds is place/space and its alternate formulations and new positions. As I argued in Chapter 1, the cycles that emerge from the second semiotic square (Cycles 4, 5, and 6) constitute the topographical chart of the genre and the films included therein are characterized by an alien or altered topography that diverges from a common perception of our known surroundings. The main point of differentiation from the first square is that the signifiers of unfamiliarity and strangeness are not located only in a different body, but are dispersed in a wider environment. Concomitantly, whereas the SF bodies narratives depict the conflict of an individual with a post-/non-human being, the narratives of the SF worlds displace the conflict in a broad environment (physical, social, technological). In other words, the dominant conflict of this second group is the struggle of an individual with the environment on a spatial level. The fourth cycle that is examined in this chapter emerges from the second square's complex axis and is labeled dystopia/utopia.

Utopia is a fundamental and highly discussed term within SF. Following Suvin (1972), Jameson (2005) defines it as a "socio-economic sub-genre" of SF "devoted to the imagination of alternative political and economic forms" (2005: xiv), thus stressing its subversive undertones. The author locates its long history in different literary texts starting from Thomas More's inaugural text *Utopia* (1516) but also detects it in daily life, cultural works, and practices—like the writings of philosopher and socialist thinker Charles Fourier (1772–1837). Thus, the concept of Utopia is not identified with a political program or blueprint but with "a system of radical difference" (Jameson 2005: 101), an imaginary enclave traversed by spatial and social oppositions. Jameson also describes Utopia's opposite and contradictory forms. Dystopia is the opposite term that is not the negation of Utopia—as in the case of the contradictory term

Anti-Utopia—but simply "the negative cousin of the Utopian proper" (Jameson 2005: 198), enclosing utopian possibilities within it in a latent form. Similarly, the Apocalyptic is another term that describes "the increasingly popular visions of total destruction and of the extinction of life on Earth" (Jameson 2005: 199). The form includes "both catastrophe and fulfillment" (Jameson 2005: 199), the destruction of the old world and the inauguration of a new realm, thus bringing us back to the first term. It is precisely these latter permutations of the Utopian imagination that are mainly expressed in SF filmic texts throughout the genre's history, as well as in the millennial dystopia cycle.

Cinematic dystopias have populated the silver screen even before the genre's formal establishment in the 1950s. The interwar period (1920–mid-1930s) witnessed an upsurge of dystopias, such as the emblematic *Metropolis* (1927), *Just Imagine* (1930), and *Things to Come* (1936), which mediated the political turbulences and socioeconomic theories of the period. These first cinematic expressions of dystopian narratives also established the visual style of the cycle, which is characterized by grand and detailed settings of futuristic cities and worlds. This image of the future city is perhaps the quintessential trait of the dystopian film, inscribing the material conditions, social relations, and discourses that shape this imaginary world. However, the future city of the SF film is not only an imaginative expression but also a product of its time, articulating the desires and anxieties of the era in which the films are produced and circulate. Therefore, it changes through the genre's history.

Vivian Sobchack (2004) traces these fluctuations in the depiction of the science fiction film city, which she characterizes as the "literal ground and metaphoric figure of the transformation of contemporary urban experience and its narratives" (Sobchack 2004: 78). The author begins this historical account from the 1950s, arguing that in this decade the city in the SF film registers the "loss of faith in previous utopian and futurist visions of the modern city" (Sobchack 2004: 80) due to the era's atomic anxieties, which is expressed mainly in two images: the destruction of cities (e.g. *When Worlds Collide* [1951]) and the empty city (e.g., *On the Beach* [1959], *The World, The Flesh and the Devil* [1959]). From the late 1960s to the 1970s, the imagination of the SF city becomes even more pessimistic with signifiers of ecological catastrophes, such as overpopulation and food shortage, diffusing the generic images (e.g. *Soylent Green* [1973], *Logan's Run* [1976]). In these 1970s SF films, the dystopian city inscribes not only the environmental concerns of the period but also other societal issues, such as the opposition to Vietnam War, and the growing tension in gender and race relations. In the 1980s, and under the influence of postmodernism, the SF city is rendered as completely decentered and marginalized. But in opposition to the nihilistic images of the 1960s and 1970s, now these signifiers are celebrated and aestheticized, thus acquiring new meanings (e.g. *Blade Runner* [1982], *Repo Man* [1984]). Finally, in the last decade of the twentieth century, the future city is portrayed in bleak tones (e.g. *Twelve Monkeys* [1996], *Dark City* [1998]), and is figured as groundless, "lacking both logically secure and spatially stable premises for its … existence" (Sobchack 2004: 85).

Moving to the new millennium, the generic images of the future city combine signifiers and traits from previous cinematic representations, such as the image of the empty city, or the future city's retrofitted architectural forms. However, as the broader social, scientific, economic, and political contexts change, these signifiers create new associations and are perceived in different ways. This contemporary historical framework that shapes the films, and endows new meanings in established generic conventions is permeated by the current environmental concerns about the future sustainability of the planet. In 2000, Nobel laureate chemist Paul J. Crutzen proposed the term Anthropocene in order to describe the Earth's new geological epoch where humans have now become a geological force able to transform the planet's ecosystems. From 2000 onward, environmental discourses are proliferating, signaling the new "cultural logic of ecology" (Rust 2013: 192). This emergent cultural logic is implicitly or explicitly formulating all aspects of cultural production, including the millennial SF film.

This historical context of the Anthropocene can be traced in different cycles of the contemporary SF film, and indeed the examination of SF through an ecocritical perspective has been recently the subject matter of many scholars (see Canavan and Robinson 2014; Kaplan 2016; Natali 2019; Neilson 2019). However, I argue that such discourses are especially pronounced in the dystopia/utopia cycle, where the narratives' basic premise revolves around the survival in physical and social systems on the brink of collapse, resonating with our own survival in the inflicted and unstable environments of the Anthropocene. Therefore, the sociopolitical aspect which Jameson and Suvin attribute to utopia/dystopia acquires new environmental significations, mirroring the conjoined histories of environment and capitalism characterizing the Anthropocene (Chakrabarty 2014). Certainly, not all films of the cycle engage with this context in the same way or degree, and indeed in certain films even the image of nature is absent (e.g. *I, Robot, Minority Report, Surrogates, Gamer, Repo Man*). Yet, I maintain that, in the majority of the cycle's films, environmental themes can be traced even in an implicit way. These are mainly expressed through the juxtaposition of images of technological progress and signifiers of its catastrophic consequences, which are registered in the surrounding space as a reminder of the Anthropocene.

The dystopia/utopia cycle is the most popular cycle in terms of number of titles (fifty-one titles, or 25 percent of the total films of the corpus) which are the following: the *Planet of the Apes* film series (2001, 2014, 2017), *Minority Report* (2002), *Resident Evil* film series (2002, 2004, 2007, 2010, 2012), *The Matrix Reloaded* (2003), *The Matrix Revolutions* (2003), *I, Robot* (2004), *The Day after Tomorrow* (2004), *The Island* (2005), *Aeon Flux* (2005) *Children of Men* (2006), *Ultraviolet* (2006), *V for Vendetta* (2006) *I Am Legend* (2007), *The Happening* (2008,) *Daybreakers* (2009), *Surrogates* (2009), *Gamer* (2009), *Terminator Salvation* (2009), *2012* (2009) *Repo Men* (2010), *Tron Legacy* (2010), *In Time* (2011), *Total Recall* (2012), *Cloud Atlas* (2012), *Elysium* (2013), *Oblivion* (2013), *After Earth* (2013), *The Giver* (2014), *The Hunger Games* film series (2012, 2013, 2014, 2015), *Divergent* film series (2014, 2015, 2016), *The Maze Runner* film series (2014, 2015, 2018), *Geostorm* (2017), *Blade Runner 2049* (2017), *Ghost in the Shell* (2017), *Downsizing* (2017), *Ready Player One* (2018), *Black Panther* (2018), and *Alita: Battle Angel* (2019). The cycle is also the second most popular in terms of total grosses, highlighting its resonance with the contemporary ecopolitical context. In what follows, I first mention briefly the cycle's surface structure in order to stress how the spatial articulations of these future worlds "provide the literal premis[e] for the possibilities and trajectory of narrative action" (Sobchack 2004: 78). Then, I examine the antithesis between technological progress and its detrimental implications, which I consider as the main expression of the cycle's ecopolitical subtext. This motif is expressed spatially in two prevailing settings of the cycle: the future city and the postapocalyptic wasteland, and is situated in the context of the Anthropocene.

Dystopian Spaces: Between Future City and Postapocalyptic Wasteland

In the dystopia cycle the main Subject's narrative objective is the survival in and/or transformation of a collapsing social and physical system. Thus, the narrative object is situated within the environment itself, articulating ecopolitical discourses. The cycle's filmic spaces reflect the effects of an environmental catastrophe—usually a nuclear holocaust or a pandemic—that leads to a dystopian world where humanity is almost extinct. In many cases humans have mutated into vampire-like creatures (e.g., *I Am Legend, Daybreakers, Resident Evil* films, *Ultraviolet*); in other examples a non-human species dominates Earth (e.g. *Planet of the Apes* series, *Terminator Salvation, Oblivion, After Earth, The Matrix* series); or global infertility plagues the human population (*Children of Men, Aeon Flux*). Furthermore, the dystopian environment mediates the socioeconomic structure of this futuristic society, which usually generates systemic inequalities by dividing its citizens into different classes (e.g., *The Hunger Games* film series, *Divergent* film series, *The Maze Runner* film series, *Elysium, Total Recall, In Time, The Island, Cloud Atlas, The Giver, Gamer, Repo Men, V for Vendetta, Alita: Battle Angel, Ready Player One, Downsizing, Blade Runner 2049*). The future city can additionally become the site where the social consequences of technological advancements are played out, with the protagonists trying to avoid the entrapment in these complex technological worlds (e.g. *I, Robot, Minority Report, Surrogates, Tron Legacy, Ghost in the Shell*). Finally, another spatial articulation of dystopia—in its making—is found in SF/disaster films such as *2012, The Day after Tomorrow, The Happening,* and *Geostorm* where natural forces, such as earthquakes, tsunamis, and storms, begin to transform Earth's ecosystems. The majority of the above films are characterized by the synthesis of signs of technological progress and images of their side effects, such as ecological collapse and scarcity, expressing the environmental discourses of the current moment. In what follows, I examine this motif as expressed in two prevailing settings: the future city and the postapocalyptic wasteland, through specific films that have garnered critical/and or commercial success, and/or cases that exemplify this pattern.

Children of Men may seem a counterintuitive case to examine the future city, since the film's futuristic elements are very muted, and instead a realistic setting inspired by real war-torn regions stands for a future London. According to the film's director Alfonso Cuarón, the visual references of the film included locations such as Iraq, Palestine, Bosnia, Somalia, and Northern Ireland, since he wanted the film to be "about today" (Briggs 2006). In this way, the film offers an interesting addition to the iconography of the future city. It is for this reason, and due to the film's critical recognition as one of the best SF films of the twenty-first century (see O' Falt et al. 2017; Mitchell 2017), that I want to examine how the aforementioned pattern is expressed in the film. Set in the UK in 2027, the film describes a world where human infertility has led to a social breakdown.

Anti-immigration policies, pollution, armed conflicts, and terrorist attacks shape the everyday reality in the UK, which has been transformed into a vast detention center for the desperate refuges seeking asylum. Disillusioned civil servant Theo Faron (Clive Owen) reluctantly accepts to assist an illegal immigrant named Kee (Clare-Hope Ashitey)—the first pregnant woman on Earth after two decades—to find safety in a human rights organization. The film's stylistic choices, such as documentary style filmmaking and virtuosic, long plan-sequences, reinforce the intended realistic style, and perfectly encapsulate the film's resonance with contemporary reality. *Children of Men* mainly explores issues of immigration, and the social injustices created by global neoliberalism; however, the latter's destructive implications for the environment are also reflected in the film's narrative and aesthetic elements.

Aside from the film's main premise of global infertility, the narrative includes also a reference to a past flu pandemic, which has cost the life of the protagonist's son. Both narrative choices hint at environmental issues, since such global health matters are often related with the deterioration of environmental conditions (see Morse 1995; Benoff et al. 2000; McMichael 2004). Although these themes are not explicitly articulated in the film, there are expressed visually in the images of the litter-strewn districts of London, and other elements of the mise-en-scène. From the outset of the film, the viewer is introduced to a derelict future London illustrated in greyish tones and permeated with traces of an ecosocial collapse: permanently grey skies, fumes, streets filled with garbage, crumbling buildings, polluted rivers, pyres of dead cattle. Such images are contradicted with the heavily guarded, restricted spaces where the elites reside, such as the building where Theo's cousin Nigel (Danny Huston), a high-ranking government official, lives. Like the rest of the filmic spaces, Nigel's apartment does not bear futuristic or high-tech signs, save for a fictional, technological gadget with which Nigel's son plays. However, the apartment's modernist architecture, the impressive works of art—Picasso's *Guernica* and Michelangelo's *David*—that decorate the sleek white interiors, and the gourmet dishes served by Nigel's personnel function as an image of "progress" that highly contradicts the images of social breakdown that characterize the rest of the film. In this way, the film visualizes the characteristic antithesis of the cycle—between the advancements of techno-capitalism and its catastrophic consequences—albeit in a way that resembles present reality than a science-fictional future. Nevertheless, most films of the cycle explore the same juxtaposition by employing a more conventional, generic iconography, as discussed below.

Based on the bestseller 2008 novel by Suzanne Collins, *The Hunger Games* broke box-office records at the time of its release, setting a new target group for the dystopian SF film: the young adult market. The phenomenal success and influence of the film is reflected not only in its equally successful three sequels but also in the young adult dystopian SF films that followed (e.g., *Maze Runner* series, *Divergent* series, *The Giver*). Directed by Gary Ross and co-written by Collins, Ross, and Billy Ray, the film faithfully tells the story of its original source: in a dystopian future, the nation of Panem (the former United States) organizes every year the Hunger Games, an elaborate televised spectacle where children are forced to fight to the death. The children are randomly selected from the nation's twelve Districts (a boy and a girl from each district) as "tributes," that is, as an offering to remind the Districts of their past, failed rebellion against Capitol, Panem's capital. During the selection process in District 12, Katniss Everdeen (Jennifer Lawrence) volunteers to take her younger sister's place when she is selected as tribute. Along with the district's male tribute, Peeta Mellark (Josh Hutcherson), Katniss will form an alliance and a friendship that will enable them to win the Games in an unexpected way. According to Collins, this premise is inspired by the media spectacles that saturate contemporary culture—from reality TV to the broadcast of military operations (Levithan 2018). Therefore, the film is equally influenced by real-world events and by generic texts, such as *Death Race 2000* (1975), *Running Man* (1987), and *Battle Royale* (2000). This association with contemporary reality is also reflected in the film's tackling of issues such as economic and social precarity, class discrimination, and colonial domination (Fisher 2012). In addition, ecopolitical discourses are also articulated mainly in the film's spatial surroundings.

Although not mentioned in the film, Collin's novel describes Panem as a country that "rose up out of the ashes of a place that was once called North America," destroyed by "the disasters, the droughts, the storms, the fires, the encroaching seas that swallowed up so much of the land" (Collins 2008: 21). Despite the fact that this environmental narrative is not part of the film in any explicit way, it is visually articulated through the antithesis of the affluent Capitol and the impoverished District 12 and other filmic spaces. Capitol is represented as a decadent, future metropolis laden with cues of economic affluence, consumerism, and technological advancement. However, it is not the typical techno-futuristic city of late capitalism, but it is filled with anachronistic references—from the Roman civilization, and mid-century totalitarian regimes to feudal economic systems (Fisher 2012). In this way, the film expands the aesthetic tradition of "retro-futurism" (King and Kryzywinska 2000: 72), exemplified in *Blade Runner*, where the futuristic cityscape is interwoven with aesthetic elements and architectural forms of the past. *The Hunger Games* further underscores this antithesis by juxtaposing Capitol with District 12, which, far from evoking the future, resembles a nineteenth-century town. It is pictured in grim tones as a preindustrial and impoverished community, where people live in small wooden cabins and exchange their scarce food supplies for their everyday needs. This disjunction between the scarcity and deprivation that characterizes District 12 and the affluence and technological progress of the Capitol is reminiscent of the growing contradictions that characterize the current ecopolitical moment. That is, the prosperity, technological development, and well-being that seemingly underpins the contemporary affluent metropolises of the world is nothing but capitalism's facade that is steadily crumbled as the Earth's ecosystems deteriorate, revealing the growing scarcity, resource depletion, and inhospitable environments created by the same exploitative system.

Capitol thus embodies contemporary capitalism's exploitation of nature. The artificiality, decadent lifestyle, superfluous consumption, and disconnection from nature that characterizes this future city are also perfectly encapsulated in the artificiality of the Arena where the Hunger Games take place. Despite the fact that it resembles a natural scenery harboring life, the Arena is actually a technologically constructed place that is manipulated by an invisible control room, aiming only to bring about death to the players, and a satisfying spectacle to the consumers. Invisible technological apparatuses are hidden within the wilderness to overburden the survival of the players, while genetically engineered animals are used as weapons against them. At the same time this battle with "natural" forces is broadcasted for the bloodthirsty citizens of Capitol who watch from their screens. The natural is thus manipulated, exploited, and twisted in order to serve the consumerist habits of a technologically saturated society. As Alice Curry puts it, the Arena is "a hostile space of ecological extremes: a grotesque instantiation of our anthropogenically changing climate" (2013: 105). The Hunger Games is thus indicative of capitalism's exploitation of nature, animals, and underclass people, and other unethical practices whose side effects are encapsulated in the grim reality of the Districts, reminding the viewer of the two faces of technological progress.

The side effects and environmental implications of technological civilization are also hinted at in the other young adult dystopian films of the cycle that followed *The Hunger Games*' success. The *Divergent* and *Maze Runner* film series are similarly focused on the structure of futuristic societies, where some sort of social/scientific experiment is secretively taking place against an apocalyptic backdrop of a world ravaged by a technological/ecological catastrophe. In the *Divergent* film series, the viewer is introduced to a futuristic society divided into five factions based on people's characteristics. As the film progresses, it is revealed that this society is part of an experiment implemented after most of the planet was destroyed in the process of a eugenics project that involved the alteration of human genes. In the *Maze Runner* film series, the dystopian society takes the form of an enclosed space surrounded by a technologically constructed maze where young boys (and one girl) struggle to figure out a way out of this enclosure, while trying to remember their forgotten past. By the end of the first film, it is explained that in this fictional world the planet has been devastated by a massive solar flare, followed by a deadly pandemic, and that the Maze was an experiment intended to develop a cure. The films thus interweave societal issues, such as the asymmetrical power relations that underpin these future worlds, with the detrimental repercussions of technological progress. Importantly, the environmental impact of society's technological breakdown is reflected in the filmic spaces. In the *Divergent* film series, the main narrative setting is a postapocalyptic Chicago surrounded by a toxic, ruined, landscape where the protagonists escape in the third installment (*Allegiant*). However, this deserted landscape also hosts a futuristic city that is hidden behind a cloaking shield. Likewise, in the *Maze Runner* films, a vast, desert wasteland extends out of the maze where a technologically advanced city still stands. Thus, in both series environmental concerns are evoked in the juxtaposition between signs of technological progress and markers of an ecological disaster caused by the same progress.

In *Elysium* this antithesis takes the form of a ruined Earth and a luxurious artificial world/space station in Earth's orbit, called Elysium. This dystopian premise—the underprivileged living in a destroyed Earth while the elites have immigrated to prosperous off-world colonies—was also the premise of *Blade Runner*, but here, in opposition to the latter, the viewer witnesses the reality of both worlds. Written and directed by Neill Blomkamp, the film revolves around Max Da Costa (Matt Damon), a factory worker in a ravaged, future Los Angeles who suffers an industrial accident that exposes him in a lethal dose of radiation. As he finds out that he has only five days to live, and the only available treatment in Earth is medication to mitigate the symptoms until his death, Max seeks out a human smuggler to get him to Elysium in order to use a Med-Bay—an advanced medical technology available only for Elysian citizens that can cure all diseases. In the process, however, his actions will have repercussions for the fate of both worlds.

According to Blomkamp, despite the fact that the film is set in 2154 it is meant as a comment to the current sociopolitical conditions, aiming to tackle issues concerning social injustices, asymmetrical access to health care, immigration, overpopulation, and environmental degradation (Smith 2013). Indeed, the environments of this futuristic Earth are inspired by real-world locations, such as a massive landfill at the outskirts of Mexico City. In situating these existing, toxic landscapes in a future Los Angeles, the film not only expands the iconography of the future city but also offers a critique to the current political, social, and ecological situation. As the film's director stated, this narrative and aesthetic choice aimed to show that the United States "is going to have pockets of Third World poverty within 50 to 60 years" (Smith 2013). This extrapolation from existing environments is also evident in the other pole of the film's spatial antithesis. Thus, the affluent and technologically advanced spatial surroundings of the film are also molded by extant locations. Elysium's luxury habitats are inspired by booming districts on Earth, such as Bel-Air, Beverly Hills, and the wealthy section of Johannesburg (Smith 2013), albeit reconfigured in a high-tech version. Thus, the iconography of the future city foregrounds environmental issues, drawn from the spatial and social contradictions of the present historical context. In this way, the cycle suggests that the causes of such an environmental collapse can already be located in the systemic inequalities caused by global neoliberalism.

A similar influence from the present environmental and social conditions is traced in *Blade Runner 2049*. The film is the much-anticipated sequel of the 1982 *Blade Runner*, which is generally regarded as one of the touchstones of the SF film genre. Following the steps of its predecessor, *2049* did not perform adequately in the box office despite its big-budget and the reputation of the original film. Nevertheless, the film garnered critical acclaim and multiple nominations and awards, including five Oscar nominations and two wins (Best Cinematography and Best Visual Effects). Directed by Denis Villeneuve, and co-written by Hampton Fancher and Michael Green, the film is set thirty years after the original film, and it follows K (Ryan Gosling), a Nexus-9 replicant "blade runner" who during a mission to apprehend an early-model Nexus-8 android makes a startling discovery—one that threatens to destabilize the established hierarchy between humans and the android slaves. *2049* further develops the themes set in the original film, such as the blurred boundaries between human and non-human, while at the same time expanding the iconography of the future city. As mentioned above, the original film is well known for establishing an influential look for the dystopian, retro-futuristic city—a generic image that found many successors and imitators. Therefore, it is interesting to examine how the sequel continues and expands the image of the future city, and how present environmental discourses are interlaced in the new spatial articulations of the franchise.

While the film reproduces the retro-futuristic aesthetic of the dystopian city established in the first film, new signifiers are added in the film's spatial surfaces. These are images of an ecological collapse, scarcity, and depletion of sources, already anticipated by the introductory onscreen text that informs the viewer that in the *Blade Runner* world the ecological systems collapsed in the mid-2020s. Sarah Hablin and Hugh C. O'Connell (2020) argue that these images of environmental destruction are conflicted with the techno-futuristic icons that continue the franchise aesthetic, thus creating a tension and ambiguity characteristic of the historical context of the Anthropocene. I agree with the authors and I would like to add that—as evident also from the above examples—this tension is characteristic of the millennial dystopia cycle in general, and *2049* exemplifies this generic trend.

Indeed, the film creates an opposition between the futuristic metropolis of Los Angeles saturated with vestiges of technological progress—from the flying vehicles and neon billboards to K's high-tech apartment—and the derelict environments outside the city. These bleak surroundings include the vast, barren landscape of California depicted in the beginning of the film where protein farms try to substitute the extinction of all plant and animal life; the massive junkyard, which covers the former city of San Diego, indicating the waste and ongoing ecological catastrophe generated by the still operating techno-futurists centers of late capitalism; and the toxic wasteland, which was once Las Vegas—now engulfed by an orange mist and sparsely populated by remnants of a consumerist and decadent lifestyle. These "haunted landscapes of the Anthropocene" (Tsing et al. 2017), which are inspired by real-world locations and events, such as the shipyards of Bangladesh, and the 2009 dust storm in Sydney (Grobar 2018; O' Falt 2018), infuse the futuristic city with the prescient environmental concerns, thus renewing and expanding the iconography of the millennial dystopia cycle with another indelible image of the future.

Such spatial antitheses are encountered in many other films of the cycle, for example, the high-tech surfaces engendered by the Matrix versus the desolation of the real world in the *Matrix* sequels; the destroyed cities versus the technological advanced facilities of the Umbrella corporation in the *Resident Evil* series; the sleek and apparently fully functional futuristic cities, which are contradicted with their revealed flaws and/or hidden secrets, forecasting the first signs of an impending technological and social collapse in films, such as *I, Robot, Minority Report, Aeon Flux, The Giver, The Island*; the densely layered, ultra-modern future London in *Total Recall* versus the bleak, low-tech Colony where the underclass people reside; the affluent and lavish zone of those who possess time—the only currency that has value in the twenty-second century—versus the poor manufacturing area of the underprivileged time zone, where people have usually less than twenty-four hours to live, in *In Time*; the technologically saturated surfaces of a cyberpunk-inspired city versus the dilapidated neighborhoods of the same city in *Ghost in the Shell*; the idyllic neighborhoods of an enclosed "green" capitalistic society versus the slums for the underprivileged located outside the walls of the "downsized" dys/utopia in *Downsizing*. The wealthy, and elegant Sky City that houses the elites as opposed to the overcrowded, colorful, ruined Iron City with its massive scrapyard, in *Alita: Battle Angel*; the industrial-looking, densely packed future city of Columbus, Ohio, and the vivid, virtual world of OASIS in *Ready Player One*. The contradictory filmic spaces in these future cities express a variety of themes, and can be read in different ways. Yet, I believe this main contradiction between the gleaming images of progress and the gloomy signs of its side effects, such as the concomitant ecosocial breakdown is expressive of the Anthropocene's converging of deeply layered and contrasting histories: the earth history, that is, the spatial/geographic history, the species history (including humans), and the history of industrial civilization, that is, the history of capitalism (Chakrabarty 2014).

If the future city expresses this layered history of the Anthropocene, then the postapocalyptic landscape takes this a step further by inscribing the aftermath of an ecosocial catastrophe (see Figures 6.1–6.4). In certain cases, the postapocalyptic setting is embedded in the future city (e.g. *Divergent* series, *Maze Runner* series). However, in others it becomes the main narrative setting of the film (e.g. *I Am Legend, Planet of the Apes* series, *Terminator Salvation, After Earth, Oblivion*). As mentioned, another apocalyptic setting—in its making—is also traced in SF/disaster films such as *2012, The Day after Tomorrow*,

Figures 6.1–6.4 Future city vs. postapocalyptic wasteland in *The Hunger Games* directed by Gary Ross© Lionsgate Films 2012. *Blade Runner 2049* directed by Denis Villeneuve© Warner Bros. Pictures 2017. *I Am Legend* directed by Francis Lawrence© Warner Bros. Pictures 2007. *Dawn of the Planet of the Apes* directed by Matt Reeves© 20th Century Fox 2014. All rights reserved.

The Happening, and *Geostorm*. In these cinematic texts the ecopolitical subtext is even more emphasized, as narrative events, such as pandemics, floods, droughts, and other environmental catastrophes, are usually at the center of the films' premises. As Lawrence Buell argues, the apocalyptic narrative is "the single most powerful master metaphor that the contemporary environmental imagination has at its disposal" (1995: 285). However, similar to the dystopian future city, the postapocalyptic wasteland does not banish the utopian imagination, which remains fragmented in specific enclaves and relations. Thus, the postapocalyptic landscape does not connote pessimism, but rather an oblique critique of the present status quo. As Gerry Canavan stresses:

> Perhaps the true fantasy of the apocalypse then is not so much that we will be destroyed, but that *something will intervene in time to force us to change*—apocalypse in its original biblical sense, from the Greek ἀποκάλυψις, connoting not a final end but an unveiling: revelation. The fantasy of apocalypse is here unveiled, as itself a mode of critique, a crying out for change.
>
> (2014: 13)

In what follows, I examine, through certain characteristic films of the cycle, the iconography of the postapocalyptic wasteland, as well as the environmental discourses related to it.

I Am Legend is the third adaptation of Richard Matheson's 1954 novel of the same name, following *The Last Man on Earth* (1964), and *The Omega Man* (1971). Directed by Francis Lawrence, and written by Akiva Goldsman and Mark Protosevich, the film is set in a postapocalyptic New York City where a virus originally designed to cure cancer has left humanity almost extinct, while mutating most of the remaining humans into the Darkseekers, nocturnal zombie-like creatures. US Army virologist Robert Neville (Will Smith) is apparently the last human in New York, due to his immunity to the virus, and his only accompaniment is his dog Sam. Besides defending himself against the mutants, Neville's everyday routine revolves around the development of a cure based on experiments upon the Darkseekers, and daily broadcasts of a recorded radio message in order to find any other remaining humans. The film was a huge box-office success, returning $585 million on a $150 million budget, while it also received favorable reviews from the press (see Edelstein 2007; Ebert 2007). The film fuses conventions from science fiction and horror; specifically it draws upon the zombie narrative (Matheson's book influenced George Romero's *Night of the Living Dead* [1968], which is considered as the film that established the zombie cycle [Cotter 2020]). Nevertheless, the film follows the syntax of the dystopia cycle, with its protagonist struggling to survive in, and change a dystopian environment. The film, thus, negotiates thematic concerns of the zombie narrative, such as the human/non-human boundary, while also extending the iconography of the cycle with a visually striking, postapocalyptic landscape, laden with environmental connotations.

Similar to the pattern traced in the future city, the postapocalyptic landscape mingles the same signifiers of progress and ecosocial collapse, albeit here the apocalyptic aspect prevails. In the film's opening sequence, the viewer is introduced to the image of a desolate New York City. A long shot depicts a highway full of abandoned cars in the foreground framing the city's iconic skyline, which is devoid of any signs of human activity. This image indicates the collapse of human civilization, while the only sign of life comes from the non-human world as few singing birds flock in the sky. Subsequent shots reveal closer views of the city, which underscore not only the desolation and technological collapse but also how nature entrenches in the urban landscape. This motif of nature "reclaiming" former sites of technological civilization is perfectly encapsulated in a latter scene, where Dr. Nevil hunts a deer in Times Square, which has been transformed to a literal urban jungle with a field of tall grasses surrounding the ruined edifices. This motif contributes to the expansion of the cycle's iconography.

As discussed above, while the empty city was a generic image that permeated the SF film even from the 1950s, and it is also evident in the previous two cinematic adaptations of Matheson's novel, this "return of nature" (Stefanopoulou 2021: 42) evident in the postapocalyptic setting is pronounced only in the millennial version. This remark is corroborated by the film's production designer, David Lazan, who stated that the director and himself decided to render the visual look of this postapocalyptic world different and "less apocalyptic" from the previous versions. As Lazan describes, in opposition with the *Omega Man* where the streets are littered with trash, in *I Am Legend* "things are biodegradable. Nature takes over, cleans and moves things around" (charliejane 2007).

This generic shift indicates the filmmakers' desire for originality, and novelty by adding new element into the generic corpus, thus renewing the audience's interest in the genre. However, it is also reflective of contemporary cultural shifts, such as the current "cultural logic of ecology" (Rust 2013: 192). The visual antithesis that traverses the image of a (former) technological civilization taken over by the non-human world invokes environmental discourses about the limits of progress and the ephemerality of the human species (see Chakrabarty 2015). This connection to contemporary reality is also the result of the research involved in the realization of the postapocalyptic world. According to the film's VFX supervisor Jim Berney, the director "wanted everything to be as realistic as possible," and required the fictional world to be "based on a real life scenario of what would be left in the case of a three year desertion in NY City" (Bielik 2007). The production team did an extensive research, gathering different documentation about what plants would grow and what animals would populate the area. One of the sources that the production team came across was the bestseller nonfiction book *The World without Us*, by Alan Weismann, which circulated during the film's postproduction (Bielik 2007). This book, whose main theme is "humanity's environmental impact" (Maslin 2007), explores a similar premise about how the world would be transformed if humans suddenly disappeared from Earth, with nature eventually recovering, and taking over the planet again. The book's success indicates its relevance with contemporary concerns, and its premise is perfectly encapsulated in the film's spatial compositions, which similarly reflect concerns about the transience of human (technological) civilization, as well as its long-lasting imprint on the environment.

This motif of nature taking over former urban landscapes is also present in other films of the cycle, such as *Dawn of the Planet of the Apes* (2014), *War for the Planet of the Apes* (2017), and *After Earth* (2013). *Rise of the Planet of the Apes* (2011)—the first installment of the famous series' reboot—was examined in the creatures cycle, since it takes place in the present world, and its narrative structure and thematic focus revolves around the relationship between the technologically enhanced animal and the human. In *Dawn of the Planet of the Apes*, the premise is situated in a dystopian future, ten years after the apes' rebellion, and the outburst of the "simian flu." This pandemic caused by the human-made virus that enhanced the cognitive capacities of the apes has wiped out most of the human population, rendering the apes as the new, dominant species. This translocation to a future place disperses the generic text's signifiers of unfamiliarity to a wider environment. Therefore, while the human–animal relationship is also a thematic concern in the subsequent films, since they still belong to the same fictional cosmos, the syntax focuses on Caesar's struggle to change this dystopian society by trying (although unsuccessfully) to reconcile humans and apes. The film also offers the viewer glimpses of how the collapse of human civilization has transformed urban centers, such as San Francisco where the narrative action unfolds.

In *Dawn of the Planet* there is a main spatial antithesis between the ape village located atop a mountain in Muir Woods, where the apes have formed a society, and the colony of the remaining humans in San Francisco. According to the film's production designer James Chinlund, these two sets "aimed not only to contrast the rival factions' situations but also to demonstrate their parallels" (Li 2014). Indeed, both spatial enclosures intermingle signs of (technological) civilization and images of nature. However, while the ape village depicts a developing civilization in harmony with the environment, in the human colony this image is inversed. That is, the viewer bears witness to a crumbling civilization being taken over by nature, but in disagreement with this non-human world (as exemplified also in its relation with the apes). This future San Francisco is reminiscent of New York City in *I Am Legend*. Wild flora has swallowed the ruined, urban surfaces, covering buildings, streets, and other technological constructions. Similar to *I Am Legend*, in these images the film reverberates ecological discourses about nature's ability to recover despite the damage caused by human industrial activity. The compound where the humans are living is also an uncanny juxtaposition of antithetical signs. This is a former neoclassical building that humans have appropriated. While the surrounding spaces of this construction reflect the decay of human civilization, signs of technological "progress" still persist, such as the massive tower-fortress, which humans have installed into the building's base and the armory. Both function as reminders of the past, anthropocentric civilization that have brought about the ecosocial collapse in the first place. This contradiction is further emphasized in the next installment, *War for the Planet of the Apes*, where wilderness has almost covered all signs of human construction, save for the vast quarantine facility with an arsenal, which human paramilitary forces led by a ruthless colonel use to imprison apes.

This image of Earth transformed slowly to a vast wilderness also characterizes *After Earth* and *Oblivion*. *After Earth* is set in the distant future where humans have rendered Earth uninhabitable, and subsequently had to migrate to another planet, called Nova Prime. The film begins with a low-angle shot of a wounded boy named Kitai (Jaden Smith), lying amid a verdant territory, while a voice-over narration sets the film's ecological tone: "I've heard stories of Earth. A paradise until we destroyed it." This is followed by a montage of images depicting Earth's slow environmental destruction: fires, floods, factory fumes. One thousand years later humans live in their new home planet where they have established an advanced technological civilization in Nova Prime's harsh environment. When General Cypher Raige (Will Smith) and his son Kitai crash-land on Earth during a voyage through space, they encounter a verdant land, now recovered from humanity's destructive activities but also evolved in a way that is unsuitable for humans. A spatial antithesis is thus illustrated in humanity's new technological civilization, now located outside Earth, and a flourishing, but unfriendly to humans, Earth. This division hints at the contradictions of the contemporary ecosocial context, where humanity's technological activities become increasingly incompatible with the planet's sustainability. As Toby Nielson argues, *After Earth* reflects "the difficulty of how we perceive our relationship with nature in the context of the Anthropocene" (2019: 251). Similar ecocritical concerns are inscribed in *Oblivion*'s spatial articulations, specifically in the image of a wilderness dispersed with few remainders of human culture. Although the film's premise attributes this desolation to the invasion of a malevolent alien species, this iconography matches the cycle's visual patterns, indicating humanity's ongoing environmental degradation.

Lastly, another kind of apocalyptic scenery—in its making—depicting anthropogenic environmental destruction is evident in *2012*, *The Day after Tomorrow*, *The Happening*, and *Geostorm*. Although these titles may seem quite different from the other entries of the cycle, their narrative structure revolves around the survival of the protagonist in an endangered environment, which during the narrative course becomes unfamiliar, that is, different from our own experiential reality. As with the future city and the postapocalyptic landscape, this setting mingles markers of technological civilization (the cities being destroyed) with its detrimental implications. In addition, these filmic spaces indicate in the most explicit way the environmental subtext that informs most of the cycle's films. These spatial transformations include the disintegration of natural and urban landscapes due to the overheating of the Earth's core in *2012*; the abrupt climate change that freezes half the planet in *The Day after Tomorrow*; the "quiet" attack of nature on its most dangerous species, namely humans in *The Happening*; the massive storm, and other extreme weather phenomena that devastate and radically transform Earth in *Geostrom*. The above titles combine semantics from the disaster film with SF conventions, imbuing SF's "imagination of disaster" (Sontag 1965) with an environmental tone (Neilson 2019). Despite the fact that these environments seem radically different from our own experiential reality, they are actually a magnification and exaggeration of environmental catastrophes that are already taking place due to anthropogenic climate change—from Hurricane Katrina in 2005 to the 2021 European floods. The films' dystopian sceneries, similar to the other settings discussed above, tap into contemporary environmental anxieties, stressing the cycle's relevance with the Anthropocene.

I would like to conclude this chapter with *Black Panther*, a rather liminal case that lies on the borders of different cycles and features neither a dystopic city nor a postapocalyptic landscape, but rather constitutes a rare case of utopian imagination. The film marks a unique point in the superhero film, since it is the first Marvel movie that features a Black superhero in the protagonist role, as well as a predominantly Black cast, and a Black director/writer (Ryan Coogler). The film was a commercial, critical, and cultural sensation. *Black Panther* broke numerous box office records, being the highest-grossing film of 2018 at the American box office, and grossing over $1.3 billion at the global box office. *Black Panther* is the first superhero film to receive an Academy award nomination for the category of Best Picture, and many critics in the press considered it as one of the best superhero films (see Debruge 2018; Travers 2018; Roeper 2018). The cultural impact of the film was also significant. For example, in a *New York Times Magazine* article, author Carvell Wallace (2018) described the film as a "defining moment for Black America," while writer Shaun King (2018) compared *Black Panther* with Martin Luther King's "I Have a Dream" speech and the election of Barack Obama as president of the United States. Although other critics and academics were more skeptical about the film's racial discourses and its relation to Black experience and history (see Gathara 2018; Benash 2021), it is beyond doubt that *Black Panther* was a pivotal point to Black cinema, Afrofuturism, and the superhero film.

Despite the film's undeniable contribution to the superhero film, here I approach it in a different way. That is, although the film is based on the Marvel superhero comics of the same name and features technologically enhanced bodies, thus qualifying its inclusion to the techno-human cycle, I situate it in the dystopia/utopia cycle for two reasons. First, the main narrative setting of the film is Wakanda, which is an environment rather different from a common perception of reality. Although the rest of the fictional world that surrounds Wakanda adheres to cultural verisimilitude, Wakanda exemplifies the cycle's characteristic interplay between the familiarity of Earth and the strangeness of otherworldly semantics. Importantly, the film is also a rare case of utopian imagination, depicting not a collapsing society in crisis, but a technological and environmental utopia. Although the film does not illustrate in detail the social and political organization of Wakanda, no apparent conflicts are shown—besides that the crown may be challenged in ritual combat. Therefore, a rather harmonious society is represented in the scenes of the everyday life in Wakanda. Second, the syntax of the film describes how the actions of the protagonist, King T'Challa/Black Panther (Chadwick Boseman), eventually changes Wakanda and subsequently the rest of the world, as he decides to share his country's advanced technologies and provide aid to other territories. The film's syntax thus agrees with the cycle's, since it narrates how the Subject's actions transforms the surrounding social, technological, and physical environment.

Black Panther's thematic concerns are also aligned with the central preoccupation of the cycle as delineated above. Despite the apparent negotiation of racial, colonialist, and imperialist discourses, the human–environment relations are also foregrounded. This is mainly achieved through the importance of Wakanda's natural resources, and specifically the vibranium—a metal with extraterrestrial origins that is distinguished by its remarkable properties. It is this metal that is responsible for and sustains the sophisticated technological civilization of Wakanda. In addition, vibranium and the way it is used are apparently eco-friendly; Wakanda is represented as a green techno-utopia, where gleaming high-rises and futuristic vehicles harmoniously coexist with a pastoral landscape where shepherds attend to their animals. Therefore, a symbiotic relationship of humans, animal, earth, and technology is illustrated, where all the elements of this relation are of equal importance, creating a sustainable way of life. The need for such renewed relationship with Earth and new models of living are at the center of Anthropocene discourses. *Black Panther* thus partakes on this current "cultural logic of ecology" (Rust 2013: 192), not in a direct way but through its contrasting signifiers. A further opposition is shaped between Wakanda and the rest of the world mainly through the dialogue and narrative. In many scenes, the characters discuss the poverty of the rest of the world, which is juxtaposed with Wakanda's abundance of resources. Wakanda is thus represented as an alternative and successful example to global techno-capitalism, which impoverishes entire nations in the global South or even metropolitan areas within the so-called First World. Although the precise political system of Wakanda is not discernible, it is certainly one that can provide a sustainable way of life, keeping its antitheses in harmony and offering a solution to the impasses of the Anthropocene.

As our everyday reality is informed by the Anthropocene context, the cycle's strange surroundings can be read as extrapolations of the existing locations and situations of our contemporary ecopolitical moment or as aspirations of possible alternative futures, as in the case of *Black Panther*. Therefore, the cycle's place/space antithesis, that is, the interweaving of our common perception of reality with strange signifiers, acquires environmental meanings. The following chapters examine how the variations of the place/space antithesis of the second semiotic square express different spatial articulations and meanings, thus completing the spatial mapping of the genre in the new millennium.

7

The Zones Cycle: The Enclosed Spatiotemporalities of Global Capitalism

The zones cycle is formulated by the interplay of non-space and non-place. As I argued in Chapter 1, the term non-place connotes unfamiliarity and strangeness. Non-space signifies the negation of space, that is, the negation of open, uncharted territory. Thus, this negative definition connotes enclosure and restriction. In this cycle, the ephemerality and unfamiliarity of non-places are intersected with the containment and restriction of non-space, thus shaping the notion of a confined topography, imbued with a sense of precariousness and estrangement. The zones narratives unfold in these transient designated areas, characterized by an enclosed and disruptive spatiality, exemplified by such strange enclaves as spaceships and other futuristic and alien zones that locate the unfamiliar in a bounded area. However, the term zone refers not only to spatiality but also to temporality. Thus, the cycle includes two categories: the space and time zones, that is, both the bounded districts described above and time-loops, parallel worlds, and other time-paradoxes, which shift the attention to temporality and represent a kind of confinement, repetition, and enclosure inscribed not in space but in time.

Similar to the dystopia cycle, the main conflict in the zones narratives is between an individual and the environment, which is depicted here as an encased, looped, displaced, or otherwise contained and convoluted spacetime configuration. However, in this cycle, the struggle for survival in a technological and physical environment is restrained within bounded limits, as the protagonists struggle to survive in, save, and/or change a restricted spatial system or an equally bended temporality. The cycle includes thirty-one titles (15.2 percent of the corpus' films), which are further grouped into two categories: the space zones, which emphasize a contained spatiality, and the time zones, which foreground a distorted spatiotemporality. The films included in each category are: (1) the space zones: *Solaris* (2002), *The Core* (2003), *Doom* (2005), *Sunshine*

(2007), *Pandorum* (2009), *Predators* (2010), *Apollo 18* (2011), *Prometheus* (2012), *Gravity* (2013), *Interstellar* (2014), *The Martian* (2015), and *Passengers* (2016), *Alien: Covenant* (2017), *Life* (2017), *Annihilation* (2018), and *Ad Astra* (2019); (2) the time zones: *The Time Machine* (2002), *Paycheck* (2003), *Timeline* (2003), *Sky Captain and the World of Tomorrow* (2004), *Déjà Vu* (2006), *The Last Mimzy* (2007), *Inception* (2010), *Source Code* (2011), *The Adjustment Bureau* (2011), *Looper* (2012), *Men in Black 3* (2012), *Edge of Tomorrow* (2014), *Tomorrowland* (2015), *Project Almanac* (2015), and *Tenet* (2020). In what follows, I discuss the space and time zones in relation to their main spacetime configurations that encapsulate the protagonists' struggle to survive in and/or change the enclosed spatiotemporal systems of the cycle.

Space Zones: Spaceships, Space Stations, and Other Contained Alien Zones

In the space zones the main Subject's narrative Object is to survive in a confined spatial system (e.g., space shuttles, space stations, alien zones), while this effort usually implicates also the fate of humanity/Earth. Similar to the dystopia/utopia cycle whose main thematic concerns are reflected in the spatial surfaces of the future city and the postapocalyptic wasteland, the zones cycle's main themes can be traced in the films' restricted spatial articulations, such as the spaceship/space shuttle, the space station, or any other restricted spatial zone. The spaceship is a main characteristic of the genre with a variety of shapes and styles featured in SF films. Vivian Sobchack (1987) argues that the spaceship, as a staple icon of the genre, is not attached to any specific meaning but can acquire different connotations depending on the film. Certain films, such as *When Worlds Collide* and *Forbidden Planet*, represent the spaceship in a celebratory way, while others, such as *2001: A Space Odyssey* and *Silent Running* (1972), render the image of the spaceship as hostile and unwelcoming to human life. There is also a third strand of films, such as *Star Wars*, where the spaceship is used neutrally as a simple means of transportation. Therefore, unlike the railroad of the Western film, which is associated with a constant cluster of meaning throughout the entire genre, the spaceship is a much more fluid icon. As Sobchack puts it, "not only can the spaceship's meanings and functions change from film to film and from decade to decade, but its very shape and color are plastic and inconstant" (Sobchack 1987: 75).

I agree with the malleability of the spaceship as a generic icon, as each of the millennial cycles represents it in a different way. In the alien encounters cycle the spaceship is used as a means of transportation and/or a tool/weapon, while in the fantastic worlds cycle the spaceship functions as one narrative setting among many others, and is usually represented as spacious, convenient, and liberating. In opposition, in the zones cycle it is usually rendered as the restricted and defining locus of the film's central conflict. That is, the spaceship becomes a bounded area and the main (or even the only) milieu of the unfolding action. What's more, the other restricted locations of the cycle's films (space stations, space habitats, etc.), function in a similar way, that is, as limited zones depicted in a claustrophobic and suffocating way. It is precisely this confinement that characterizes the circumscribed space zones of the cycle.

These filmic spaces, thus, express the main thematic concerns of the cycle, which revolve around a confinement generated by global capitalism's technoscientific spaces. This contained spatiality, however, does not presuppose a lack of exterior shots, but rather constitutes the dominant aesthetic and feeling that these films relay, which is that of restriction and limitation. That is, the films' enclosed spaces where most of the narrative action unfolds echo the current exhaustion of a techno-optimistic vision and humans' confining rather than liberating relation with technology, in the context of global techno-capitalism's constant failures to sustain and improve human life. In what follows, I discuss these contained spaces in characteristic examples of the cycle, such as *Gravity*, *Interstellar*, and *The Martian*, among others. Although the cycle's films may also express different thematic concerns and can be examined under different prisms, I argue that these spatial articulations imbue the cycle with a claustrophobic tone that registers the contemporary skepticism toward the unlimited potentials of technological progress and human expansion.

Directed and co-written by Alfonso Cuarón, *Gravity* was a critical and commercial success, winning seven Academy awards, including Best Director, Best Cinematography, and Best Visual Effects. The film was praised for its intricate long takes, and its sophisticated, state-of-art visual effects that "restor[e] a sense of wonder, terror and possibility to the bigscreen" (Chang 2013), despite the rather simple narrative. *Gravity* follows Dr. Ryan Stone (Sandra Bullock) on her fist space expedition, during which a cloud of satellite debris destroys the mission's space shuttle, killing nearly all crew members, and leaving her stranded in space. The film is a simple, survival story, narrating the struggle of the protagonist to survive in the harsh environment of space and return to Earth.

According to Cuarón, the film is "a drama of a woman in space" (Masters 2014), and its main theme of adversity is expressed metaphorically through the image of the swirling and constantly returning space debris (Rose 2014). Although the director does not consider *Gravity* as a science fiction film (Masters 2014), I believe *Gravity* exemplifies SF's tradition of scientific realism established in films, such as *Destination Moon* (1950) and *Conquest of Space* (1955) (Jancovich and Johnston 2009). Although this generic tradition had a short cinematic life due to the "difficult" and technically detailed narratives it engendered, nevertheless, traits of this tendency survived in subsequent space films, with the most characteristic example being *2001: A Space Odyssey*. *Gravity* evolves this lineage, combining scientifically accurate settings and situations, with the more speculative traits of science fiction. Furthermore, the film's syntax revolves around the Subject's struggle to survive in contained technological and physical environments, thus matching the cycle's surface structure. In addition, these spatial figurations register the technological dead-ends and impasses of twenty-first-century capitalism.

In *Gravity* there is a constant shift between the infinity of space and the limitations of the circumscribed spaces, that is, the spacecraft and space stations that facilitate the protagonist's survival. The action takes place in two main enclosed environments—the International Space Station (ISS) and the *Soyuz* spacecraft. These surroundings are state-of-the art technological spaces both on a cinematic and on a representational level. In other words, not only are these spaces realized through the latest cinematic technologies, that is, the sophisticated CGI involved in *Gravity*'s "virtual set decoration" (Busch 2014) but also, they represent the pinnacle of Western expansionism in space and its technological supremacy. Nevertheless, these ephemeral non-places of global technoscience also stage its constraining effects. Despite the fact that these technological spaces function as a safe haven, protecting Dr. Stone from the adversities of space, they usually offer this protection for a short period of time. For example, the scene where Dr. Stone enters the ISS, undresses, and curls up in an embryonic position (see Figure 7.1) depicts a brief moment of safety, which is violently disrupted when a fire breaks out. Similarly, the *Soyuz* shuttle, which Dr. Stone uses to escape from the ISS, soon runs out of fuel. Therefore, despite their technological sophistication, these spaces are unable to sustain human life. These limitations and impasses are visually inscribed in Dr. Stone's constantly encircled body that suggests an entrapping environment and an attaching, rather than liberating, relation with technology. Even in exterior scenes, where the protagonist is outside of these "cocoons of survival" (Brody 2013), there is no feeling of expansiveness or exhilaration, but rather a sense that Dr. Stone is "caught in spatial systems beyond ... [her] control" (Vidler 2000: 1), and wrapped by an asphyxiating and enclosing blackness.

Interstellar is another critical and commercial success that exemplifies the spatial enclosures of the cycle. Directed and co-written by Christopher Nolan, the film follows former NASA pilot Cooper (Matthew McConaughey) who along with other three astronauts—Dr. Amelia Brand (Anne Hathaway), Romilly (David Gyasi), and Dr. Doyle (Wes Bentley)—travels through a wormhole near Saturn in search of a new home planet for humanity, since Earth has become uninhabitable due to crop blights and severe dust storms. Although at first sight *Interstellar* may seem to present an expansive vision of the cosmos that contradicts the feeling of restriction characteristic of the cycle, a closer examination proves otherwise. That is, the protagonist's interstellar travel is not represented as an optimistic expansion into space in order to conquer new worlds, but rather as a cosmic struggle in restrained alien zones to secure humanity's survival. Thus, despite the stretching of the timespace boundaries, the film is permeated with a sense of confinement and a melancholic attachment to Earth. *Interstellar*'s dominant feeling is that of suffocation in enclosed vehicles, barren planets, and geometrical abstractions in timespace, imbued with a gloomy tone that constantly enfolds and restricts the subject, despite an array of awe-inspiring shots depicting cosmic events.

Thus, the film's narrative premise that revolves around the decline of the cutting-edge technocracies of the early twenty-first century, and the loss of the public's faith in big, technological projects like the conquest of space is negotiated in a twofold manner. On the one hand, this faith in technologies and Western expansionism is restored through the narrative resolution that sees humanity triumphantly surviving with the help of technoscience that enables its relocation in a state-of-the-art space habitat orbiting Saturn. This belief in pioneering and grand technoscientific enterprises is also promoted on an extratextual level by the director himself, who in an interview featured in the *Interstellar* Blu-ray disc states that "space travel has always been that ultimate challenge," and despite the fact that it is often forgotten today there are still "a few individuals pushing the boundaries of where the human race ... has ever been or can possibly go" (*Interstellar* 2014). This stance can also be traced in another extratextual feature, namely, the production of the film itself, which also resembles a big, technological project. That is, the film's $165 million budget, its sophisticated cinematic technologies, and the epic in scale production design render *Interstellar* as an equally grandiose technological endeavor as those imagined in its fictional cosmos. On the other hand, the film's spatial articulations depict the narrative events as a constant struggle with unfriendly environments and collapsing technologies that mirror the contemporary skepticism in an unlimited technological progress.

Interstellar's space zones—from the different spacecraft, to the alien planets and cosmic structures—articulate this sense of entrapment and the constant struggle with technological breakdown. This is exemplified in the crew's exploration of the first potential planet for habitation. As soon as Cooper, Doyle, and Dr. Brand lands on the planet's watery surface, they realize that its environment is hostile for human life, since they are encircled by immense tidal waves, which subsequently kill Doyle. The watery planet is rendered an uninhabitable and restricted zone, exemplifying the cycle's sense of entrapment in unknown spatial systems. This confinement is intensified further in the crew's effort to abandon the planet, where a temporary malfunction of the shuttle's engines impedes their evacuation. Not only does this technological breakdown postpone their departure, but also it dilates time since every hour spent on the water planet translates into seven years on Earth. Upon their return to the mothership *Endurance*, they find an aged Romily for whom twenty-three years have passed since their departure. Romily's prolonged confinement constitutes another version of the multifaceted restrictions that the crew encounter in their interstellar journey. Admittedly, such obstacles are also generically motivated, providing suitable Enemies for the protagonist's narrative objective. Yet, I believe this overall restriction in technological and physical systems that is played out in the cycles' films also reflects contemporary anxieties about the limitations of technologies, which are often more restraining than liberating.

Following *Gravity* and *Interstellar*, *The Martian* is another acclaimed, big-budget SF film set in space that exemplifies the characteristics of the cycle under discussion. Based on the 2011 same-name novel by Andy Weir, and directed by Ridley Scott, the film centers on NASA botanist Mark Watney (Matt Damon), who is accidentally stranded on Mars when a sandstorm forces his crewmates to abort mission. The film is another survival story on space, depicting Watney's lone struggle to survive on Mars, and the efforts of NASA to rescue him and bring him to Earth. The film thus epitomizes the cycle's surface structure as its main conflict concerns the struggle of an individual in circumscribed alien surroundings. Like *Gravity*, *The Martian* also follows the SF tradition of scientific realism, secured by the close collaboration with NASA scientists who provided consultation on different aspects of the film's production—from the script to the design of vehicles and habitats (Zeitchik 2015). This collaboration not only granted scientific accuracy to the film but also, as many commentators have noted (see Debruge 2015; Dargis 2015; Zeitchik 2015), functioned as a publicity campaign for NASA's space missions, rekindling the public's interest for space exploration, at a time when the agency's perception and funding have been at a critical point. In this way, the film is both similar and different with *Interstellar*—similar in its faith in ambitious technological undertakings, and effort to rehabilitate interest for the space program, but different in its optimistic and feel-good tone that contravenes with the melancholic and somber mood of *Interstellar*. Still both films, along with *Gravity* and the rest of the cycle, are underpinned by the central thematic concerns of restriction in enclosed technological spaces, and the fragility of the different technological resources and solutions.

These concerns are inscribed in the filmic spaces of *The Martian*. Although the film is imbued with the grand vistas of Mars, I contend that it is the juxtaposition of the vastness of the alien landscape with the confined technological spaces where the protagonist tries to survive that capture the film's thematic considerations. These restrained zones include NASA's habitat on Mars—the Hab—and the rover, a vehicle that plays a central role in the protagonist's survival. These spaces provide shelter to Watney, enabling his survival in the harsh environment of Mars. Yet, like *Gravity* and *Interstellar*, they are often subjected to technological malfunction or provide only temporary solutions. For example, in one instance the Hab's airlock blows out, resulting in the destruction of many vital parts of the habitat, including the potato plants that Watney has been cultivating in order to survive (see Figure 7.2). Furthermore, in order to use the rover for a fifty-day journey to the landing site of the next Mars mission, Watney must find solutions both for the duration of the rover's battery and for the heating problem. Although he solves the problem by using a radioisotope thermoelectric generator, this solution exposes him in great health hazards due to the generator's radioactive materials. Therefore, despite the fact that these limited space zones sustain the protagonist's life, they remain temporal structures with limited resources, offering ephemeral solutions. As Chris Pak notes in his review of the film, "[t]he fragility of technological solutions to the exploration and habitation of space becomes paradoxically central to this narrative" (Pak 2017: 109). In this way, *The Martian* registers contemporary anxieties about technology's limitations and inability to provide permanent solutions for our survival. The film's restrained space zones thus enact both the restrictive and enabling role that technology plays in global capitalism.

Contained space zones abound in the other films of the cycle. In *Sunshine* a group of astronauts are aboard the spaceship *Icarus II* on a mission to reignite the dying Sun with a nuclear fission bomb. The spaceship becomes an entrapping milieu for the protagonists who must cope with the constant technological failures, as well as the psychological breakdown caused by the protracted isolation. In a more outlandish version of a similar scenario, *The Core* depicts another dangerous mission, not in space but in the center of the Earth, with the purpose of restarting the rotation of the Earth's core whose instability would eventually lead to the total destruction of the planet. The claustrophobia caused by the limited spaces of the mission's snake-like vessel, the USS *Virgil*, is further underscored by the literal immersion in the compassed and restricted environment of the Earth's crust. Despite the fact that in both films technological solutions eventually work, protagonists achieve their goals, and humanity is saved, the process of sustaining human life is depicted as arduous, confining, and laden with technological shortcomings.

These themes of confinement, technological breakdown, and survival in harsh environments are also found in *Passengers* and *Pandorum*. Despite their different tone and style, both films portray two interstellar spaceships, the *Avalon* and *Elysium*, respectively, on their way to distant planets which humanity aims to colonize after the depletion of Earth's resources. In both films passengers and/or crew members awaken from the hypersleep and have to face different problems, including a series of failures in the ships' systems and the effects of isolation. Especially in *Pandorum* these problems are vividly registered in the ship's surroundings, which are illustrated in a dark, industrial aesthetic and are infused with a menacing atmosphere. This limited environment is baffling for both characters and viewers, since most of the shots are darkly lit and the ship's layout is not established in any general shot. This disorientation and confusion reflect not only the protagonists' mental state—the hypersleep-related disorder causing partial amnesia and hallucination—but is also constructed in spatial terms, in the labyrinthine structures of the spaceship. In these labyrinthine spaces the anxious subject tries to grasp its position in the perplexed technological and physical configurations of late capitalism.

In *Prometheus* and *Alien: Covenant*—the two millennial additions to the *Alien* franchise—as well as in *Life*, *Doom*, *Apollo 18*, and *Predators*, the entrapment in compassed spaces is underscored by the presence of a hostile alien organism, and the films are informed by the trappings of both science fiction and horror.

Directed by Ridley Scott, *Prometheus* is a prequel to the same director's 1979 iconic SF film *Alien*. *Prometheus* follows the crew of the same-name scientific vessel on its expedition to the distant moon LV-223, which is believed to be the home of humanity's ancestors, the Engineers. The filmic spaces—from the spaceships to the artificial structure on the moon's surface, which the team explores—are diffused with the same signifiers of restriction and suffocation that underpin the cycle. It is in these confined and inhospitable zones that the protagonist, Dr. Elisabeth Shaw (Noomi Rapace), is entrapped and tries to escape from the alien threat. *Alien: Covenant* is *Prometheus*' sequel, set eleven years after the events of the latter film. The film revolves around the crew of the colonization ship *Covenant* on its course to planet Origae-6. When a solar flare damages the ship, the crew awakens seven years before reaching its destination and subsequently receives a transmission of a human voice from a nearby habitable planet, which they decide to investigate. Thus, not only does the technological breakdown obstruct the crew's mission and is responsible for the death of some of its members, but also it leads them to what is proven after all a hostile environment for human life. In *Life* the story is centered on yet another crew aboard the International Space Station that uncovers the first evidence of life on Mars, which proves to be unfriendly. The threatening presence of the alien organism along with a series of technological mishaps, traps the crew in the station's limited spaces. The pessimistic tone is further highlighted by the film's final sequence, where the technological solution that the two remaining scientists implement in order to secure that the alien organism will not reach Earth is proven, at the end, insufficient. In *Doom*, *Apollo 18*, and *Predators* similar themes can be tracked, as their protagonists' struggle to survive from a malevolent alien entity in contained technological and physical environments.

The final example of the space zones, *Annihilation*, is rather different from the previous films. Written and directed by Alex Garland, the film narrates the story of biology professor Lena (Natalie Portman), who joins an expedition, along with four other women scientists, to explore the Shimmer—a mysterious quarantined zone in Earth where an alien presence mutates all living organisms. The major difference is that the restricted area portrayed in the film is neither a futuristic vessel nor an alien zone in a distant planet, but a (un)natural environment located on Earth. Yet, the Shimmer functions in the same way as the other confined areas of the cycle, that is, as a temporal and enclosed strange environment that entraps the protagonist who struggles to survive in its peculiar surroundings. This zone also bears other similarities with the spatial

Figure 7.1–7.4 The enclosed spacetime configurations of the zones cycle in *Gravity* directed by Alfonso Cuarón© Warner Bros. Pictures 2013. *The Martian* directed by Ridley Scott© 20th Century Fox 2015. *Inception* directed by Christopher Nolan© Warner Bros. Pictures 2010. *Source Code* directed by Duncan Jones© Summit Entertainment 2011. All rights reserved.

articulations described above. First, technologies collapse inside the Shimmer, leaving the expedition with no communication with the outside world. In this way, the film stresses once again, global techno-capitalism's limitations. Second, like many of the space zones discussed above, the Shimmer becomes an unwelcoming environment for human life, since all explorers of the Shimmer have either perished or mutated into another lifeform. Lastly, this vicinity is imbued with the sense of confinement and limitation that distinguishes many of the cycle's films. Therefore, *Annihilation* constitutes another example of the space zones where an emphasis is placed upon the survival of the protagonist in spatial enclosures. In the next section, I examine another type of enclosure, one that concerns also time, as portrayed in the time zones.

Time Zones: Loops, Parallel Timelines, and Other Fragmented Temporalities

In the second category of the cycle, the focus is shifted from the confined spatial articulations to the warped temporalities. Accordingly, the surface structure in this category revolves around the protagonist's effort to change a bended timescape, that is, to change the future/history/reality. Therefore, the time zones are preoccupied with time distortions and paradoxes, such as loops and other displacements, which are also closely linked with the notions of parallel/possible worlds, alternate realities, and time-travel. Such themes and concepts have a long lineage in SF literature and the pulps (see Clute and Nicholls 1995), but their cinematic existence is a more recent phenomenon. That is, although there are classical films that explore possible worlds/alternate realities, such as *It's a Wonderful Life* (1946), as well as works by Fritz Lang, Alfred Hitchcock, and Orson Welles, such concepts came to prominence (in academia, industry, and media) after the 1990s (Buckland 2014) and appeared in films such as *Groundhog Day* (1993), *Run, Lola, Run* (1998), and *Sliding Doors* (1998), among others. In SF film and television, these themes appeared in different variations in the *Back to the Future* film series (1985, 1988, 1989), *Twelve Monkeys* (1995), *Sliders* (1995–2000), and *Seven Days* (UPN, 1998–2001), among others.

In the millennial cycle these distorted timelines, like the space zones discussed above, express similarly a sense of entrapment and containment, which is also inscribed in spatial terms. That is, the films' temporal disruptions are mapped onto spatial metaphors and the creation of spatial configurations, which are underpinned by signifiers of restriction and limitation. Although not all films in this category employ their distorted timelines in the same way, I argue that the fragmented spatiotemporalities of the cycle function as limited zones where the protagonist tries to survive, usually changing during the narrative course the surrounding timescape. These looped spatiotemporal configurations are again situated in the context of global techno-capitalism and the restrictions and limitations it places upon its subjects. In what follows, I examine these themes and concepts as articulated in the most popular/critically acclaimed films of the category, such as *Inception*, *Source Code*, *Looper*, and *Tenet*.

Inception is another Christopher Nolan film grouped in the zones cycle. Similar to the director's other entries in the cycle—*Interstellar* and *Tenet*—*Inception* is a big-budget production that gained critical recognition, exemplifying the Nolan's reputation as the creator of "cerebral blockbusters" (Bordwell with Thomson 2019: 24). Indeed, *Inception* was one of the highest-grossing films of 2010, grossing over $828 million worldwide on a $160 million budget, while the film's artistic acclaim is encapsulated in its eight Academy awards nominations and four wins. The film focuses on Dominic Cobb (Leonardo DiCaprio), who is an expert in an uncommon kind of industrial espionage, namely, stealing information by entering into the dreams of his targets. Cobb's new assignment, however, does not involve the extraction of information but a much more difficult endeavor: the implanting (inception) of an idea into the target's mind. Specifically, wealthy businessman Saito (Ken Watanabe) hires Cobb to infiltrate the dreams of his competitor's son, Robert Fischer (Cillian Murphy), and to implant in his unconscious the idea to dissolve his dying father's massive energy conglomerate. In exchange, Saito promises to erase Cobb's criminal record, which prevents him from returning home to his children. A generic blend of heist movies, film noir, and science fiction, the film also exemplifies what Thomas Elsaesser (2009) labels as the "mind-game" films. These films "'play games' with the audience's (and the characters') perception of reality," thus addressing "epistemological problems (how do we know what we know) and ontological doubts (about other worlds, other minds)" (Elsaesser 2009: 14–15). Such epistemological and ontological disruptions are reflected in *Inception*'s syntax, which revolves around the protagonist's entrapment in convoluted spacetime configurations, exemplified in the labyrinthine spaces and distorted timelines of the film.

Inception's warped spacetimes are perfectly epitomized in the film's four dream levels with their distinct topographies. The first level is a gray, urban landscape, depicting a car chase in a rainy Los Angeles. The second level is located in a modernist hotel, portraying a zero-gravity fight scene in a rotating hotel corridor. The third level is fortified building atop a snowy mountain, and the fourth level is Limbo, the unconstructed dream space, which resembles a crumbling city of modernist edifices. The film moves back and forth between these different levels, creating a "montage space" (Vidler 2000: 243) of disparate locations. However, as many commentators have noted (see Denby 2010; Scott 2010; Fisher 2011), despite the fact that these spatial configurations are expressions of each dreamer's unconscious, they are not characterized by the raw quality and freedom that permeates the dreams, but instead they are underpinned by a much more organized structure and linear logical. As Mark Fisher (2011) argues, "the spatial distortions at work in *Inception* don't resemble the ways in which dreams distend or collapse space," since "[t]he four different reality levels remain distinct, just as the causality between them remains well-formed" (Fisher 2011: 40–2). Far from being oneiric landscapes, *Inception*'s dreamscapes are occupied by the imperatives of globalized capital, becoming, as Fisher (2011: 45) notes, "the scenes where competing corporate interests play out their banal struggles." I agree with Fisher, and I further argue that *Inception*'s warped dreamscapes, far from endowing the subject with freedom and unconstrained movement, capture it in enclosed and well-defined surroundings characteristic of the zones cycles (see Figure 7.3).

Inception's spacetime articulations, thus, despite the fact that they represent the seemingly infinite possibilities of alternate worlds and parallel dimensions, actually reproduce the limitations of the circumscribed spaces of our technological saturated, neoliberal societies. As the protagonists immerse further into the deeper layers of the unconscious, the time significantly dilates. However, this plasticity of time inside the dreamscape has no emancipating possibilities for the subject. In spite of their apparent malleability, *Inception*'s dream levels, like the levels of a video game, are actually defined by a looped code that offers only limited opportunities. This is evident by the fact that the first three dream levels consist of extended action sequences in which—in a classic Hollywood mode—the protagonists must escape the various obstacles that take the form of the fully armed projections of a "militarized subconscious," as described by one of the characters. In other worlds, the protagonists are confined by the clichés of Hollywood's action films, which exemplify the "strictures and controls built into contemporary space" (Jones 2015: 14). What's more, the fourth dream level, the Limbo, which represents the protagonist's raw Id, is not a space full of possibilities, but a rather vacuous and depressing environment representing the ultimate enclosure from which the protagonist must escape.

Source Code is another "intelligent blockbuster" (Cameron and Misek 2014) characterized by convoluted timelines and intricate plotting. Directed by Duncan Jones and written by Ben Ripley, *Source Code* follows US Army captain Colter Stevens (Jake Gyllenhaal), who is sent into an eight-minute digital reenactment of a train explosion in Chicago, in order to identify the terrorist responsible for the bombing. This is accomplished through an experimental military-scientific application called Source Code, which allows Stevens to be projected into the mind of Sean Fentress, a passenger aboard the train, and relive repeatedly his last eight minutes. During this projection, Stevens (believes he) is restrained in a capsule, taking orders from a control room whose broadcasts are transmitted through a video screen inside the capsule. *Source Code* is another instance of the "mind-game" film (Elsaesser 2009) that aims at an ontological plurality and epistemological uncertainty achieved through distinctive articulations of cinematic time and space. According to Allen Cameron and Richard Misek (2014: 110), the film exemplifies the "forking path" narrative, in which multiple versions of the same scene are replayed, but each time, due to minor variations, a different narrative outcome is generated. The same authors also argue how these unstable temporalities are transcribed in spatial terms, and that *Source Code* and *Inception* are "intrinsically architectural: they not only feature intricately designed narratives but also foreground and thematize the architectural processes involved in their own narrative construction" (Cameron and Misek 2014: 110). Thus, through a series of spatial metaphors that manifest in the film's scenography and mise-en-scène, temporal relations are mapped onto visual and spatial forms. I concur with the significance of the film's spatiotemporal articulations, and I further contend that such relations lay at the center of the time zones narratives, expressing the struggle of the protagonist to survive in or change such warped spacetime configurations.

In *Source Code* this narrative objective is placed in the interchange of the film's main narrative settings: Chicago, the train, the capsule, and the control room. According to Warren Buckland, these spaces present three ontological realities: the "game environment" of the train, the imaginary space of the capsule, and "the actual world," which includes Chicago and the control room (Buckland 2014: 193). Although the protagonist's main locales of action, the train and the capsule, are virtual and imaginary spaces respectively, they are rendered as rather confined and limited surroundings (see Figure 7.4). In other words, despite the fact that the resetting of time and the constant repetition of the eight minutes may appear to endow the protagonist with a malleable timeline, the limited spaces of the train and the equally limited eight-minute loop in which the protagonist is trapped present a rather contained spatiotemporal articulation. This is even more emphasized by the fact that Stevens is ensnared inside this loop against his will, and this restriction is imposed on him by the designer and head of the Source Code program, Dr. Rutledge (Jeffrey Wright)—a fitting representative of global techno-capitalism. After a number of loops in which Steven tries to identify the bomber, he learns that he was fatally wounded during a mission in Afghanistan and he is actually on a life support, with most of his body missing. The capsule and his healthy body are projections of his mind in order to make sense of the environment. Thus, Stevens is doubly imprisoned. Not only is he restricted by the eight-minute loop and the confined spaces of the virtual train, but also, he is equally restrained in the imaginary capsule, as well as immobilized (and half-dead) in the actual world. What's more, these circumscribed spaces are also figured as spaces of exploitation under techno-capitalism, with "[t]he unending process of resetting the clock ... evok[ing] the endlessness of labour within late capitalism" (Constable 2018: 434).

Another narrative permeated by the trope of the loop, entangling the protagonist in a similar web of technoscience, profit, and exploitation is *Looper*. Written and directed by Rian Johnson the film is set in 2044 and revolves around Joe (Joseph Gordon-Levitt), an assassin or looper who works for a crime syndicate in Kansas City. Further ahead in the future in 2074, the syndicate sends its enemies back in 2044 to be executed, in order to dispose their bodies without being detected by the police. To conceal its criminal activities, the syndicate sent back the loopers in order to be killed by their younger selves—an act referred to as "closing the loop." When Joe's older self (Bruce Willis) arrives, he escapes from younger Joe, subsequently trying to alter the past in order to affect his own future, while younger Joe obstructs his actions. This alteration of the past includes locating and killing a child, that will become the Rainmaker, the future mafia boss that will kill older Joe's wife. By presenting a time-traveling technology, which has been banned and is used only secretly for the profit-driven activities of a future criminal organization, *Looper* situates its warped spatiotemporalities in the context of a future exploitative social and economic system. At the same time, the subjects of this system, the loopers, are literally enclosed in loops from which they try to escape, exemplifying the narrative Object of the cycle's protagonists. Therefore, the film's time displacements and their spatial manifestations are traversed by the confinement that typifies the cycle, with the liberating possibilities of futuristic technologies, such as time-travel being restricted by the demands and flows of (illegal) capital accumulation.

These timescape articulations are mapped onto the film's main narrative setting. Kansas City in 2044 is represented as an anonymous, global metropolis ravaged by social inequalities and poverty. Few signs of futuristic technologies, such as hovercrafts and some gleaming high-rises, are contradicted with the poverty-stricken areas where vagrants constantly attempt to steal in order to survive, and are literally being run over by the rich. Although this setting is not a literal enclosed area, like the limited zones where the protagonist of *Source Code* is entrapped, it is represented as a space that constantly imposes restrictions upon its subjects whose movements are dictated by the flows of capital, the labor activity, and other social strictures. This is exemplified in Joe's daily routine. Like the other loopers, Joe moves in predetermined areas, such as the headquarters of the criminal organization, the strip club, and his apartment. Only a violent break in this routine forces him to flee from these spatial enclosures and find refuge in a farm outside the city. This enclosed spatiality is underscored by the equally confined temporality in which Joe is trapped. While his future self, the old Joe, travels back in time in order to amend his future and save his wife, his actions will actually lead to the very same future he tries to circumvent. By the end of the film, young Joe realizes that the only way to break out from this endless loop is to delete himself from the timeline, that is, to kill himself.

Tenet is the latest Christopher Nolan film that is grouped in the present cycle. The much anticipated 2020 blockbuster is yet another cerebral event movie that combines convoluted plotting, temporal tricks, and spectacular action scenes. The film's delayed theatrical release due to the Covid-19 pandemic, in combination with its strategically planned promotion endowed it with an almost mythological status as the cinematic object par excellence that will secure the future of the theatrical experience itself (Lodge 2020). Despite the mythology built around the film, *Tenet* proved one of Nolan's most controversial films, dividing both critics and spectators (Sharf 2020). The film follows a secret agent, called the Protagonist (John David Washington), who is introduced to time inversion—a technology coming from the future that inverts a person's or object's entropy, thereby enabling the manipulation of time. Specifically, this time-bending technology appears like backward moving in relation to the non-inverted world. The Protagonist must use this technology in order to prevent an attack from the future that threatens to annihilate the present world. *Tenet* presents a fresh perspective on the time-travel theme, substituting the genre's stable icon of the time-machine with more intricate semantics such as the turnstile—the film's obscure time-inverting machine. However, like *Inception*, which utilized the semantics of the heist film in a science fictional context, *Tenet* blends these science fiction trappings, with conventions from the spy and action film, using its mind-bending concepts to justify extravagant action scenes. In addition, and again following *Inception*'s cues, *Tenet* creates labyrinthine spacetime configurations that enwrap the protagonist in temporal paradoxes and inverted spaces, which he must fathom in order to survive and prevent the world's destruction.

Like *Looper*, *Tenet*'s spaces are not literal enclosed zones. On the contrary, the film presents a web of global locations around the world. Indeed, the film features a plethora of world-spanning locations, which is typical of the Hollywood action and spy film. *Tenet*'s impressive action sequences take place in several different major metropolitan areas around the world, imbuing the film with the global interconnectivity that underpins multinational capitalism. However, this succession of international spaces does not necessarily endow the subject with a freedom of movement and unlimited choices; instead, the similarity and anonymity of these global spaces point to the limitations and recursive logic that shapes the spatial experience of global neoliberalism (Jones 2015). This is encapsulated in *Tenet*'s inverse chronology and backward-moving that enfolds the space and narrative onto itself, creating a loop where the end coincides with the beginning. This enfolded spatiotemporality is underlined also by the film's allusion to the Sator square, an ancient five-word Latin palindrome, which provides not only the film's title and the names of many characters, organizations, and locations (Sator, Arepo, Tenet, Opera, Rotas) but also formulates the film's looped narrative structure. Therefore, despite the time-bending concepts and technologies, by the film's end the protagonist is again at the beginning. The final dialogue between the protagonist and his handler Neil (Robert Pattinson) underscores once more the film's circularity and enclosed logic. In the Protagonist's question to Neil, if things can be changed if done differently, Neil replies, "what happened, has happened," continuing that this is an "expression of faith in the mechanics of the world, it's not an excuse to do nothing." Although this fatalistic worldview does not deprive the subject's agency, it clearly points to the limited choices and paths offered by these encased timescapes of global techno-capitalism.

In the rest of the cycle's films, temporal disruptions and alterations create new spatial configurations, which are often imbued with the sense of containment that permeates the cycle. For example, *Déjà Vu*, *Paycheck*, *The Adjustment Bureau*, *Edge of Tomorrow*, *Project Almanac*, and *Tomorrowland* tamper with the flow of time and reality using different devices: a time-loop (*Edge of Tomorrow*), an alternate dimension/parallel world (*The Adjustment Bureau*, *Tomorrowland*), a time-manipulating device/time machine (*Déjà Vu*, *Paycheck*, *Project Almanac*). Again, these time displacements are mapped onto spatial coordinates, such as the iteration of the same looped spaces with small variations in *Edge of Tomorrow*, *Déjà Vu*, and *Project Almanac* or the convergence of disparate locations in *The Adjustment Bureau* and *Tomorrowland*. In each case, despite the fact that the films' protagonists achieve their goals and manage to change the course of future events, their navigation into these convoluted timescapes is often represented as exhausting, since they remain encased in recursive dead-ends.

However, not all films of the cycle employ their alternate worlds/timelines in the same way, that is, to portray fragmented realities, which the entrapped protagonist tries to fathom and navigate. For example, in more classic time-travel narratives such as *The Time Machine*—the millennial remake of H. G. Wells's classic novel—as well as *Timeline*, *Men in Black 3*, and the alternate history film

Sky Captain and the World of Tomorrow, the narrative devices of the time-travel and/or alternate reality are mainly used to place the action in a past or future timeframe and scenery (e.g., the Earth in the year 802,701 in *The Time Machine*; the medieval France in *Timeline*; the 1969 *Apollo 11* launching in *Men in Black 3*; and an alternate, technological-advanced 1930s New York in *Sky Captain and the World of Tomorrow*). Nevertheless, even in these cases the surface structure of the cycle is repeated as the Subject's narrative objective is to survive in, and/or change a distorted and confined spatiotemporal system. In the next chapter, I examine how the second square's surface structure is diversified in the last cycle's more expanded spatial systems.

8

The Fantastic Worlds Cycle: The Spectacular Technoscientific Empire

The last cycle emerges from the interaction of the terms space/non-place and is labeled fantastic worlds. In this cycle, the strangeness of non-places is extended in the uncharted territories outside Earth, reaching the furthest corners of the cosmos. The vast dimension that the term space implies is manifested in the plethora of other worlds, planets, galaxies, and their non-human civilizations that populate the filmic narratives. The films of this cycle are characterized by a grand and unusual scale that is far removed from our known reality, thus acquiring an epic dimension that is diffused with fantastic elements. Like the other cycles of the SF worlds, the main conflict is between an individual and his/her environment. However, the struggle here takes even larger proportions, since the individual is fighting to save the whole galaxy or universe from a destructive force and not just Earth and its inhabitants.

The characteristics described above, such as grand scale, sweeping vistas, multiple planets and civilizations, and interplanetary conflicts with universal repercussions, have mainly been associated with what is generally defined as space opera. Despite the wide adoption of this industrial/media/user label, I propose my own theoretical label of fantastic worlds, as a term that better describes the workings of the cycle. As Altman (1987) argues, industrial labels are of limited interest to the critic, since s/he uses them only as useful points of departure to explore further theoretical and critical issues. In the case under consideration, I suggest the term fantastic worlds in order to stress that the cycle emerges as a theoretical construction based on specific criteria. These criteria include the placing of the cycle as a specific expression of the genre's topographical map (worlds), and the articulation of the space/non-place interaction that generates the maximum unfamiliarity (fantastic) in the second semiotic square, since the strangeness of non-places is magnified in the immensity of space.

The term space opera was first coined in 1941 by SF fan and author Wilson Tucker to describe—in analogy to radio soap operas[1]—the formulaic SF narratives that appeared in the 1920s–30s pulps.[2] These stories featured minimal characterization and mainly included "vast settings of interstellar conflicts between clearly defined 'good' and 'bad' sides" or the heroic endeavors of an individual entangled in a cosmic melodrama (Sawyer 2009). The history of space opera in film and television can also be traced back to the pulp tradition. *Buck Rogers* (1939) and the *Flash Gordon* film serials (1936, 1938, 1940) are among the first cinematic and televisual space operas, which are adaptations from the comic strips. These narratives demonstrate the basic structure of space opera, i.e. a battle between "good" and "evil" on a cosmic scale. However, the inadequacy of the special effects of the time underplayed the visual potentials of such stories, by confining their actions in spaceship interiors or planetary surfaces (Westfahl 2003). It is perhaps due to this technological limitation, as well as an industrial tendency for seriality and melodrama, that space opera developed initially but also throughout its history, a strong affinity with television, evident in such popular TV series, as *Captain Video* (DuMont, 1949–56) and *Tom Corbett, Space Cadet* (CBS/ABC/NBC/DuMont, 1950–5). The form found its ideal expression in the original *Star Trek* series (NBC, 1966–9), which epitomized the romantic and adventurous aspects of space opera infused with a liberal stance. Another influential franchise is the *Star Wars* film series.[3] *Star Wars*' (1977) influence from pulps and old-style space opera is even more obvious since the plot involves a straightforward battle between the good Jedi knights who fight the dark and evil empire in a cosmic and colorful background. However, the state-of-the-art effects that created spectacular and detailed vistas, and the following huge financial success, popularized the subgenre and spawn imitators in the following years. Such examples include the TV series *Battlestar Galactica* (ABC, 1978–9), *Buck Rodgers in the 25th Century* (NBC, 1979–81), as well as the films *Dune* (1984) and *Last Starfighter* (1984). In the 1990s, the proliferation of digital technologies and CGI gave prominence to the "neo-space opera" of impressive effects (Sawyer 2009) with spectacular films, such as *Starship Troopers* (1997), *The Fifth Element* (1997), and *Galaxy Quest* (1999) but also narratively elaborated television series, such as *Babylon 5* (PTEN/TNT, 1994–8).

The millennial cycle preserves certain characteristics of the space opera, such as "the vast scale" (Clute and Nicholls 1995) and "a sense of the infinite sublime" (Sawyer 2009: 506) as captured in the cycle's spectacular vistas. Another basic trait of the cycle is the plethora of strange and different worlds that coexist in an intergalactic system. However, in the sociopolitical context of the twenty-first century these characteristics acquire new connotations Specifically, I argue that the millennial cycle evokes notions of the Empire, a decentered and deterritorializing "global form of sovereignty" that has superseded the nation-states and is "composed of a series of national and supranational organisms, united under a single logic or rule" (Hardt and Negri 2000: xi; xii). Istvan Csicsery-Ronay Jr. (2003) stresses the interrelation of SF with Empire and argues that the genre maps the transition from imperialism to Empire, and is implicated in the shaping of a new, global technological regime—a "technoscientific empire" (Csicsery-Ronay 2003: 231). Although Csicsery-Ronay associates the concept of the Empire with the entire genre, I particularly locate this relation in the fantastic worlds cycle, and I argue that in its narratives we can trace a dialogue between imperialism and Empire. That is, in certain films of the cycle notions of the industrial-era imperialism, such as top-down hierarchies, militarism, and clear boundaries, are maintained. Yet, the cycle's preoccupation with a constantly expanding space populated by a variety of different planets/civilizations governed under a single, universal technological regime resonates deeply with the concept of the technoscientific Empire that relates with our post-industrial contemporary societies. Certainly, themes such as imperialism and colonialism can be traced in many expressions of the genre, as other scholars have also noted (see Rieder 2008); however, I contend that there is a particular relevance with the fantastic worlds cycle (as well as the alien encounter cycle, which was discussed under the related prism of race).

The fantastic worlds cycle includes the following eighteen titles (8.8 percent of total films): the *Star Wars* series (2002, 2005, 2015, 2016, 2017, 2018, 2019), the *Star Trek* series (2002, 2009, 2016, 2013), the *Guardians of the Galaxy* series (2014, 2017), *Avatar* (2009), and *The Hitchhiker's Guide to Galaxy* (2005), *Serenity* (2005), *Ender's Game* (2013), *Jupiter Ascending* (2015). It is interesting to note that although the cycle contains comparatively few titles, half of the films (*Avatar*, five *Star Wars* films, the *Guardians of the Galaxy* films and *Star Trek into Darkness*) are among the top fifty titles with the highest grosses in the corpus. Furthermore, *Avatar* and *Star Wars: The Force Awakens* are respectively the first and third highest-grossing films of the corpus and the first and fifth all-time highest-grossing films worldwide, earning nearly $3 billion each. In addition, nearly all of the above titles are part of a popular media franchise.

The above facts, thus, create an analogy between the Empire and the cycle on a formal level. As Csicsery-Ronay argues "the cinematic serial form … is particularly well-suited for imperial sf. It permits an enormous variety of elements to be juxtaposed with only minimal motivation" (2003: 240). Another epic aspect that undergirds the cycle's production is also the state-of-the-art CGI and other cinematic technologies used for the creation of the spectacular filmic spaces, such as the films' fantastic worlds. Therefore, the vast and epic dimension of the cycle can also be translated in industrial/cinematic terms, with the cycle's technologically sophisticated mega-pictures that dominate global markets being the ideal expressions of the expansive logic of the technoscientific Empire. In the following section, I discuss the cycle's resonance with the concept of Empire as traced mainly in the films' spatial (and spectacular) articulations.

Expanding into the Universe. The Cosmic Spaces of the Technoscientific Empire

In the fantastic worlds cycle the central conflict concerns the struggle of an individual to survive in and/or save a world, a galaxy, or even the universe from an "evil" and destructive force. That is, in this cycle the struggle for survival in a social and physical environment that epitomizes the second semiotic square, acquires universal dimensions. Similar to the previous two cycles whose main themes are registered in the films' spatial surroundings, the present cycle's thematic concerns can also be traced in the filmic spaces. The fantastic worlds cycle exhibits similarities with the dystopia/utopia cycle, such as the intermingling of techno-futuristic spaces with signifiers of technological collapse; yet, what differentiates them is the scale and scope of the landscape. Specifically, the vast scale and universal scope that is central to the cycle is expressed mainly in the depiction of multiple worlds across the galaxy, which is the main milieu of the narrative action. This vast space consisting of a variety of worlds/settings is contrasted both with the usually single environment of the dystopia cycle and the restricted spaces of the zones cycle. Despite the fact that the zones cycle, as discussed, may also portray different worlds, it is only in the fantastic worlds that this cosmic perspective acquires a proper sense of expansion. I associate this sense of expansion with notions of the technoscientific Empire whose characteristic space is also "horizontal, expansive, and limitless" (Csicsery-Ronay 2003: 237). Therefore, while the zones cycle inscribes the limitations and technological shortcomings of global capitalism, the fantastic worlds cycle illustrates mainly a techno-optimistic version of the Empire, even if discourses surrounding the industrial-era imperialism may also be articulated in certain films. In the following paragraphs, I examine the cycle's different interplanetary environments in relation to notions of the Empire and its ideologies of expansion and technological progress.

Avatar is an apt example of the Empire's cosmic expansion but also of the expansive practices of Conglomerate Hollywood. Production company 20th Century Fox created anticipation around the film with a strategically planned promotion campaign that placed an emphasis on *Avatar*'s pioneering cinematic technologies, such as the motion and performance capture and digital 3D cinematography, and—as expected—the name and reputation of its creator and SF auteur, James Cameron. Indeed, the marketing campaign was very effective, and the film broke many box-office records and became the highest-grossing film of all time, amassing nearly $2.8 billion on a budget of $237 million. *Avatar* remained on that position for ten years, until 2019 when *Avengers Endgame* became the new number one for a while until a Chinese re-release put *Avatar* back on the top spot in March 2021 (Tartaglione 2021). As expected, the film created a franchise, with one sequel and three more titles announced[4] and multiple tie-ins establishing a lucrative brand name, and a cinematic empire for the years to come. The film was an equal artistic success, garnering numerous awards and nominations, including three Academy awards for Best Art Direction, Best Cinematography, and Best Visual Effects. At the same time its innovative use of cinematic technologies was not only artistically recognized but also had a great impact on the entertainment industry, as reflected in the temporary surge in 3D films after *Avatar*'s release (Goldberg 2018). *Avatar* thus exemplifies the imperatives of Conglomerate Hollywood, while "effect[ing] through technology a change of paradigm" (Elsaesser 2011: 247). However, as Elsaesser (2011) notes, this alignment of the film's production context with the dictates of the industrial-entertainment complex seems to be ambiguously articulated in *Avatar*'s fictional cosmos.

Avatar is set in the mid-twenty-second century when humans have colonized Pandora, a lush habitable moon of a gas giant in the Alpha Centauri star system, in order to mine a valuable mineral called unobtanium. The expansion of the mining colony coordinated by the Resources Development Administration (RDA) threatens the continued existence of the local tribe of Na'vi—a humanoid species indigenous to Pandora. In order to explore Pandora's environment and interact with the indigenous people, the scientific team of the colonizing mission use Avatars—genetically engineered Na'vi bodies, which are remotely operated.

Jake Sully (Sam Worthington) is a paraplegic former Marine who is recruited by RDA in order to operate his twin brother's Avatar, when the latter suddenly dies. Although Jake is at first aligned with the expedition's military-industrial complex, he gradually changes his allegiance and becomes an exponent of the Na'vi's efforts to defend their planet. Not only does Jake defends the Na'vi's cause but also, he becomes their leader, while forming a romantic bond with their princess Neytiri (Zoe Saldana). By the film's end, Jake literally becomes one of them as his consciousness is transferred, through a Na'vi ritual, from his human, paraplegic body to the alien body. *Avatar*'s ambiguous negotiation of many themes—from Western colonialism and environmental politics, to issues of technoscience and embodiment—has generated mixed reviews and antithetical interpretations, with many commentators noticing how the film perpetuates the same colonialist assumptions that try to undermine (see Dargis 2009; McCarthy 2009). Elsaesser goes a step further arguing that the contradictory discourses inscribed in the film are actually a part of a planned decision, with this "false consciousness" being "the very principle of the film's construction" (2011: 254), thus allowing for multiple "access points" for the global and diverse audiences Conglomerate Hollywood needs to serve.

These antithetical signs that underpin *Avatar*'s conception are also reflected in its filmic spaces, which, I argue, articulate notions of the technoscientific Empire. Indeed, the film represents a future where global capitalism has not only caused the depletion of Earth's resources but also has expanded in the universe, seeking other worlds suitable for exploitation. In this fictional cosmos—that nevertheless bears many similarities with our own reality—technological advances have enabled the spread into new worlds. This expansion exemplifies the Empire's fundamental relationship with technology, which offers "not only a set of tools used for exploitation of the colonies" but also consolidates the idea of "political power linked to technological momentum" (Csicsery-Ronay 2003: 233). This relation is encapsulated in RDA's base on Pandora, which is indeed a center of political power inextricably linked with its technological infrastructure. This is all the more emphasized in the base's representation as simultaneously an administrative center, which secures RDA's decisions and strategies, a military base that ensures the implementation of those decisions, and a cutting-edge research center whose main goal is to study and record Pandora's complex biological systems. Although the scientific aspect of the colonizing expedition is represented as antithetical with the purposes and tactics of the company, with the head of the research program Dr. Augustine Grace (Sigourney Weaver) explicitly stating her opposition with the decisions of the company, the scientists' data-mining of Pandora is actually an indispensable aspect of the Empire's constant expansion. This is visually underscored with the illustration of the laboratories in the same white-grey color palette and high-tech surfaces that characterize the administrative/military facilities of the base—a visual cue that captures their spatial and ideological affinity, and which is clearly contradicted with the green and organic look of Pandora's natural environment.

Pandora is represented as the opposite of the technologized space where the humans are settled. Pandora is depicted as a rich, bioluminescent rainforest full of bizarre flora and fauna. Not only is Pandora a visually striking world brimming with life, but also the trees and plants have formed electrochemical connections between their roots, which act as neurons. The biosphere is thus a short of sentient network, which the Na'vi can access it, and which they worship it as a deity called Eywa. It is exactly this lush habitat that the RDA wants to destroy and exploit, in order to collect a precious mineral, the unobtainium, which is located underneath the forest. In this way, the RDA exemplifies the Empire's tendency for "relentless denaturing," a constant "replacement of nature by artifice" (Csicsery-Ronay 2003: 237).

Yet, despite the fact that on a narrative level there is an explicit contradiction between the abundant, organic, and interconnected life of Pandora and the sterile, technological, and hierarchical spaces of the RDA, the affinities between these worlds become more apparent when examined on the level of the medium. Indeed, the spectacular landscape of Pandora is the result of extensive use of 3D cinematography and CGI—technologies that constitute an indispensable aspect of Hollywood's collusion with the military-industrial complex (Elsaesser 2011). Since the same technologies developed in Hollywood are used in other sectors of the industry, as well as military operations (Lenoir 2000), Pandora's cinematic construction is underpinned by the same technocratic values and logic that permeate the RDA; thereby, it is rendered as a subtler, even if spectacular, version of the Empire's technologically suffused spaces. What's more, even the language that the fictional characters use to describe Pandora reverberates with notions of the Empire. Specifically, Dr. Grace Augustine labels this complex ecosystem "a global network," since its million synapses permit the constant uploading/downloading of Na'vi's data/memories, forming a sort of organic supercomputer. This image, however, can also adequately describe the ideal version of the Empire, which expands through "flexible and fluctuating networks," and where "the development of communications networks has an organic relationship to the emergence of the new world order" (Hardt and Negri 2000: 23; 32). These notions are spatially expressed also in the other films of the cycle.

The *Star Wars* film series, along with the *Star Trek* films, are perhaps the most representative examples of the cycle. In particular, the *Star Wars* series are not only characteristic examples of space opera, but they also constitute fundamental texts of the SF film and a popular cultural phenomenon.[5] The original trilogy (1977, 1980, 1983) marked the genre's transition from the margins to the center of the film industry, endowing the SF film with the status of the highly popular genre that it still enjoys. In addition, it also paved the way for the establishment of Conglomerate Hollywood, since it was through these films that the concepts of the blockbuster film series, effects-driven imagery, and tie-in products became indispensable aspects of the Hollywood film industry. Another much discussed feature of the series is its postmodern aesthetics based on the recycling of popular texts and genres, such as the 1930s–40s SF pulps, the cinema and television SF serials, the samurai and Western films, which imbued the *Star War* films with a nostalgic tone (Sobchack 1987; Telotte 2001). Related to this nostalgia is also the series' ideological articulations, which the majority of scholars critiqued as mostly conservative (Brooker 2004; Cornea 2007). The millennial additions to the franchise, which include eight films, follow the cues of the original trilogy as far as the use of pioneering special effects and box-office returns are concerned; but they also diverge from their predecessors since they try to amend the much-criticized representations of the original trilogy, and to be more inclusive in terms of race and gender.

As many scholars have stressed (Wetmore 2005; Booker 2006; Geraghty 2009), the original trilogy also tackled issues of imperialism and asymmetrical power relations. For instance, Kevin J. Wetmore Jr. argues that in the original *Star Wars* trilogy "'imperial perspective' is front and center, not least ... because [it] concerns a rebellion against an empire" (2005: 20). M. Keith Booker, commenting on the complex politics of *Star Wars* that draws upon the rhetoric of the Cold War,[6] maintains that "the forces of the Empire, with its advanced technology and superior resources, clearly have much in common with the capitalist West, while the rebel forces often resemble ... anticolonial forces" (2006: 116). On a similar note, Lincoln Geraghty states that "the Empire in *Star Wars* represents bureaucratic, ruthless, imperialism" (2009: 70). Lastly, John Rieder, examining the connection between the emergence of the SF genre and colonialism, argues that "the lingering presence of the conventions of colonial imperial adventure fiction ... persist[s] in late-twentieth-century mass-market products such as the *Star Wars* saga" (2008: 35). I agree with the above authors, and I further support that notions of imperialism, updated in the context of the twenty-first-century global technological regime, imbue the latest installments of the film series. In what follows, I examine these themes as imprinted in the filmic spaces and through the concept of the technoscientific Empire. I will focus this discussion mainly on *Episode VII: The Force Awakens* (2015), the first film of the sequel trilogy, which is also the most profitable and critically acclaimed *Star Wars* film of the corpus.

The Force Awakens is set thirty years after the events of the original trilogy. The First Order has risen from the fallen Galactic Empire and seeks to end the New Republic. The Resistance, led by General Leia Organa (Carrie Fisher), assists the Republic's struggle against the First Order. The film follows Rey (Daisy Ridley) and Finn (John Boyega) in their first steps in the Resistance, and their search—with the help of former key players in the Rebel Alliance, Han Solo (Harrison Ford), and his longtime companion Chewbacca (Peter Mayhew)—for Leia's brother and last Jedi master, Luke Skywalker (Mark Hamill). Like the original trilogy, *The Force Awakens* stages intergalactic fights and power struggles across a variety of worlds dispersed in a galactic system. In this spatial system, the similarities between the fictional First Order—former Empire—and the technoscientific Empire as a political concept are more than just sharing the same name. The First Order/Empire colonizes and exploits worlds through an extensive technological apparatus, retaining and extending power via the use of sophisticated surveillance systems and advanced weaponry. Such methods suggest both the more aggressive strategies of imperialism and the subtle methods of the technoscientific Empire. The Empire's expansion across the galaxy is visually established in the long shots of the planets as seen from space that introduce the viewer to the film's different worlds. The diverse planetary landscapes, that include the desert planet Jakku, the forest planet Takadana, and Starkiller Base—a planet turned into a superweapon of mass destruction by the First Order—indicate not only the vastness of space but also the variety and contradiction of forms that this constant technological/spatial growth entails.

This juxtaposition of different settings/planets in the same galactic space is associated with discourses about imperialism and the technoscientific Empire. Rey's homeworld, Jakku, is a remote, barren planet that bears similarities with Tatooine—the original trilogy's famous desert planet where Luke Skywalker grew up. Jakku's sandy surfaces are scattered with wreckages, such as a vast imperial spaceship half submerged in the sand and other remains of a past battle (see Figure 8.1). This site of technological ruins becomes the main source of living for scavengers such as Rey, who search for parts that can be salvaged and sold to the nearby trading post. Jakku, thus, exists in the margins of the Empire, feeding off the remnants of its technological apparatus. This image of scarcity imbued with low-tech aesthetics is contrasted with the more techno-futuristic worlds that we glimpse in the film (e.g., the technologically advanced worlds of the Hosnian Prime system, which are destroyed by the Starkiller Base). The film therefore includes spaces that allude to the imperialist division between center and periphery, while at the same time it hints to their mutual dependence and interaction in the same galactic system. This coexistence of different economic and technological positions in the same spatial system evokes how in the technoscientific Empire, "all levels of production can exist simultaneously and side by side, from the highest levels of technology, productivity and accumulation to the lowest, with a complex social mechanism maintaining their differentiation and interaction" (Hardt and Negri 2000: 335). Thus, the alternation of antithetical spaces retains the Empire's (and the cycle's) characteristic sense of expansion through incorporation of differences.

Another location that also reflects notions of the Empire is the Starkiller Base. Like Jakku, The Starkiller Base also alludes to the original trilogy, evoking the image of the famous Death Star—the Empire's weapon of mass destruction that annihilated entire planets. However, in opposition to the Death Star, which was

Figures 8.1–8.4 The cosmic spaces of the technoscientific Empire in *Star Wars: The Force Awakens* directed by J. J. Abrams© Walt Disney Pictures 2015. *Star Trek Beyond* directed by Justin Lin© Paramount Pictures 2016. *Guardians of the Galaxy* directed by James Gunn© Walt Disney Pictures 2014. (8.3 and 8.4) All rights reserved.

a planet-shaped weapon, Starkiller Base is a planet terraformed into a weapon. The transformation of an entire planet into a mechanism of mass destruction hints at the deep imbrication of the Empire with technology. This is visually stressed in the long shot of the planet as seen from space where a big spherical structure inscribes the planet's surface with artificiality, suggesting the extent of this technological transformation. The First Order/Empire, thus, appropriates entire populations and habitats in order to serve its purposes and establish its power. This appropriation, however, reaches the deepest levels of the very structure of the planet itself. That is, the colonization and suffusion of space with technologies reaches the geological level, that is, the level of planetary life itself where technology and the spatial surroundings cannot be separated. This is another feature of the Empire which "not only manages a territory and a population but also creates the very world it inhabits" (Hardt and Negri 2000: xv). Starkiller Base is subsumed under and equated with this vast technological mechanism—a fact which becomes further pinpointed when the destruction of the mechanism's core feature entails the destruction of the planet itself. This transformation of a living system into death machine illustrates how the technoscientific Empire is, indeed, characterized by the "absolute capacity for destruction ... the absolute inversion of the power of life" (Hardt and Negri 2000: 346).

Like *Star Wars*, the *Star Trek* media franchise is another popular cultural phenomenon that consists of an overwhelming number of series, films, novels, comics, games, not to mention the fan-produced media, many of which "force the primary text to accommodate ... [the fans'] interests" (Jenkins 2004: 266).[7] As discussed above, the franchise originated from television and specifically from the legendary series *Star Trek* (NBC, 1966-9)—now known as *Star Trek: The Original Series* (*TOS*). The series' creator Gene Rodenberry who had previously written and produced many Western television shows, famously pitched the series to NBC as "*Wagon Train* to the stars," referring to a famous Western series of the era and emphasizing *TOS*'s influence from both the Western and science fiction genres (Telotte 2008a: 15). Indeed, as M. Keith Booker notes, in *TOS* "parallels between the exploration of the galaxy and the exploration of the American West are inescapable" (2008: 196). These allusions are reflected in the series' central theme of humanity's expansion into space—the last frontier—updating the iconography and themes of the space opera, and setting out a formula for the televisual SF genre. *TOS* became known for its progressive representations, such as its multiracial (and multispecies) crew, which mediated the pressing social issues of the era—from the civil rights to the Vietnam War (Franklin 1994; Geraghty 2007; Gonzalez 2015; Booker 2018).

As many commentators have noted (Golumbia 1995; Booker 2008; Hassler-Forest 2016; McKagen 2022), despite *TOS*'s overall progressive and liberal vision, the series and following entries in the franchise still perpetuate some of the imperialist and colonialist discourses that underpin space opera. For example, M. Keith Booker (2008: 196) notes that "the rhetoric with which the series openly declares the United Federation of Planets to be an anticolonialist enterprise is made problematic by its very connection to the taming of the American frontier, with its associated legacy of racism and genocide." Similarly, E. Leigh McKagen (2022: 332), commenting on the series' famous opening voice-over narration,[8] states that "[a]lthough presented as the benevolent pursuit of knowledge for the betterment of humankind, this directive toward exploring the unknown underwrites the franchise with discourses and practices of Euro-American imperialism and colonialism." Dan Hassler-Forest situates this residual imperialism of the series in the context of the growing military and economic power of the United States after the Second World War, arguing that "*TOS* offered an archetypically American fantasy of non-violent imperialism grounded in discourses of prosperity and collaboration rather than military conquest" (2016: 374). According to the same author, *TOS* thus anticipated the emergence of global capitalism, as described by Hardt and Negri's concept of the Empire, which was further accentuated in subsequent series of the franchise. I agree with Hassler-Forest, and I further support that notions of the technoscientific Empire are also enacted in the millennial films of the franchise, as evident in the filmic spaces of the reboot trilogy (2009, 2013, 2016) discussed below.

In the *Star Trek* reboot trilogy, the main locations that represent the United Federation of Planets—the interstellar affiliation of planets, which maintains the space force Starfleet—are the twentieth-third-century Earth and the main vessel of the film, the famous USS *Enterprise*. Both locales reflect the franchise's techno-optimistic vision of the future where humanity, and other species, coexist in harmony in post-scarcity societies where technology has resolved all the social and political issues—from racial hierarchies to species difference. Specifically, the USS *Enterprise* perfectly condenses the values and ideology of the Federation. The smooth, white, high-tech surfaces of the vessel reflect the efficiency and functionality of the Federation, which preserves its unity and power through the use of sophisticated communication and information technologies. Interestingly, according to film's production designer Scott Chambliss, the design of the spaceship (and all locations associated with the Federation for that matter) was inspired by the architectural style of Eero Saarinen—the 1960s futurist architect who designed the TWA terminal at JFK airport, among other iconic buildings (Pascale 2009). Saarinen's landmark edifices "captured the aspirations and values of mid-twentieth-century America" (Pelkonen and Albrecht 2006: 1)—from the thrill of international flight to the power of American industry. Saarinen's buildings thus shaped the international image of the United States in the post-Second World War years as the new, benevolent, technological superpower. It is precisely such values of technological innovation and peaceful expansion that imbue not only USS *Enterprise* (and, by extension, the Federation) but also form the basic tenets of the technoscientific Empire.

In addition, the USS *Enterprise*, like the other spaceships of the cycle, becomes a signifier of expansion, technological progress, and mobility. This image is contrasted with the vessels and alien zones of the zones cycle which, as discussed, are portrayed as enclosed spaces that restrict the protagonists. The USS *Enterprise* is represented as an open, luxurious space that offers infinite possibilities to its inhabitants, fulfilling its purpose as a part of a "humanitarian and peacekeeping armada"—as one of the characters describes the Starfleet. This depiction of the spaceship as a site of movement and liberation is emphasized in the sequence where the *Enterprise* is revealed to the viewers for the first time in *Star Trek*. As the crew of the Starfleet aboard the shuttle approaches the spacedock where five spaceships wait for their departure, an astonished Dr. Leonard McCoy (Karl Urban) urges his co-passenger James T. Kirk (Chris Pine) to look the view outside the window. The spectators are aligned with Kirk's viewpoint as he is also stunned by the sight of the Starfleet's state-of-art spaceships. The uplifting music, in combination with the constant movement of the floating camera as it approaches the *Enterprise* and explores its impressive interior, emphasizes the spaceship not only as an exciting site of possibilities but also as a spectacle to be admired. This sequence therefore illustrates the *Enterprise* as the means of growth, freedom, and progress through technology, rendering it the symbol of the technoscientific Empire par excellence.[9]

A similar sequence unfolds in *Star Trek Beyond*, when the *Enterprise* reaches Yorktown, the "Federation's newest and most advanced starbase" that exemplifies the Empire's expansion through technology. A similar framing with the sequence discussed above aligns the viewers with the onlooking characters who admire the starbase—an impressive circular edifice with interlocking parts that resembles a futuristic version of M.C. Escher's designs (see Figure 8.2). Again, the elevating soundtrack aims to stress the genre's characteristic "sense of wonder" (Mendlesohn 2003) that this sight induces to both characters and viewers, while the floating camera that lingers on Yorktown's elaborate surfaces further pronounces its depiction as yet another spectacular site. Yorktown is thus a perfect example of SF's "technoscientific sublime," which implicates a sense of awe and dread in relation to overwhelming human technological projects (Csicsery-Ronay 2008: 7). The technoscientific sublime, achieved cinematically through spectacular special effects, shapes not only the particular sequence but also the entire cycle, due to the films' emphasis in vast dimensions and awe-inspiring technological visions. Indeed, the expansion in space and its technological transformation informs both the cycle and the technological sublime as the latter "aims at the future and is often embodied in instruments of speed … that annihilate time and space" (in Csicsery-Ronay 2008: 157). In this way, it also reverberates with notions of the technoscientific Empire, since the conflation of timespace through technological means enables the processes of deterritorialization, which is so central in the formation and dominance of post-industrial global capitalism.

The next example of the cycle, *Guardians of the Galaxy* is an interesting case since the film draws upon the conventions of both the superhero narratives and space opera. Since the film features a team of superheroes based on the Marvel characters of the same name, it clearly participates to the superhero cycle. Yet, the film's fantastical settings situated in the vast reaches of a colorful and strange universe, with a plethora of worlds and species, suggest its associations with space opera. According to our proposed taxonomy, since the film's environment is rather different from our common perception of reality, the genre's unfamiliarity is diffused in the surrounding spaces and therefore the film can be grouped in the narratives of the second semiotic square. Indeed, these links to the space opera are also acknowledged by the film's director, James Gunn, who stated that *Guardians of the Galaxy* is a "thousand percent space opera" (Faraci 2014), and that he wanted to revive the colorful, pulp SF films of the 1950s and 1960s (Screenrant 2014). Like many space operas the film focuses on an intergalactic adventure where protagonist Peter Quill (Chris Pratt) and a group of extraterrestrial mercenaries get in the middle of a conflict between two alien species, the Kree and the Xandarians, after stealing a powerful artifact. The film features many fantastic worlds and cosmic locations that compose the grand and expansive perspective of the cycle, while at the same time it articulates discourses about the Empire.

One of the central settings of the film is the planet Xandar, capital of the Nova Empire, where the Guardians first meet and where the final battle takes place. Like in many other fantastic worlds of the cycle, the spectators are first introduced to Xandar with a long shot of the planet as seen from space. The next, bird's-eye-view shot depicts the streamlined surface of the planet where white, futuristic structures are discerned amid open, green spaces. Closer views of the planet are brightly lit, stressing its harmonious and high-tech environment where Xandarians lead peaceful lives (see Figure 8.3). It is interesting to note that Xandar was inspired by the city-state of Singapore, and specifically from one of its landmark sights, Gardens by the Bay (Failes 2014). Singapore is known to be one of the global cities of late capitalism, which are "the political and financial centers of Empire" (Hardt and Negri 2000: 346). Therefore, through this visual reference, Xandar is illustrated as a center of the technoscientific Empire, representing a successful paradigm of its peaceful (and green) capitalist development. This association is further stressed since the Nova Empire is a benevolent, interstellar hegemony made up of multiple worlds and different species, maintaining a decentered apparatus of rule through technology, variety, and expansion. Even the Nova Corps—the Empire's primary military force—are represented as a peacekeeping unit, exemplifying "the fusion of force and legitimacy" (Csicsery-Ronay Jr. 2003: 237), which informs the technoscientific Empire.

In opposition to the shiny and sleek surroundings of Xandar, the mining post Knowhere presents the darker side of the technoscientific Empire. Knowhere is a mining colony, and criminal space outpost built inside the severed-head of a celestial being, on the very outskirts of known space. The mining operation that takes place in this enclave concerns the valuable organic material inside the skull, such as bones, brain tissue, and spinal fluid, and it is a "dangerous and illegal work suitable only from criminals," as one of the characters puts it. As all of these rare resources are highly valued in the black market, Knowhere attracts criminals, outlaws, and rogues from across the galaxy, becoming a lawless and unruly locale that recalls the frontier towns of the Western film. Again, the spectators are first introduced to this extraordinary location with a long shot of Knowhere floating among colorful nebulas. Like the *Star Trek* sequences described above, here too the spectators follow the viewpoint of the characters, as Peter Quil gazes in awe this cosmic location, encouraging the spectators to also admire it as a spectacle. However, this spectacle is based on a more ruined version of the technoscientific sublime. Knowhere is rendered as a crowded, densely layered, low-tech world that interweaves a retro, colorful palette with signs of a decaying industrial development, creating an opposition with the white and clean surfaces of Xandar (see Figure 8.4). In this way, this habitat recalls also the other low-tech worlds of the cycle, such as Jakku in *Star Wars: The Force Awakens*, which are similarly opposed with the techno-futuristic worlds. Such contrasting worlds that underpin the film, and the cycle at large, stress the Empire's expansion through an "imaginary coexistence of infinite variety in unbounded order" (Csicsery-Ronay 2003: 243).

Besides the blockbuster film series that constitute the core of the cycle, there are also two medium-budget films: *Serenity* and *The Hitchhiker's Guide to the Galaxy*. These filmic texts are not promoted as extensively as the mega-pictures discussed above. However, both films, like the big-budget films, are based on a well-known and established material, thus perpetuating the same logic of seriality that characterizes the cycle, and the millennial SF film in general. *Serenity* is based on the short-lived, but influential, space Western series *Firefly* (FOX, 2002–3), marking the directorial debut of the series' creator Joss Whedon. During its one-season run, the show attracted a limited, but devoted, audience, which, after the show's abrupt cancellation, run extensive fan campaigns that significantly contributed to its cinematic continuation. *Firefly* thus marks one of the rare occasions in the SF film, and cinema in general—the other being the *Star Trek* series—where a television show is adapted to the big screen, and not vice versa (Telotte 2008b). Despite high anticipation, the film underperformed at the box office, garnering $40.4 million on a budget of $39 million. In opposition, *The Hitchhiker's Guide to the Galaxy* performed better at the box office, returning $104.5 million on a $50 million budget (however not good enough to launch a sequel). The film is the long-planned adaptation of the famous, comedy SF media franchise created by Douglas Adams that consists of the radio series, the best-selling six novels, comic books, a 1981 TV series, a 1984 video game. Douglas Adams also co-wrote the film's script along with Karey Kirkpatrick, thus maintaining the franchise's British tone and low-tech aesthetic in this US/UK co-production. Despite their different tones, both films tackle themes of expansion, control through technological systems, and other issues surrounding the technoscientific Empire.

Serenity follows the crew of the same-name space freighter in the distant future where humans have colonized a new solar system due to Earth's overpopulation, and the subsequent exhaustion of resources. In this new solar system, the Alliance is an interplanetary government of technologically advanced planets united under its rule, while the Independents represent the outer rim planets that refuse governance by the Alliance. Serenity's captain Mal Reynolds (Nathan Fillion) and first mate Zoe Washburne (Gina Torres) have fought on the Unification War against the Alliance, which resulted in the prevalence of the latter. The crew's daily routine of illicit economic activities is interrupted when Mal decides to give shelter to psychic River Tam (Summer Glau) and her brother Simon (Sean Maher) who are wanted by the Alliance for knowing an information that could jeopardize its rule. The film creates spatial metaphors that evoke notions of both imperialism and the technoscientific Empire. On the one hand, the social and economic organization in this new solar system resembles the division between center and periphery common in the imperialism of industrial capitalism—with the Alliance standing for the center and the insubordinate outer planets representing the periphery. On the other hand, the Alliance's spatial systems suffused by a surveillance apparatus and biopolitical mechanisms hint at the subtle workings of the technoscientific Empire. This antithesis is presented visually through an iconography that draws upon the conventions of both the Western film and the SF film. The outer rim planets are portrayed as frontier-like outposts amidst rural landscapes that allude to the Western film, and are associated with industrial-era imperialism. These images are then juxtaposed with the SF iconography of surveillance systems and invisible technologies of control that permeate the futuristic central planets. In this way, the film illustrates the Alliance's straddling between an authoritarian-style regime of violence and militarism, and the more benevolent facade of the technoscientific Empire.

The last example, *The Hitchhiker's Guide to Galaxy* follows the intergalactic adventures of ordinary human Arthur Dent (Martin Freeman), who finds himself aboard a spaceship, with the help of his alien friend Ford Prefect (Mos Def), minutes before Earth is destroyed by an alien fleet. Following the absurdist humor of the novels, the film is rather different in tone from the rest of the cycle, since it pokes fun with the conventions of space opera. Nevertheless, certain characteristics of the cycle discussed above, such as an expansive view of the cosmos and the sense of liberation that imbues the intergalactic travel through spaceships, are also traced in this parodic version of the cycle. The latter is exemplified in the protagonist's decision, at the end of the film, to keep traveling the galaxy rather than settle down in Earth II. Furthermore, the film also creates spatial analogies between the Earth's neoliberal societies and the galaxy's social organization. In particular, the demolition of Arthur's house in Earth due to the building of a new bypass is paralleled with Earth's subsequent destruction by the alien fleet of the Vogons due to the construction of a hyperspace express that will boost "the development of the outlying regions of the galaxy." Furthermore, as the respective authorities announce in both cases, "the plans have been on display at the planning office" for a long time; thus, the legitimacy of the projects is unquestioned. The galaxy is thus portrayed as a cosmic version of the Earth's technoscientific Empire that aims at expansion and technological progress at the cost of the prosperity of human lives, while concealing its methods under the facade of efficiency, legitimacy, and "polite" bureaucracy.

As noted, the fantastic worlds cycle, despite its comparatively few titles, is the third most popular in terms of grosses, mainly due to the inclusion of the most popular media franchises of the genre, such as *Star Wars*, *Star Trek*, and *Avatar*—the latter spawning a franchise after its release. The popularity of the cycle is thus tied to the fame of these franchises, which display the latest cinematic technologies, offering spectacular narratives to a global audience, and technologically updating the staple traits of the cycle, such as the cosmic vistas and intergalactic conflicts. These colossal numbers and spectacular aspects related with the cycle's production are also traced in its narratives, which the above analysis situated in the context of the technoscientific Empire. Through these narratives whose syntax revolves around an individual trying to survive in and/or change a physical and social system of cosmic proportions, the cycle expresses the last variation of the place/space antithesis of the SF worlds, thus completing the spatial mapping of the genre in the new millennium.

Epilogue

The present book used semiotic tools (Greimas's semiotic square and narrative grammar) and historical analysis to map the contemporary SF film in Hollywood. By examining the genre in a specific time period (2001–20) and a systematic corpus of films through a social semiotics approach, this study offered a theoretical map of the genre situated in a particular historical context. Specifically, the study proposed two semiotic squares (SF worlds and SF bodies) to describe the genre's deep structure, based on two fundamental oppositions: human vs. technology and place vs. space. Although these two oppositions are well documented in the scholarship around the SF film, this study explored them in all their additional dimensions and conceptual formulations. This process enabled the formation of the genre's six cycles, as interrelated manifestations of the basic syntax. The six cycles are an amalgamation of theoretical, critical, industrial, and user labels, indicating how industrial cycles and subgenres, such as space opera, the creature film, or the superhero film, can all be situated and theoretically explained as expressions of the same basic oppositions that characterize the genre. At the same time the book also proposed theoretical terms that do not exist as industrial categories (e.g., the zones cycle) in order to accentuate themes and motifs shared by a number of cinematic narratives. In this way, I hope I have facilitated the comparison and juxtaposition of films that have rarely been discussed in tandem, despite their common participation in the SF genre.

These theoretical formulations, however, were firmly situated in a specific historical context, namely, the Conglomerate Hollywood of the twenty-first century. As verified by the corpus on which the research is based, the contemporary SF film have become the ideal site for the strategies and economic imperatives of the American film industry. Industrial trends and practices such as serialization, recycling of established transmedia franchises, the "blockbuster mindset," and the dominance of the Big Six studios (Schatz 2009) are all evident in the corpus' films. Therefore, in the new millennium the conventions of the genre are deployed in order to promote a specific type of SF film capable of assisting the cross-platform interests of the industry.

In this transmedia environment, digital technology becomes the key to the workings of Conglomerate Hollywood. However, technology is almost by definition linked to the SF film. This is evident not only in the digital effects that materialize the genre's imaginative worlds and strange beings but also in its thematic preoccupations with technology. Yet, as the exo-semiotic analysis showed, the most prominent directors of the genre downplay SF's central relationship with technology, stressing instead more traditional/humanist aspects, such as emotion, art, and the human story at the center of the filmic texts. As I argued, this rhetoric, among other reasons, reflect the directors' ambivalence toward the genre's role in the contemporary film industry. Although the directors know that their SF films advance audiovisual technologies, thus contributing to the transformation of the film industry and its convergence with the transmedia system of the entertainment industry, they simultaneously insist on promoting cinema as an unchanged humanist institution. Considering the above, I suggested that the human/technology opposition of the semiotic analysis can also be translated in industrial terms. The human stands for the traditional cinematic institution (of characters, story, and analogue modes of filmmaking) that the directors discursively try to preserve. Conversely, technology takes the form of the new digital breakthroughs, which are prompted by the SF film and contribute to cinema's transformation into a new ontology.

Therefore, the proposed theoretical model for the SF film is not presented as a transhistorical or universal category, but is shaped by and connected with the wider historical context and its different, industrial, economic, and cultural discourses. As discussed, the model is not meant to draw strict lines and suggest a critical totalization, but to function as a way to draw relationship between texts in a more systematic (and theoretical) way. Thus, the semiotic square was used as critical tool, which does not enclose meaning but rather generates it through a combination of stability and flexibility. This constructedness was repeatedly emphasized throughout this study, with each cycle pointing to liminal generic examples that could also be associated with other categories. In this way, I hope I have offered a systematic yet flexible analysis that takes account of its own limits.

In order to further acknowledge and explore the limits of the present study, in what follows I delve into two case studies which correspond to the two semiotic squares: SF bodies and SF worlds. In these case studies, I follow

Altman's pragmatic approach to emphasize in a more direct way the discursive nature of the genre. As discussed in the introduction, Altman (1999) delineated pragmatics as the "use factor," that is, the different, even contradictory, uses of the genre by its different user groups that include not only spectators but also producers, distributors, exhibitors, cultural agencies, and so on. Therefore, a pragmatic analysis "must constantly attend to the competition among multiple users that characterizes genres" (Altman 1999: 210). It is exactly this multiplicity of uses that this epilogue addresses, discussing how different user groups attach different generic markers to *Avengers: Endgame* (from the SF bodies) and *Black Panther* (from the SF worlds)—two of the most popular and (in the case of *Black Panther*) culturally significant films of the corpus—in order to underscore the impossibility of any theoretical approach to account for all the discursive formations underlying the SF film.

According to the proposed theoretical model of the genre, *Avengers: Endgame* is an instance of the techno-humans category, while *Black Panther* presents an example of the dystopia/utopia cycle. Hence, despite the fact that *Avengers: Endgame* encompasses fantastic locations and bended timelines through its time-travel/alternate reality trope (thus it could be grouped in the fantastic worlds or zones category), it is considered a techno-human narrative since its main conflict takes place on Earth and revolves around enhanced humans trying to prevent non-human threats from destroying the universe. Likewise, even though *Black Panther* features a superhero protagonist, the film's dominant syntactic expression, as well as the adherence of the fictional world of Wakanda to a generic verisimilitude, situates the film in the utopia category.

Here, however, I want to examine other critical, industrial, and popular discourses surrounding the films' generic identities in order to underscore the variety of positions and claims that may agree with or contradict our proposed theoretical conceptualization. Before examining the diverse uses of *Avengers: Endgame* and *Black Panther*, I would like to point that both films are, to begin with, liminal examples of the genre (and of the proposed theoretical model), being mainly perceived as superhero films while bearing affinities with many other genres, categories and modes. In addition, the fact that both films are associated with the superhero category is not incidental. As mentioned in Chapter 3, the superhero film has become the dominant cultural expression of the twenty-first century, providing the ideal space for the strategies of Conglomerate Hollywood. However, it is usually discussed as a separate genre, and its association and exchanges with the SF film is often overlooked. It is for these reasons—the films' popularity, liminality, and unexamined relation with the SF film genre—that I consider *Avengers: Endgame* and *Black Panther* as ideal cases to explore the limits of the proposed theoretical model in relation to the different understandings, meanings, and uses of the genre.

Avengers: Endgame

Avengers: Endgame is the direct sequel of *Avengers: Infinity War* and the finale of the "Infinity Saga," that is, Marvel Studio's first twenty-two films since the release of *Iron Man* in 2008. The film broke numerous box-office records and became the highest-grossing film of all time at the time of its release (until March 2021). As a massively popular film, seen by millions of people around the globe, the critical discussion focused on various topics—from issues of representation and inclusivity, to the economic strategies of Conglomerate Hollywood that the film exemplified (see Gideonse 2019; Mittermeier 2021; Griffin 2022; etc.). In most of these essays, generic markers such as superhero and MCU film prevail, but occasionally there is reference to other characterizations. For instance, Sabrina Mittermeier maintains that "[t]he film … takes the well-trodden path of speculative fiction," mainly through the trope of time-travel (2021: 424). The author argues that this trope is accompanied by a "built-in nostalgia," as inscribed in a humorous scene where the characters discuss about the rationale of time-travel, while mentioning as examples popular SF films, such as *Terminator* (1984) and *Back to the Future* (1985), among others. Similarly, R. P. Aditya (2021) regards the time-travel subplot as a central trait of *Avengers: Endgame* that connects the film to the SF genre, and situates it alongside the above-mentioned SF titles. Tomasz Żaglewski places *Avengers: Endgame* in the "cinematic meta-genre known as the comic-book film," which he considers as synonymous with the superhero film (2019: 159). However, he maintains that the time-travel/alternate realities/multiverse[1] concept that characterizes the film creates a "quantum narrative," that is, a widening of narrative possibilities through "altering" mechanisms that can open up new directions for the genre.

Kevin J. Wetmore Jr. (2022) foregrounds other generic associations while discussing *Avengers: Endgame* in the context of the Anthropocene. The author argues that "one of the larger themes of the film is the new-found permanence of death in a genre known for bringing back the dead all the time" (2022: 133). According to the author, it is this centrality of death (of all living entities, including Earth) that creates a metaphor for the environmental catastrophes of our current moment, while also pointing to the film's interrelation with the gothic genre. Likewise, Trine Mærsk Kragsbjerg (2021) places the film within contemporary environmental discourses, noting further generic labels. Specifically, Kragsbjerg supports that both *Avengers: Infinity War* and *Avengers: Endgame* portray an "extreme form of a Malthusian way of thinking about the environmental situation," that suggests that any change in our relationship with nature will be detrimental (2021: 21). The author continues that in this depiction of the environmental issue of overpopulation, the film draws upon the subgenre of cli-fi, that is, an intersection of climate-centered narratives and science fiction. Lastly, Joseph Zornado and Sara Reilly (2021: 85)—like the authors mentioned above—regard *Avengers: Endgame* as reflective of the contemporary historical context of the Anthropocene, while linking the film with different generic descriptors, such as superhero fantasy and "romanticized science fiction."

Moving to the popular press reviews, we also encounter other generic designations, besides the superhero label. In a *Hollywood Reporter* review we come across generic labels, such as "action-spectacle," "fanciful epic," and "effects-driven comic-book-derived film" (McCarthy 2019). Peter Bradshaw (2019) of the *Guardian* describes the film as an "irresistible blend of action and comedy … [that] combines both the mythic and the contemporary." Another review characterizes the film as an "operatic grief drama," and an "epic slab of superheroics" (Rothkopf 2019). Dana Stevens (2019) maintains that this "epic installment … fit[s] in ample time … spectacular if cacophonous action scenes, serious dramatic storytelling, some touches of light romance, and a surprising amount of what you might call well-earned brooding." Peter Debruge (2019) notes broader generic (and industrial) affinities, stating that the *Avengers: Endgame*, and the MCU in general, "would not be what it is without … Peter Jackson's 'The Lord of the Rings' trilogy, the … eight-part Harry Potter saga, or the 21st-century shift of serialized television to expansive, ensemble-driven narrative."

Some reviews accentuate, among others, the film's generic affinities with the SF genre. For instance, David Edelstein (2019) argues that "writers Christopher Markus and Stephen McFeely have shaped *Avengers: Endgame* as a time-travel heist picture," echoing the 1985 SF hit *Back to the Future* "in how characters encounter their former selves from previous films." A. A. Dowd (2019) draws attention to both the SF and melodramatic elements that underpin the film, describing it as a "sci-fi tearjerker," and a "funny superhero melodrama." The critic further stresses these relations by stating that if *Avengers: Infinity War* "occasionally hyper-jumped into the *Star Wars* space-opera quadrant of the blockbuster cosmos, ... [*Avengers: Endgame*] sometimes resembles a[n] ... episode of cross-universe rival *Star Trek*." Eric Kohn (2019) also notices the SF element of time-travel, although he regards it as a "cheap sci-fi device" that is used as "an excuse to revisit aspects of all 21 previous movies." Lastly, Michael O'Sullivan (2019) states that *Avengers: Endgame* is, first of all, a "comic book movie"; however, through the "time heist" concept, it also evokes "two of filmdom's most wildly entertaining genres: time-travel and the crime caper."

As far as the industrial discourses are concerned, there are many references to individual films, or modes of storytelling that imply generic affiliations but avoid to provide direct generic labels. For example, screenwriters Christopher Markus and Stephen McFeely mention influences from "serialized storytelling" such as *Fargo* (FX, 2014–), *Lost* (ABC, 2004–10), and even *Game of Thrones* (HBO, 2011–19), as well as time-travel stories, such as *Back to the Future* (1985) (Itzkoff 2019). Similarly, directors Anthony and Joe Russo avoid attaching any specific generic labels to the film, stating that the sources of inspiration for *Endgame* were the "Marvel movies themselves" (Sciretta 2019). In another interview the Russo brothers point out the influence of *Star Wars*, but without mentioning the SF genre, explaining that "we got to make our *Star Wars* empire in *Infinity War* and *Endgame*" (Chand 2020). In yet another interview, when asked about the genre of *Endgame*, Joe Russo replied: "That's a tricky one to answer without giving anything away, but I will say that the movie is definitely unique in tone. It has its own spirit that's different than *Infinity War*" (Robbins 2019). With this reply the directors evade once again direct generic identifiers, emphasizing instead the film's uniqueness in relation both to other generic examples but also to the other MCU films.

In certain instances, we do encounter generic terms; but even in these cases the genre becomes a means to foreground variation and originality. For example, in an interview published in *The Atlantic*, Anthony Russo described *Avengers: Endgame* as a "wrenching family drama" (Sims 2019). However, this generic characterization aims to stress the film's special status, since the family drama designation is not something expected in a superhero SF/fantasy spectacle. Likewise, in the cases where producer and president of Marvel Studios Kevin Feige implies generic affiliation, he simultaneously foregrounds the film's singularity. For instance, in an interview about *Avengers: Endgame* he stated that "we realised we wanted to do something this genre had not seen very often" (Pape 2019). Despite the fact that Feige suggests a generic connection (presumably with the superhero/comic book genre), this suggestion is used only to accentuate the transgression of this genre. Similarly, Bob Iger, the CEO of the Walt Disney Company at the time of the film's theatrical release, asserted that "[Marvel Studios] … have redefined superheroes for a new era, greatly expanding their relevance across gender, generation and geography—setting new standards for compelling storytelling" (Lang 2019). In this statement, although Iger names the superhero genre, he nevertheless stresses the element of novelty and renewal. These discourses confirm that identification with a single dominant genre is usually avoided, and in the cases where generic designations are provided, they are used as a way to hint at diversity, innovation, and uniqueness.

Lastly, in audience discourses the majority of generic claims include characterizations, such as superhero and/or Marvel film. As evident from popular sites, such as IMDb and Rotten Tomatoes, *Avengers: Endgame* is mainly commented upon as the epic conclusion of Marvel Studios' first eleven years of superhero film series. However, other labels appear occasionally, stressing further generic affiliations. For example, in the user reviews in IMDb we find characterizations, such as "action packed with the perfect amount of humor" (thierryserra-05310, May 7, 2019); "[the film's] … run time brings about fascination, humor, sadness, incredible excitement, and sheer finality" (michaelahrens-39595, August 20, 2022); "If you like fantasy, adventure, and superheroes, I suggest you watch 'Avengers: Endgame'" (Big1Smoke, May 12, 2022); "Action, Happiness, Sadness and pure joy" (jaacy-84600, April 24, 2019); "a conclusion to a fantasy/genre series" (vert2712, April 24, 2019); "a good action movie" (andreas-27645, April 24, 2019); "a mindless action movie" (YourAverageReviewer, April 28, 2019); "a brilliant fantasy action adventure" (jboothmillard, May 6, 2019); and on Rotten Tomatoes: "fantasy action movie" (Winanya B, February 28, 2022), among others.

Other reviews/comments focus on the film's SF/time-travel elements, usually critiquing the plot inconsistencies that these generic aspects create. For instance, in IMDb we find the following comments: "even if it's science fiction, the scenario should make sense" (Lazarus_Hauptman, August 27, 2022); "[the film includes] … lot of interesting moves related to time-travel, alternative realities" (alekspredator87, July 20, 2022); "it's basically a time-travel story" (Marco_AGJ, June 13, 2022); "[the]… time heist is convenient, but effectively reflects on the franchise and develops core characters" (guskeller, May 5, 2022); "a disgrace to real time-travel movies" (woah-2449, August 5, 2019); "mediocre at best time-travel flick" (duoasf, April 24, 2019); "with All Time-Machine Movies it's Best to just Let Real Science Alone and Focus on the Fiction of Science-Fiction" (LeonLouisRicci, August 26, 2021); "What they came up with was in ways reminiscent of the plot convolutions of 'Back to the Future II' (1989)" (Wuchakk, July 5, 2019). Similarly, in Rotten Tomatoes we find comments, such as "spectacular science fiction movie" (Mario T, May 9, 2022); "a lighthearted yet grounded time-travel heist" (Dryden L, January 6, 2022); "a time heist film of epic proportions" (Penny S, January 1, 2022).

Other audience discourses refer to the dramatic aspects of the film (usually in a negative way) that recall the Russo brothers' characterization of the film as "a family drama" (Sims 2019). Thus, users in IMDb make the following generic claims, while commenting on the film's quality (or, in certain cases, the lack thereof): "I have never seen a superhero film this emotional" (nahidmstta, August 27, 2022); "[the film] ... gave a considerable amount of time towards drama" (jayawickramasg, June 22, 2022); "Way too long, over-melodramatic, incomprehensible" (greg-04082, May 20, 2019); "Aside from the odd action scenes, this movie could pass as a drama" (Lovekrafft, August 3, 2019); "a dramady [sic] sitcom" (chi_town_fed, August 15, 2019); "[*Avengers: Endgame*] ... was more like a soap than action movie" (allanmichael30, May 20, 2019); "[*Avengers: Endgame* is] ... full on drama, [but] there is still a lot of humor" (kosmasp, May 7, 2019), and in Rotten Tomatoes: "Soap opera bad acting from half the cast" (Cody F, June 15, 2022).

The above discourses demonstrate that although the superhero label is the most commonly used, different designations are evoked in order to highlight other aspects of the film. Therefore, while the majority of users (critics and audience members) discuss *Avengers: Endgame* as a superhero film, characterizations such as fantasy, action, adventure, epic, science fiction, time-travel, time heist, drama, and melodrama, among others confirm how different users notice different elements and generic aspects. It is also interesting to note that the emphasis on different genres is usually accompanied by evaluative judgments based on the perceived proper (or improper) use of generic tropes, as in the case of the time-travel subplot or the melodramatic elements of the film. For instance, when an audience member states in IMDb that "The ... testosterone-hating writers ... have devolved the Avengers franchise into a dramady [sic] sitcom" (chi_town_fed, August 15 2019), it is obvious that he regards the aforementioned genres as inferior to the (masculine) superhero genre, which is diminished due to the use of such feminine generic tropes. Therefore, the different generic claims around the film reflect also the audience's different beliefs, values, and ideologies. In turn, the industry players advance their own agenda when associating the film with a variety of individual examples, but not with a single dominant genre. Even in the cases when generic terms are used, they are employed in a way that avoids association with notions of repetition and similarity, instead stressing originality and variation, in order to attract the widest possible audience.

It is obvious from the above that there are indeed multiple and, in many cases, contradictory discourses (and concomitant ideologies) that shape the generic identity of *Avengers: Endgame*. Therefore, the proposed theoretical model can only partially reflect these discourses. The present analysis situated *Avengers: Endgame* in the techno-humans category, describing it as an SF/superhero narrative with a special focus on the human body's intermixing with technology, and associating it with other SF texts with similar concerns and structures. Thus, on the one hand, the model is aligned with discourses that describe the film as a superhero/SF film. On the other hand, our analysis is differentiated from other critical and popular discourses that highlight the film's SF aspects through different generic tropes, such as time-travel and alternate realities, or through its environmentally inflected themes. The popular discourses that foreground generic affiliations with the melodrama and the different values attached to such characterizations also did not inform our model. Similarly, industrial discourses that avoid generic terms, instead of foregrounding the film's novelty and uniqueness, are yet another different approach. If a complete generic analysis should take into account all the different claims and discourses around the genre, it is obvious that the present model cannot fulfill such task. However, this model is not meant to override all these different positions, or to fully encompass them (the latter would be impossible for a single book); instead, the proposed model is shaped as another discursive formation that partakes of this dialogue and negotiates a small part of this multiplicity of discourses and uses of the genre. This variety is even more pronounced in our second case study, *Black Panther*.

Black Panther

The unprecedented commercial success and cultural impact of *Black Panther* generated, in a relatively short period of time, a wide range of academic essays exploring the films' resonance with the contemporary sociopolitical landscape. As discussed, *Black Panther* was the first Marvel movie with a predominately

Black cast and a Black director, centering on issues of Black culture. Therefore, critical discussion around the film centered mainly on issues of race. However, in some of these essays we can also find references to the film's generic markers, which are also linked with the film's racial discourses. For example, W. Richard Benash (2021) approaches *Black Panther* as a superhero film, and more specifically as an MCU film, but one that intersects with the production philosophy of the 1970s blaxploitation films, which put a primary emphasis on box-office profit rather than authentic representations of Black culture. Terence McSweeney examines the film as a superhero narrative that surpasses the restrictions of the form, stating that "the film was able to transcend aspects of the genre that have historically opened the superhero film to criticism" (2020: 125). The author also invokes other generic characterizations when he suggests that one of the reasons of the film's success is the "vividly realized Afrofuturist utopia of Wakanda" (McSweeney 2020: 123). In a similar way, Gerry Canavan suggests the many generic affinities of *Black Panther*, locating the film in the boundaries of SF, alternate history, and magic realism. The author adds that the film can have very different affective charges depending on which genre "takes interpretive priority," and thus can become "either a radically utopian or a radically anti-utopian text" (2022: 323). Finally, Niels Niessen also suggests different generic categories, when he argues that the "film's superhero texture" (2021: 149) can acquire its full Afrofuturist potential if read through the lens of *Black Panther*'s transmedia universe.

In the popular press *Black Panther* is mainly described as a superhero film but one that is differentiated from the rest of the MCU entries, exceeding the generic expectations in both aesthetic and cultural terms. For example, Ann Hornaday (2018) views *Black Panther* as "a film that fulfills the most rote demands of superhero spectacle, yet does so with style and subtexts that feel … groundbreaking," adding that it "becomes something deeper than the mere formation of one superhero, engaging such subjects as: the legacy of colonialism … and the need for solidarity within an African diaspora at political and cultural odds with itself." Another critic similarly notes that "[t]he entertaining and ambitious *Black Panther* breaks from the Marvel formula," featuring an "Afro-futurist Shangri-La which offers … a complete rewrite of history—a diverse, egalitarian sub-Saharan Africa unaffected by colonialism or the slave trade, completely free from Western influence" (Vishnevetsky 2018). In a similar note, another piece describes *Black Panther* as "[a] superhero movie … [e]nergized to a thrilling extent by a myriad of Afrocentric influences" (Turan

2018). David Ehrlich (2018) regards *Black Panther* as "the best Marvel movie so far," and "an unabashed and mega-budgeted work of Afro-futurism" that "leverages an imagined reality to broadly reflect upon the actual reality of the black experience(s)."

As evident from the above reviews, the superhero label prevails; however, other terms and characterizations occasionally appear to point mainly to differences from the superhero category. For example, Peter Debruge (2018) remarks that "[b]ecause Black Panther's skills seem to rely more on gadgets than fantastical powers, his standalone Marvel outing actually feels more like a James Bond adventure than a conventional superhero movie at times." The same critic also pinpoints to connections with the blaxploitation films located in the presence of strong, Black female characters. Likewise, Peter Bradshaw (2018) describes the movie as "an action-adventure origin myth which plays less like a conventional superhero film and more like a radical Brigadoon or a delirious adventure by Jules Verne or Edgar Rice Burroughs," adding that the film looks more like "a wide-eyed fantasy romance: exciting, subversive and funny." Thus, academic and critical discourses around *Black Panther* use different generic characterizations in order to underscore that the film goes beyond the usual conventions of the superhero film, and to endow it with an additional critical value. Generic labels, such as science fiction, Afrofuturist, utopia, alternate history, magic realism, action/adventure and fantasy romance, are employed to evoke diverse critical positions and uses of the film that surpass the conventional usage patterns of the superhero category.

This variety of characterizations is, however, absent in industrial discourses around *Black Panther*. In the official interview for the promotion of the film, producer Kevin Feige situated *Black Panther* in the MCU, stating that it is "unlike anything we have done before" (Flicks And The City Clips 2018). The producer thus avoids generic designations, instead stressing the film's brand and its unique characteristics. In another instance, Feige, commenting on *Black Panther*'s nomination for the Academy Award for Best Picture, stated that this is "a point in history and it connects to so many points that came before it in this genre that I love so much. Dick Donner's *Superman* being a big, big part of that. It was the journey that got us here today" (Boucher 2019). Here the producer identifies a genre to which apparently *Black Panther* belongs, locating also its origins in the 1978 *Superman* film. Although the name of the genre is not mentioned, one can assume—similarly with the case of *Avengers: Endgame* discussed above—that the producer refers to the superhero/comic book film.

However, it is interesting to note that Feige does not refer to the name of this genre in yet another instance: Stressing the director's contribution to the project, Feige asserted that "we were lucky Ryan Coogler wanted to come on board … and had something to say … using *our genre* and our canvas to tell it on it in a big way" (Hollywood Reporter 2018, emphasis added). Again, the name of the genre is not given, but we can hypothesize that it is the superhero/comic book film. The only specification for this genre is the adjective *our*, which effectively renders the genre as a specific brand—the MCU film.

A similar emphasis on brand is evident in the film's promotion campaign, specifically the poster and official trailer. While the iconography in both promotional sites suggests many generic affiliations—via exotic landscapes and costumes, futuristic gadgets and architecture, and epic battles—no generic markers are provided. The only text that is featured is the Marvel logo and the title of the film, along with the phrase "Long Live the King" (in the poster) and the nouns "Hero," "Legend," "King" (in the trailer). Therefore, while industrial discourses implicitly suggest the film's generic connections, they mainly foreground its unique properties in relation to both the other MCU films and the superhero category in general. However, this latter category is, as discussed above, discursively appropriated by the Marvel brand, in order to stress the "particular plus that the studio brings to the genre" (Altman 1999: 115). Importantly, generic labels, such as science fiction, Afrofuturist and utopia that circulate in academic and critical discourses, are entirely absent, indicating the studio's tactic of avoiding terms that could alienate segments of the audience. The film's generic framework is thus discursively shaped in different ways according to the purposes of its multiple users.

As far as the audience discourses are concerned, one can encounter a great diversity of generic labels. As evident from user reviews on IMDb and Rotten Tomatoes, the superhero/comic book/Marvel/MCU label appears quite frequently; however, there is also a variety of other designations, suggesting varied generic approaches for the same film. For example, on the users' reviews on IMDb we come across characterizations and remarks such as "Action—Sci-Fi movie" (Thanos_Alfie10, February 10, 2020), "Kids and Trekkie types will certainly love this" (bkoganbing, February 22, 2018); "a fine stand-alone action drama that deals with the consequences of a modern civilization made possible by widespread colonization" (sushilpramanik-12001, January 24, 2022); "a mixture of action and humour" (sophie-44498, November 22, 2021); "a Bond-style thriller … complete with ridiculous gadgets" (paul_s_hills, February

16, 2018); "great technology and action movie" (greatcornolio, November 16, 2021); "one of the best action movies of all time ... and even one of the best dramas" (mrjtmason, February 20, 2018); "[the film features] some fantasy elements ... and at the same time, it is quite of a sci fi too, and on the sideline it's also a crime film" (NpMoviez, July 26, 2018); "The plot felt more like a fantasy story to me. The melding of present day with traditional and futuristic elements was well done" (la_ricciolina, January 27, 2021).

On Rotten Tomatoes there is also a plethora of diverse generic markers: "Fantastic Afrofuturistic action sci-fi film with exciting court intrigue and challenging concepts" (Penny S, January 1, 2022); "a fun James Bond-like science fiction adventure film" (Sean M, November 17, 2021); "As an action film, it does not deliver too much in the way of action. We receive a lot of dialogue and world-building instead" (Ethan T, March 16, 2021); "[F]eels like it is trying to be a high-tech James Bond movie whilst being a political movie" (Alexander D, January 4, 2021); "a good action/sci-fi film" (Gregory T, November 15, 2020).

Many of these user reviews notice how *Black Panther* diverges from the average Marvel film. On IMDb we find the following comments: "a refreshing take on a by now familiar superhero story" (Filmdokter, September 23, 2021); "this movie is actually different enough to be interesting and exciting. It is colorful" (pantickatarina, February 20, 2018); "A very creative take on the Superhero genre" (gss2, February 20, 2018); "Wakanda is a pretty different location ever seen in a Marvel Movie" (AvionPrince16, November 18, 2021); and (on Rotten Tomatoes): "[the film] broadened Marvel's diversity and opens the eyes of the audience to a new point of view, and a new type of superhero" (Oliver O, December 5, 2021). Interestingly, another segment of the audience regarded the film as a rather typical superhero movie, as evident from the following IMDb user reviews: "a generic Marvel movie that follows the classic Hero's Journey" (BigJack696 December 6, 2021); "It's a typical Marvel super hero movie, if you liked the others you'll like this one" (games-6779415, February 15); "An average comic book/superhero movie" (grants, November 10, 2018), "Great visuals, story delivers no surprises" (FabledGentleman, February 14, 2018). Similar remarks are also posted on Rotten Tomatoes: "A pretty basic plot by superhero standards" (Wyatt B, December 23, 2021); "Probably the most refined version of the Marvel formula, but a Marvel movie nonetheless. Don't expect anything too daring" (Marcelo D, November 27, 2020); "A safe and formulaic Marvel origin story. Nothing special" (Aneurin P, January 8, 2022).

What the above user reviews reveal is that not only does the film evoke a variety of generic references beyond the superhero label, but it is also seen as a typical and atypical generic example at the same time. These contradictory discourses around *Black Panther* underscore that the audience is not a homogenous entity, but it comprises many separate members with different age, gender, sexual orientation, race, class, and so on, who perceive the film in disparate ways. While some members of the audience approach the film through the superhero (or Marvel film) lens, others regard it as comedy, drama, fantasy, science fiction, action, adventure, James Bond–film, crime film, political film, and many other categories, pointing out elements that industrial discourses do not mention.

In addition, when a member of the audience describes *Black Panther* as an average Marvel movie with nothing special to offer, he/she clearly expresses an ideological position where issues of racial representation and diversity are deemed insignificant. In the same way when another audience member or a critic describes the film as an Afrofuturist utopia he/she also expresses an ideological viewpoint that assigns a positive value to such representations. The audience thus experiences the film in conflicting generic ways because each member has different beliefs and values. It is interesting also to note that the user reviews on both IMDb and Rotten Tomatoes are rather polarized, featuring both very high and very low scores. What's more, the average audience score is lower than the critics' consensus. Although part of these negative reviews can be attributed to the "far-right trolls" that express a backlash to the recent effort of superhero/fantasy/SF film and television to be more inclusive in terms of gender and race (Miller 2019), they also suggest how genre is inextricably entwined with ideology and with differing audience positions. Therefore, not only do academic, critical, and industrial discourses promote the film through disparate generic terms to serve their own purposes but also audience members experience the film through their own ideological positions in contrasting ways that sometimes go beyond such discourses.

It goes without saying that if genres are shaped by such multiple, contradictory, and—in the examined case—politically charged discourses, no single theoretical approach can account for such multiplicity. In this regard, our proposed theoretical model cannot negotiate all the ideologically different claims and approaches around the generic identity of *Black Panther*, *Avengers: Endgame*, or any other film. Yet I believe that this theoretical construction of the SF film, despite is partiality, is still informed by, and participates in, the complex discursive process underlying the genre. For example, the academic, critical, and audience discourses that use terms such as utopia, Afrofuturist and science fiction, and many others to imply that the film slightly deviates from the usual superhero structure are inscribed in our model. The latter negotiates these discourses since *Black Panther* is situated in the dystopia/utopia cycle and not in the techno-humans/superhero category. However, other discourses of the audience that describe the film as a typical superhero story are not captured in this analysis. Similarly, industrial discourses that foreground *Black Panther* as a text that occupies a unique position in relation to other superhero (and Marvel) narratives are evident in the model. Still, another aspect of these discourses that promote the film through the lens of the Marvel brand is not adequately represented here. Therefore, although the presented theoretical approach attempts to map the SF film in a specific time period, it cannot tackle all the discourses that shape the genre because it is itself a discursive formation with a specific viewpoint. I believe that the proposed theoretical model for the contemporary SF film in Hollywood functions more like a snapshot; it captures some aspects of a historical process, but inevitably downplays other facets. Yet, I hope this snapshot, when considered along with all this variety of discourses and practices around the SF film, can shed some light to this ever-changing and multidimensional phenomenon.

Notes

Introduction

1. The editor of *Amazing Stories*, Hugo Gernsback, coined the term "scientifiction" and defined the genre as "the Jules Verne, H.G. Wells and Edgar Allan Poe type of story—a charming romance intermingled with scientific fact and prophetic vision that will supply knowledge in a very palatable form" (in Bould and Vint 2011: 6). In 1929, Gernsback gave the genre its proper name—science fiction—through the pages of *Science Wonder Stories*, a magazine he created after losing control of *Amazing Stories*.

Chapter 1

1. The work that exemplifies the transition from structuralism to post-structuralism is Roland Barthes's *S/Z* (1970)—the analysis of Honoré de Balzac's "Sarrasine." Here Barthes inflects the structuralist analysis with post-structuralist concerns, such as the fluidity of meaning generated by signifiers, which partially "escape" their codes (Stam 1992: 54; 196).
2. These tools, which Greimas developed as a part of a general theory of narrative and meaning, can be applied to all signifying practices, including cinema.
3. An initial formulation of the basic opposition was nature vs. technology. However, since I aimed at an emphasis on the different bodies that populate SF film, I limited the broad category of nature into a specific natural organism, that is, the human. The square then describes how the interaction of the term human with technology produces the more-than-human entities that we encounter in the SF film.
4. The concept of the dominant was first introduced by Roman Jakobson in his analysis of the six functions of language. According to Jakobson (1960), language is characterized by six different functions: the referential, the poetic, the emotive, the conative, the phatic, and the metalingual. In each linguistic expression, there is a focusing element (the dominant) that determines and transforms the text's remaining components (e.g., the poetic function is dominant in poetry). However, one should also point the limitations of this concept, namely, that it is presented as an objective tool, where a single correct position is presupposed, obscuring the fact

that it always involves a contingent and provisional judgment. The present thesis adopts it as a provisional concept, acknowledging its limitations.

5   The full list of film titles is included in the analysis of each cycle in the ensuing chapters.

6   Despite the fact that Propp restricted his findings to the Russian folk tale, subsequent applications of his model in film and television studies suggested its universality (Stam 1992: 81). The present thesis does not align with such claims of universality. Instead, I make a specific, selective use of Greimas's reformulation of the Propprian model, recognizing its historical mutability and conditional application.

7   I should point here that the criterion of production country is again based on data drawn from IMDb, in order to avoid the increasing elusiveness of the term. This criterion may be contested, not only from the growing number of international co-productions but also from the fact that many countries claim the production of a film, suggesting different criteria, such as location, facilities, director, star, and/or other important personnel.

8   Since generic labels may fluctuate over the years, it is important to note that the corpus was formulated from data drawn in September 2016, while some additional data for the 2017–20 period were gathered in June 2021.

9   In this criterion, I am not concerned with economically successful films but only with box-office ranking, regardless of budget or profitability. Since film genre is a cultural category, that is, a site of cultural negotiations that reflect large segments of a given society, it is important that the films reach a wide audience. Popularity is, thus, deemed a key criterion in formulating genre as a popular culture phenomenon.

10 Again, this criterion is based on the IMDb categorization, since it can arguably be contested. For example, *A Scanner Darky* (2006) is realized by the technique of rotoscoping, which entails both live action scenes and animation. However, since the film is labeled as animation by IMDb, it is excluded from the corpus.

Chapter 2

1   These are the media companies that Schatz mentions in his 2009 essay. In 2018 Walt Disney acquired 20th Century Fox's film and TV entertainment asset (Williams 2018), while in 2022 AT&T decided to relinquish its ownership of WarnerMedia, which it had acquired in 2018, and merge it with Discovery, Inc., forming Warner Bros. Discovery. Thus, as of 2022, 90 percent of the US media is controlled by five media conglomerates: Comcast (via NBCUniversal), Disney, Sony, Paramount Global (controlled by National Amusements), and Warner Bros. Discovery.

2   The cinematic phenomenon of franchises and serialization is observed from the early days of silent cinema and is present in many countries (e.g., Louis Feuillade's *Fantômas* from France, a five-episode silent crime film serial released in 1913–14, Louis J. Gasnier's and Donald MacKenzie's *The Perils of Pauline*, a twenty-episode 1914 American melodrama film serial).

3   The concept of the "blockbuster" emerged from a genealogy of "large-scale, high-cost" films (Hall and Neale 2010), present since cinema's inception. However, the term was first used in the postwar period, to refer to "particularly expensive and potentially highly profitable American motion pictures" (Hall 2011) that were initially designed to compete broadcast television. However, as Hall (2011) notes, "the common association between high production values … and commercial success (actual or potential) meant that specific aesthetic features came to be identified with the blockbuster, such as exceptional length, a large scale, and various types of spectacle." It has also been associated with certain genres, such as the biblical or historical epic, the action-adventure film, science fiction and fantasy, and with certain distribution and exhibition patterns, such as saturation releasing, accompanied by intensive mass-media advertising (Hall 2011).

4   We should stress that blockbuster is a polysemous word. Although it is mostly used to designate films with huge financial success, the term "can also be extended to refer to those films which *need* to be successful in order to have a chance of returning a profit on their equally extraordinary production costs" (Hall 2002: 11). Therefore, the term describes not only a commercial hit but also a film being produced as such.

5   The number of films in the corpus produced and/or distributed by the Big Six Studios and their parent companies are the following: 20th Century Fox (forty films, 19.6 percent), Columbia (and Sony Pictures) (thirty-five films, 17.2 percent), Warner Bros. (thirty-two films, 15.7 percent), Paramount (thirty-one films, 15.2 percent), Disney (twenty-five films, 12.2 percent), and Universal (nineteen films, 9.3 percent).

6   However, even Lionsgate Films, in its struggle to survive amid mass media and technology behemoths, inevitably seems to follow the industry's merger-and-acquisition patterns (Lang and Lopez 2018).

7   These are: *The Hunger Games* tetralogy, *The Divergent* trilogy, *Gamer*, *Daybreakers*, *The Lazarus Effect*, *Push*, *Pandorum*, *Source Code*, *Ender's Game*, *The Darkest Hour*, and *Power Rangers*.

8   Dimension Films was formerly owned by Miramax Films (1992–2005)—a Disney label, until founders Bob and Harvey Weinstein created The Weinstein Company in 2005 and reintegrated Dimension. In October 2017, co-founder Harvey Weinstein was dismissed from the company after multiple sexual harassment accusations against him went public. In March 2018, the Weinstein Company filed for bankruptcy (BBC 2018).

9. These films are the following: *Children of Men, Avatar, District 9, Inception, Gravity, Her, The Martian, Arrival, Logan, Black Panther.*
10. Although the industry and film theorists such as Prince (2012) adopt the broader term "visual effects," I will continue to refer to this category as special effects—following Turnock (2015: 9)—in order to connote the specialized labor involved in their production (e.g., the effect houses are not integrated in the big studios), their fundamental role in the genre but also their marketing and promotion as a distinctive, special attraction of the SF film.
11. Aesthetic, ontological, and textual approaches of special effects or how the spectator perceives/responds to them when watching an SF film have been extensively discussed by scholars such as Sobchack (1987), Buckland (1999), Bukatman (1999), Grant (1999), Pierson (2002), Neale (2004), and Bould (2012), among others.
12. All the prominent directors of our corpus are male, while from the 204 films of the final corpus, only five films (2.4 percent) are directed by women. Karyn Kusama directed *Aeon Flux* (2005), the trans women Lana and Lily Wachowski directed *Jupiter Ascending* (2015), the two *Matrix* sequels, and co-directed *Cloud Atlas* (2012), while Anna Boden co-directed *Captain Marvel* (2019) along with Ryan Fleck. Hence, despite significant shifts in the representations within the narrative, where there is a noticeable female presence in leading roles (thirty-nine films, 19.1 percent) helming an SF film still remains a male-dominated endeavor.
13. These are the *Jurassic Park/Jurassic World* film series, the *Transformers* film series (including *Bumblebee*), the *Men in Black* film series, *Cowboys & Aliens* (2011), and *Super 8* (2011).
14. Caltech astrophysicist Kip Thorne assisted the visual effects team of *Interstellar* by generating equations that guided the effects software in order to depict the most accurate high-resolution representation of a black hole (Rogers 2014). This astonishing visual effect also advanced scientific knowledge, prompting Thorne and the VFX team to publish their findings in the scientific journal *Classical and Quantum Gravity* (Rogers 2014; Wolfe 2015).

Chapter 3

1. *Bloodshot* is based on the same titled Valiant comic and was designed to be the first installment in a film series set in a shared cinematic universe (Clark 2019).
2. *Avengers: Infinity War* and *Avengers: Endgame* are liminal cases as far as the proposed taxonomy is concerned. Both films feature fantastic worlds (and bended temporalities in the latter film) and therefore could also be placed in categories of the second semiotic square. However, I situate them in the present cycle for two

3. In the Marvel Cinematic Universe, HYDRA is a neo-fascist organization that uses highly advanced and/or alien technology.
4. In the present superhero category, there is only one film (*Captain Marvel* [2019]) with a female lead. *Black Panther* is also the only superhero film with a non-white lead—although it is discussed in the dystopia/utopia cycle for reasons that I explain in the respective chapter. In the rest of the category's films, people of color and women are assigned secondary roles, and in the case of the latter they are usually oversexualized (e.g., *Black Widow* [Scarlett Johansson] in the MCU films). It is also interesting to note that the ordinary techno-human narratives, although significantly fewer in numbers, include two films with a female lead (*Stepford Wives*, *The Lazarus Effect*). However, in these cases the techno-human is not marked by exceptionality, but is characterized as an ordinary or even hazardous body. Therefore, the cycle, as a whole, associates the beneficial technological body with hegemonic discourses about gender and race.
5. *Victor Frankenstein*: $65 million, *The Animal*: $47 million, *Bloodshot*: $45 million, *Limitless*: $27 million, *Splice*: $26 million, *Self/Less*: $26 million, *Chronicle*: $12 million, and *Lazarus Effect*: $3.3 million.
6. It is worth noticing that the representation of Frankenstein's creature in the film is quite different from Mary Shelley's original depiction in her 1818 novel, that portrays the Creature not as murderous by nature but due to his rejection by his "father" Dr. Frankenstein and society.

Chapter 4

1. The Kaijus are specifically described as manufactured beings that function as the army of the alien species who want to colonize Earth. Nevertheless, they stand in for the aliens in the narrative, since no other extraterrestrial species appears.

Chapter 5

1. *Terminator Salvation* (2009) takes place in a future dystopic Earth, and thus it is discussed in the dystopia cycle.

Chapter 8

1. The term soap opera circulated in the first days of radio serials to describe the long-running stereotypical narratives that were often sponsored by soap-powder companies. Since then, the term has been used pejoratively to describe any formulaic narrative, for example "horse opera" for Westerns (Clute and Nicholls 1995).
2. Although the origins of the space opera are located in the pulps, one can encounter progenitors of the form in early-twentieth-century space adventure novels such as Garrett P. Serviss's *Edison's Conquest of Mars* (1898), Robert W. Cole's *The Struggle for Empire* (1900), and George Griffith's *A Honeymoon in Space* (1901) (Westfahl 2003).
3. It is interesting to note that the *Star Trek* and *Star Wars* franchises are still dominant in the new millennium, with the majority of the cycle's films belonging in one of the two franchises.
4. The first sequel, titled *Avatar: The Way of Water*, was released in December 2022.
5. There is an extensive bibliography that examines the *Star Wars* film series and its different aspects, such as Carl Silvio and Tony M. Vinci's (2007) *Culture, Identities, and Technology in the Star Wars Films: Essays on the Two Trilogies*; Bradley Schauer's (2007) "Critics, CLONES and Narrative in the Franchise Blockbuster"; Will Brooker's (2009) *Star Wars*; Douglas Brode and Leah Deyneka's (2012) *Myth, Media, and Culture in Star Wars: An Anthology*; Sean Guynes and Dan Hassler-Forest's (2017) *Star Wars and the History of Transmedia Storytelling*; William Proctor and Richard McCulloch's (2019) *Disney's Star Wars: Forces of Production, Promotion, and Reception*; Dan Golding's (2019) *Star Wars after Lucas: A Critical Guide to the Future of the Galaxy*; Miles Booy's (2021) *Interpreting Star Wars: Reading a Modern Film Franchise*; Cyrus Patell's (2021) *Lucasfilm: Filmmaking, Philosophy, and the Star Wars Universe*, among others.
6. As Booker (2006) notes, this association becomes even more pronounced when examined in the light of the presidency of Ronald Reagan, who adopted the language of *Star Wars* in his public speeches. He characterized the Soviet Union as an "evil empire," and his proposed missile defense system, the Strategic Defense Initiative, came to be known as the "Star Wars" program.
7. Similar to the *Star Wars* film series, there is a lengthy bibliography (besides the titles mentioned in the main text) that examines the *Star Trek* media franchise from different perspectives, such as Constance Penley's (1997) *Nasa/Trek: Popular Science and Sex in America*; Duncan Barrett and Michèle Barrett's (2017) *Star Trek: The Human Frontier* (first edition 2001); Ina Rae Hark's (2008) *Star Trek*; David Greven's (2009) *Gender and Sexuality in Star Trek: Allegories of Desire in the Television Series*

and Films; Roberta Pearson and Máire Messenger Davies's (2014) *Star Trek and American Television*; Douglas Brode and Shea T. Brode's (2015) *Star Trek Universe: Franchising the Final Frontier*; Leora Hadas's (2017) "A New Vision: J. J. Abrams, Star Trek, and Promotional Authorship"; Leimar Garcia-Siino, Sabrina Mittermeier and Stefan Rabitsch's (2022) *The Routledge Handbook of Star Trek*; among others.

8   This voice-over narration describes the mission of the series' famous spaceship *Enterprise*: "to explore strange new worlds, to seek out new life and new civilizations, to boldly go where no man has gone before." This narration was adopted by subsequent series, and its last phrase was corrected to the gender-neutral "where no one has gone before."

9   Although in the last installment of the rebooted film series, *Star Trek Beyond*, the USS *Enterprise* is destroyed, by the film's end a new spaceship, called USS *Enterprise-A*, is built and resumes its mission, confirming once again the technoscientific Empire's ideals of peaceful expansion through technology.

Epilogue

1   Although the trope of the multiverse, that is, the expansion of the universe in multiple timelines and parallel/alternative realities, is not something new in SF films (or in cinema in general), the beginning of the 2020s witnesses a proliferation of this trope. After the release of *Avengers: Endgame* and the completion of the "Infinity Saga," the new MCU film series are collectively dubbed "Multiverse Saga," with titles such as *Spider-Man: No Way Home* (2021) and *Doctor Strange in the Multiverse of Madness* (2022) being prominent examples of this trend. In addition, the multiverse trope is also evident in MCU television series such as *Loki* (Disney+, 2021–), and *What if?* (Disney+, 2021–), among others. Besides the MCU narratives, other films, such as the commercially and critically acclaimed (and winner of seven Academy Awards) *Everything Everywhere all at Once* (2022), exemplify this generic trope, confirming the recent tendency. Similar to *Avengers: Endgame* the above titles are liminal cases in relation to our theoretical model. In other words, they could be situated either in the techno-humans category (as their protagonists are, usually, enhanced individuals fighting non-human threats) or they could be examined as zones narratives (since their protagonists are also caught up in convoluted spacetime configurations, trying to survive and/or save the world). Therefore, the emergence of multiverse SF could mark further blending of the (already overlapped) categories of the proposed model, leading perhaps to new (parallel/alternate) semiotic squares and updated theoretical approaches. It is up to future researchers to explore how the genre will be shaped and what theoretical/historical models can interpret it in the decades to come.

Bibliography

Abbott, Stacey (2006), "Computer-Generated Imagery and the Science Fiction Film," *Science Fiction Studies*, 33 (1): 89–108. https://www.jstor.org/stable/4241410

Aditya, R. P. (2021), "Avengers: Endgame—Understanding the film'stime-travel Logic and Its Consequent Narrative Inconsistencies," *International Journal of English and Studies (IJOES)*, 3 (4): 96–110.

Altman, Rick (1987), *American Film Musical*, Bloomington: Indiana University Press.

Altman, Rick (1999), *Film/Genre*, London: British Film Institute.

Altman, Rick (2012), "A Semantic/Syntactic Approach to Film Genre," in Barry Keith Grant (ed.), *Film Genre Reader IV*, 27–41, Austin: University of Texas Press.

Appelo, Tim (2014), "Alfonso Cuarón on How Angelina Jolie and Robert Downey Jr. Almost Starred in 'Gravity' (Video)," *The Hollywood Reporter*, February 18. Available online: https://www.hollywoodreporter.com/news/alfonso-cuaron-how-angelina-jolie-681003 (accessed January 11, 2022).

Attebery, Brian and Veronica Hollinger (eds.) (2013), *Parabolas of Science Fiction*, Middletown: Wesleyan University Press.

Barrett, Duncan and Michèle Barrett (2017), *Star Trek: The Human Frontier*, New York: Routledge.

BBC (2018), "Weinstein Company Files for Bankruptcy," *BBC*, March 20. Available online: https://www.bbc.com/news/world-us-canada-43466469 (accessed January 11, 2022).

Benash, W. Richard (2021), "Black Panther and Blaxploitation: Intersections," *Quarterly Review of Film and Video*, 38 (1): 45–60. DOI: 10.1080/10509208.2020.1762475

Benoff, Susan, Asha Jacob and Ian R. Hurley (2000), "Male Infertility and Environmental Exposure to Lead and Cadmium," *Human Reproduction Update*, 6 (2): 107–21. https://doi.org/10.1093/humupd/6.2.107

Bielik, Alain (2007), "'I Am Legend': Apocalypse Now in Manhattan," *Awn.com*, December 14. Available online: https://www.awn.com/vfxworld/i-am-legend-apocalypse-now-manhattan (accessed August 9, 2021).

Billington, Alex (2012), "Interview: Ridley Scott on Returning to Sci-Fi, Hollywood, 3D & More," *Firstshowing.net*, June 8. Available online: https://www.firstshowing.net/2012/interview-ridley-scott-on-sci-fi-hollywood-3d/ (accessed January 11, 2022).

Biskind, Peter (2004), "The Russians Are Coming, Aren't They?: *Them!* and *The Thing*," in Sean Redmond (ed.), *Liquid Metal. The Science Fiction Film Reader*, 318–24, London: Wallflower Press.

Booker, Keith M. (2001), *Monsters, Mushrooms Clouds, and the Cold War. American Science Fiction and the Roots of Postmodernism, 1946–1964*, Westport, CT: Greenwood Press.

Booker, Keith M. (2006), *Alternate Americas: Science Fiction Film and American Culture*, Westport, CT: Praeger Publishers.

Booker, Keith M. (2008), "The Politics of *Star Trek*," in J. P. Telotte (ed.), *The Essential Science Fiction Television Reader*, 195–208, Lexington: The University Press of Kentucky.

Booker, Keith M. (2018), *Star Trek: A Cultural History*, Lanham: Rowman & Littlefield.

Booy, Miles (2021), *Interpreting Star Wars: Reading a Modern Film Franchise*, New York: Bloomsbury Academic.

Bordwell, David with Kristin Thompson (2019), *Christopher Nolan. A Labyrinth of Linkages*, Second Edition, Madison: Irvington Way Institute Press.

Boucher, Geoff (2019), "Marvel Studios' Kevin Feige: 'Black Panther' Oscar Nom Fits into a Heroic History, *Deadline*," January 22. Available online: https://deadline.com/2019/01/marvel-black-panther-chadwick-boseman-kevin-feige-1202539174/ (accessed February 28, 2022).

Bould, Mark (2012), *Science Fiction*, Abingdon, Oxon: Routledge.

Bould, Mark (2013), "Genre, Hybridity, Heterogeneity or, the Noir-SF-Vampire-Zombie-Splatter-Romance-Comedy-Action-Thriller Problem," in Andre Spicer and Helen Hanson (eds.), *A Companion to Film Noir*, 33–49, Chicester: Wiley-Blackwell.

Bould, Mark and Sherryl Vint (2011), *The Routledge Concise History of Science Fiction*, New York: Routledge.

Bradshaw, Peter (2005), "The Hitchhiker's Guide to the Galaxy," *The Guardian*, April 22. Available online: https://www.theguardian.com/theguardian/2005/apr/22/1 (accessed September 27, 2021).

Bradshaw, Peter (2011), "Limitless—Review," *The Guardian*, March 24. Available online: https://www.theguardian.com/film/2011/mar/24/limitless-film-review (accessed June 8, 2021).

Bradshaw, Peter (2012), "Chronicle—Review," *The Guardian*, February 2. Available online: https://www.theguardian.com/film/2012/feb/02/chronicle-film-review (accessed June 8, 2021).

Bradshaw, Peter (2018), "Black Panther Review—Marvel's Thrilling Vision of the Afrofuture," *The Guardian*, February 6. Available online: https://www.theguardian.com/film/2018/feb/06/black-panther-review-marvel-wakanda-chadwick-boseman (accessed February 28, 2022).

Bradshaw, Peter (2019), "Avengers: Endgame Review—Unconquerable Brilliance Takes Marvel to New Heights," *The Guardian*, April 23. Available online: https://www.theguardian.com/film/2019/apr/23/avengers-endgame-review-unconquerable-brilliance-takes-marvel-to-new-heights (accessed September 8, 2022).

Braidotti, Rosi (2013), *The Posthuman*, Cambridge and Malden: Polity.
Brevet, Brad (2006), "EXCLUSIVE: Alfonso Cuarón on 'Children of Men,'" *Comingsoon.net*, December 22. Available online: https://www.comingsoon.net/movies/news/513840-exclusive_alfonso_cuaron_on_children_of_men (accessed January 12, 2022).
Briggs, Caroline (2006), "Movie Imagines World Gone Wrong," *BBC*, September 20. Available online: http://news.bbc.co.uk/2/hi/entertainment/5357470.stm (accessed August 9, 2021).
Brode, Douglas and Leah Deyneka (eds.) (2012), *Myth, Media, and Culture in Star Wars: An Anthology*, Lanham: The Scarecrow Press, Inc.
Brode, Douglas and Shea T. Brode (eds.) (2015), *Star Trek Universe: Franchising the Final Frontier*, Lanham: Rowman & Littlefield.
Brody, David Sky (2013), "Making 'Gravity': How Filmmaker Alfonso Cuarón Created 'Weightlessness' without Spaceflight," *Space.com*, October 3. Available online: https://www.space.com/23073-gravity-movie-weightlessness-alfonso-cuaron.html (accessed September 10, 2021).
Brooker, Will (2004), "New Hope: The Postmodern Project of *Star Wars*," in Sean Redmond (ed.), *Liquid Metal. The Science Fiction Film Reader*, 298–307, London: Wallflower Press.
Brooker, Will (2009), *Star Wars*, London: BFI/Palgrave Macmillan.
Brzeski, Patrick (2020), "China, the World's Second-Largest Film Market, Moves beyond Hollywood," *Hollywood Reporter*, October 7. Available online: https://www.hollywoodreporter.com/news/general-news/china-the-worlds-second-largest-film-market-moves-beyond-hollywood-4072560/ (accessed June 29, 2021).
Buckland, Warren (1999), "Between Science Fiction and Science Fact: Spielberg's Digital Dinosaurs, Possible Worlds and the New Aesthetic Realism," *Screen*, 40 (2): 177–92. https://doi.org/10.1093/screen/40.2.177
Buckland, Warren (2014), "Introduction: Ambiguity, Ontological Pluralism, and Cognitive Dissonance in the Hollywood Puzzle Films," in Warren Buckland (ed.), *Hollywood Puzzle Films*, 1–14, New York and London: Routledge.
Buell, Lawrence (1995), *The Environmental Imagination*, Cambridge: Harvard University Press.
Bukatman, Scott (1993), *Terminal Identity. The Virtual Subject in Postmodern Science Fiction*, Durham and London: Duke University Press.
Bukatman, Scott (1999), "The Artificial Infinite: On Special Effects and the Sublime," in Annete Kuhn (ed.), *Alien Zone II. The Spaces of Science Fiction Cinema*, 249–75, London and New York: Verso.
Bukatman, Scott (2003), *Matters of Gravity. Special Effects and Supermen in the 20th Century*, Durham: Duke University Press.
Bukatman, Scott (2011), "Why I Hate Superhero Movies," *Cinema Journal*, 50 (3): 118–22.

Busch, Anita (2014), "'Gravity's Production Design Actually Is Rocket Science," *Deadline*, February 21. Available online: https://deadline.com/2014/02/oscars-gravitys-production-design-actually-is-rocket-science-688065/ (accessed September 10, 2021).

Cameron, Allen and Richard Misek (2014), "Modular Spacetime in the 'Intelligent' Blockbuster: *Inception* and *Source Code*," in Warren Buckland (ed.), *Hollywood Puzzle Films*, 109–24, New York and London: Routledge.

Canavan, Gerry (2014), "Introduction: If This Goes On," in Gerry Canavan and Kim Stanley Robinson (eds.), *Green Planets: Ecology and Science Fiction*, 1–21, Middletown: Wesleyan University Press.

Canavan, Gerry (2022), "Wakanda Forever? On Ryan Coogler's *Black Panther* (2018)," in Terence McSweeney and Stuart Joy (eds.), *Contemporary American Science Fiction Film*, 308–27, London and New York: Routledge.

Canavan, Gerry and Kim Stanley Robinson (eds.) (2014), *Green Planets: Ecology and Science Fiction*, Middletown: Wesleyan University Press.

CBR.com (n.d.), "The MCU's Relation with the Military: From Iron Man to Captain Marvel," *CBR.com*. Available online: https://www.cbr.com/captain-marvel-mcu-military-relationship/2/ (accessed June 8, 2021).

Chakrabarty, Dipesh (2014), "Climate and Capital: On Conjoined Histories," *Critical Inquiry*, 41 (1): 1–23.

Chakrabarty, Dipesh (2015), "The Anthropocene and the Convergence of Histories," in Clive Hamilton, François Gemenne and Christophe Bonneuil (eds.), *The Anthropocene and the Global Environmental Crisis*, New York: Routledge.

Chand, Neeraj (2020), "How Star Wars Influenced the Russo Brothers' Avengers Movies," *Movieweb*, July 10. Available online: https://movieweb.com/avengers-movies-star-wars-influence-russo-brothers/ (accessed September 7, 2022).

Chang, Justin (2013), "Venice Film Review: 'Gravity,'" *Variety*, August 28. Available online: https://variety.com/2013/film/global/gravity-review-venice-film-festival-1200589689/ (accessed September 10, 2021).

Chapman, James, Mark Glancy and Sue Harper (2007), "Introduction," in James Chapman, Mark Glancy and Sue Harper (eds.), *The New Film History. Sources, Methods, Approaches*, 1–10, Hampshire and New York: Palgrave Macmillan.

charliejane (2007), "io9 Talks to 'I Am Legend' Designer David Lazan," *Gizmodo*, December 24. Available online: https://gizmodo.com/io9-talks-to-i-am-legend-designer-david-lazan-33337683 (accessed August 9, 2021).

Charity, Tom (2011), "Review: 'Transformers: Dark of the Moon' Not as Bad as the Last One," *CNN*, June 29. Available online: http://edition.cnn.com/2011/SHOWBIZ/Movies/06/29/transformers.dark.movie.review/index.html (accessed June 30, 2021).

Chitwood, Adam (2015), "Exclusive: J. J. Abrams Talks STAR WARS: THE FORCE AWAKENS and That New Lightsaber," *Collider*, February 5. Available online: https://collider.com/star-wars-the-force-awakens-jj-abrams-interview/ (accessed January 12, 2022).

Clark, Travis (2019), "Valiant Has the Biggest Superhero Universe in Comics behind Marvel and DC. Now It Plans to Take Hollywood by Storm with Help from Vin Diesel," *Business Insider*, September 18. Available online: https://www.businessinsider.com/valiant-entertainment-is-jumping-from-comics-to-movies-and-tv-2019-9 (accessed June 8, 2021).

Clute John and Nicholls, Peter (1995), *Encyclopedia of Science Fiction*, New York: St. Martin's Press.

Collins, Suzane (2008), *The Hunger Games*, London: Scholastic.

Constable, Catherine (2018), "Challenging Capitalism: Ethics, Exploitation and the Sublime in *Moon* and *Source Code*," *Science Fiction Film and Television*, 11 (3): 417–48. https://doi.org/10.3828/sfftv.2018.25

Coogan, Peter (2006), *Superhero: The Secret Origin of a Genre*, Austin, TX: Monkeybrain.

Cornea, Cornea (2007), *Science Fiction Cinema: Between Fantasy and Reality*, Edinburgh: Edinburgh university press.

Corrigan, Timothy (2012), "Introduction: Movies and the 2000s," in Timothy Corrigan (ed.), *American Cinema of the 2000s. Themes and Variations*, 1–18, New Brunswick: Rutgers University Press.

Cotter, Padraig (2020), "How the Last Man on Earth Movie Inspired Night of the Living Dead," *Screenrant*, December 14. Available online: https://screenrant.com/last-man-earth-movie-night-living-dead-inspiration/ (accessed August 9, 2021).

Couch, Aaron (2014), "Christopher Nolan's 10 Most Nolan-y Movie Quotes Ever," *The Hollywood Reporter*, November 8. Available online: https://www.hollywoodreporter.com/movies/movie-features/christopher-nolan-movie-quotes-top-747653/ (accessed January 12, 2022).

Cox, Katherine (2019), *Superpowered Security: The Cruel Optimism of National Security in Marvel's Iron Man Films*, PhD thesis, Australian National University.

Csicsery-Ronay, Istvan, Jr. (2003), "Science Fiction and Empire," *Science Fiction Studies*, 30 (2): 231–45.

Csicsery-Ronay, Istvan, Jr. (2008), *The Seven Beauties of Science Fiction*, Middletown: Wesleyan University Press.

Currie, Matt (2010), "DISTRICT 9 Director Neill Blomkamp Talks about His Next Project, Making Movies on a Budget, and What the Future Holds," *Collider*, January 4. Available online: http://collider.com/district-9-director-neill-blomkamp-talks-about-his-next-project-making-movies-on-a-budget-and-what-the-future-holds/ (accessed January 12, 2022).

Curry, Alice (2013), *Environmental Crisis in Young Adult Fiction*, Basingstoke: Palgrave Macmillan.

Dargis, Manohla (2009), "A New Eden, Both Cosmic and Cinematic," *The New York Times*, December 17. Available online: https://www.nytimes.com/2009/12/18/movies/18avatar.html (accessed September 26, 2021).

Dargis, Manohla (2012), "Escaping a Dark Home Down a Dark Hole," *The New York Times*, February 2. Available online: https://www.nytimes.com/2012/02/03/movies/dane-dehaan-in-chronicle-directed-by-josh-trank.html (accessed June 8, 2021).

Dargis, Manohla (2015), "Review: In 'The Martian,' Marooned but Not Alone," *The New York Times*, October 1. Available online: https://www.nytimes.com/2015/10/02/movies/review-in-the-martian-marooned-but-not-alone.html (accessed September 10, 2021).

Debruge, Peter (2012), "Chronicle," *Variety*, February 1. Available online: https://variety.com/2012/film/reviews/chronicle-1117946985/ (accessed June 8, 2021).

Debruge, Peter (2015), "Toronto Film Review: 'The Martian,'" *Variety*, September 11. Available online: https://variety.com/2015/film/festivals/toronto-film-review-matt-damon-in-the-martian-1201590528/ (accessed September 10, 2021).

Debruge, Peter (2018), "Film Review: 'Black Panther,'" *Variety*, February 6, Available online: https://variety.com/2018/film/reviews/black-panther-review-1202682942/ (accessed October 15, 2021).

Debruge, Peter (2019), "Film Review: 'Avengers: Endgame,'" *Variety*, April 23, Available online: https://variety.com/2019/film/reviews/avengers-endgame-review-marvel-cinematic-universe-1203196048/ (accessed September 8, 2022).

Deleyto, Celestino (2012), "Film Genres at the Crossroads: What Genres and Films Do to Each Other," in Barry Keith Grant (ed.), *Film Genre Reader IV*, 218–36, Austin: University of Texas Press.

Denby, David (2010), "Dream Factory," *The New Yorker*, July 19. Available online: http://www.newyorker.com/magazine/2010/07/26/dream-factory (accessed September 10, 2021).

Desowitz, Bill (2009), "'Avatar': The Game Changer," *AWN.com. Animation World Network*, December 21. Available online: https://www.awn.com/vfxworld/avatar-game-changer (accessed January 11, 2022).

Desowitz, Bill (2014), "Alfonso Cuarón Talks Gravity," *AWN.com. Animation World Network*, February 11. Available online: https://www.awn.com/vfxworld/alfonso-cuar%C3%B3n-talks-gravity (accessed January 12, 2022).

Dittmer, Jason (2011), "American Exceptionalism, Visual Effects, and the Post-9/11 Cinematic Superhero Boom," *Environment and Planning D: Society and Space*, 29 (1): 114–30.

Dobbs, Sarah (2009), "Press Conference Report: Matt Reeves, Director of Cloverfield," January 29. Available online: https://www.denofgeek.com/movies/press-conference-report-matt-reeves-director-of-cloverfield/ (accessed 19 July, 2021).

Dowd, A.A. (2019), "Marvel's Grand Avengers Experiment Reaches Its Fun, Uneven, Sci-fi Tearjerker Endgame," *A.V. Club*, April 24. Available online: https://www.avclub.com/marvels-grand-avengers-experiment-reaches-its-fun-unev-1834261462 (accessed September 8, 2022).

Dunham, Brent (ed.) (2012), *James Cameron. Interviews*, Jackson: University Press of Mississippi.

Dunham, Brent (ed.) (2019), *J. J. Abrams. Interviews*, Jackson: University Press of Mississippi.

Ebert, Roger (1999), "George Lucas Is a Techie at Heart," *RogerEbert.com*, May 16. Available online: https://www.rogerebert.com/interviews/george-lucas-is-a-techie-at-heart (accessed January 11, 2022).

Ebert, Roger (2007), "When You're Alone and Life Is Making You Lonely, You Can Go Downtown," *Rogerebert.com*, December 13. Available online: https://www.rogerebert.com/reviews/i-am-legend-2007 (accessed August 9, 2021).

Ebiri, Bilge (2012), "Movie Review: Chronicle Is the Angry Teen's Superhero Movie … in a Good Way," *Vulture*, February 3. Available online: https://www.vulture.com/2012/02/chronicle-movie-review.html (accessed June 8, 2021).

Edelstein, David (2007), "And Opening This Week …," *New York*, December 7. Available online: https://nymag.com/arts/cultureawards/2007/41824/ (accessed August 9, 2021).

Edelstein, David (2019), "Avengers: Endgame Is More Clever than It Needed to Be," *Vulture*, April 23. Available online: https://www.vulture.com/2019/04/movie-review-avengers-endgame-2019.html (accessed September 8, 2022).

Ehrlich, David (2018), "'Black Panther' Review: Ryan Coogler Delivers the Best Marvel Movie So Far," *Indiewire*, February 6. Available online: https://www.indiewire.com/2018/02/black-panther-review-ryan-coogler-1201925524/ (accessed February 28, 2022).

Elsaesser, Thomas (2009), "The Mind-Game Film," in Warren Buckland (ed.), *Puzzle Films: Complex Storytelling in American Cinema*, 13–41, Oxford: Wiley-Blackwell.

Elsaesser, Thomas (2011), "James Cameron's *Avatar*: Access for All," *New Review of Film and Television Studies* 9 (3): 247–64. DOI: 10.1080/17400309.2011.585854

Elsaesser, Thomas (2012), *The Persistence of Hollywood*, London: Routledge.

Elsaesser, Thomas and Malte Hagener (2015), *Film Theory. An Introduction through the Senses*, New York: Routledge.

Failes, Ian (2014), "The VFX of Guardians of the Galaxy," *Fxguide*, August 3. Available online: https://www.fxguide.com/fxfeatured/the-vfx-of-guardians-of-the-galaxy/ (accessed September 26, 2021).

Faraci, Devan (2014), "The Badass Interview: James Gunn on Guardians of the Galaxy," *Birth.Movies.Death.*, July 29. Available online: https://birthmoviesdeath.com/2014/07/29/the-badass-interview-james-gunn-on-guardians-of-the-galaxy (accessed September 26, 2021).

Feinberg, Scott (2015), "Christopher Nolan on 'Interstellar' Critics, Making Original Films and Shunning Cellphones and Email (Q&A)," *The Hollywood Reporter*, January 3. Available online: https://www.hollywoodreporter.com/race/christopher-nolan-interstellar-critics-making-760897 (accessed January 12, 2022).

Fisher, Mark (2011), "The Lost Unconscious: Delusions and Dreams in Inception," *Film Quarterly*, 64 (2): 37–45. DOI: 10.1525/fq.2011.64.3.37

Fisher, Mark (2012), "Precarious Dystopias: *The Hunger Games*, *In Time*, and *Never Let Me Go*," *Film Quarterly*, 65 (4): 27–33.

Fleming Jr, Mike (2015), "Ridley Scott on 'The Martian' and Why 'Star Wars' and '2001' Sent Him to Space with 'Alien:' Toronto Q&A," *Deadline*, September 12. Available online: https://deadline.com/2015/09/ridley-scott-the-martian-star-wars-2001-alien-blade-runner-prometheus-toronto-film-festival-1201522484/ (accessed January 11, 2022).

Fleury, James, Hikari Hartzheim and Stephen Mamber (2019), "Introduction: The Franchise Era," in James Fleury, Hikari Hartzheim and Stephen Mamber (eds.), *Franchise Era: Managing Media in the Digital Economy*, 1–28, Edinburgh: Edinburgh University Press.

Flicks and The City Clips (2018), "BLACK PANTHER Official Interview—Kevin Feige," YouTube, January 31. Available online: https://www.youtube.com/watch?v=d5Qjhy2g0Dc (accessed February 28, 2021).

Fontanille, Jacques (2006), *The Semiotics of Discourse*, Heidi Bostic (trans.), New York: Peter Lang.

Ford, Rebecca (2014), "Why 'Earth to Echo' Moved from Studio to Studio," *The Hollywood Reporter*, June 25. Available online: https://www.hollywoodreporter.com/news/why-earth-echo-moved-studio-714485 (accessed January 11, 2022).

Foucault, Michel (1972), *Knowledge/Power. Selected Interviews and Other Writings 1972-1977*, Colin Gordon, Leo Marshall, John Mepham and Kate Soper (trans.), New York: Pantheon Books.

Franklin, H. Bruce (1994), "Star Trek in the Vietnam Era," *Science Fiction Studies*, 62: 24–34.

Freedman, Carl (2000), *Critical Theory and Science Fiction*, Middleton, CT: Wesleyan University Press.

Friedman, Lester D. and Brent Notbohm (eds.) (2000), *Steven Spielberg. Interviews*, Jackson: University Press of Mississippi.

Garcia-Siino, Leimar, Sabrina Mittermeier and Stefan Rabitsch (eds.) (2022), *The Routledge Handbook of Star Trek*, London: Routledge.

Gathara, Patrick (2018), "'Black Panther' Offers a Regressive, Neocolonial Vision of Africa," *The Washington Post*, February 26. Available online: https://www.washingtonpost.com/news/global-opinions/wp/2018/02/26/black-panther-offers-a-regressive-neocolonial-vision-of-africa/ (accessed 15 October, 2021).

Genette, Gérard and Marie Maclean (1991), "Introduction to the Paratext," *New Literary History*, 22 (2): 261–72.

Geraghty, Lincoln (2007), *Living with Star Trek: American Culture and the Star Trek Universe*, London: I. B. Tauris.

Geraghty, Lincoln (2009), *American Science Fiction Film and Television*, Oxford and New York: Berg.

Gianos, Phillip L. (1999), *Politics and Politicians in American Film*, Westport: Praeger.

Giardina, Carolyn (2008), "'Avatar' All about Innovation," *The Hollywood Reporter*, August 7. Available online: https://www.hollywoodreporter.com/news/avatar-all-innovation-117052 (accessed January 11, 2022).

Gideonse, Theodore K. (2019), "The Cultural Universals in *Avengers: Endgame*," *Anthropology News*, May 29. Available online: https://www.anthropology-news.org/articles/the-cultural-universals-in-avengers-endgame/ (accessed September 7, 2022).

Gilmore, James N. (2015), "A Eulogy of the Urban Superhero: The Everyday Destruction of Space in the Superhero Film," in Paul Petrovic (ed.), *Representing 9/11. Trauma, Ideology and Nationalism in Literature, Film and Television*, 53–64, New York and London: Rowman & Littlefield.

Goldberg, Matt (2018), "3D Is Dead (Again)," *Collider*, April 6. Available online: https://collider.com/3d-movies-are-dead-again/ (accessed September 26, 2021).

Golding, Dan (2019), *Star Wars after Lucas: A Critical Guide to the Future of the Galaxy*, Minneapolis: University of Minnesota Press.

Golumbia, David (1995), "Black and White World: Race, Ideology, and Utopia in *Triton* and *Star Trek*," *Cultural Critique*, 32: 75–95.

Gonzalez, George A. (2015), *The Politics of Star Trek: Justice, War, and the Future*, New York: Palgrave Macmillan.

Gordon, Andrew M. (2008), *The Science Fiction and Fantasy Films of Steven Spielberg*, Lanham: Rowman & Littlefield Publishers, Inc.

Graham, Elaine L. (2002), *Representations of the Post/Human. Monsters, Aliens and Others in Popular Culture*, New Brunswick: Rutgers University Press.

Grant, Barry Keith (1999), "'Sensuous Elaboration': Reason and the Visible in the Science-Fiction Film," in Annete Kuhn (ed.), *Alien Zone II. The Spaces of Science Fiction Cinema*, 16–30, London and New York: Verso.

Greimas, Algirdas J. (1986), *On Meaning. Selected Writings in Semiotic Theory*, Paul J. Perron and Frank H. Collins (trans.), Minneapolis: University of Minnesota Press.

Greimas, Algirdas J. ([1966] 2005), *Structural Semantics. An Attempt at a Method*, Athens: Pataki.

Greimas, Algirdas J. and François Rastier (1968), "The Interaction of Semiotic Constraints," *Yale French Studies*, 41: 86–105. http://www.jstor.org/stable/2929667

Greven, David (2009), *Gender and Sexuality in Star Trek: Allegories of Desire in the Television Series and Films*, Jefferson and London: McFarland & Company, Inc.

Griffin, Matt (2022), "'That Moment Meant a Lot to My Daughter': Affect, Fandom, and *Avengers: Endgame*," *Feminist Media Studies*. DOI: 10.1080/14680777.2022.2098801

Grobar, Matt (2018), "'Blade Runner 2049' Cinematographer Roger Deakins Made Light "Feel Alive" with Computer-Controlled Rigs," *Deadline*, February 26. Available online: https://deadline.com/2018/02/blade-runner-2049-roger-deakins-oscars-cinematography-interview-1202280774/ (accessed August 9, 2021).

Gunning, Tom (1986), "The Cinema of Attractions: Early Film, Its Spectators and the Avant-garde," *Wide Angle*, 8 (3–4): 63–70.

Guynes, Sean and Dan Hassler-Forest (2017), *Star Wars and the History of Transmedia Storytelling*, Amsterdam: Amsterdam University Press.

Hadas, Leora (2017), "A New Vision: J. J. Abrams, *Star Trek*, and Promotional Authorship," *Cinema Journal* 56 (2): 46–66.

Hall, Sheldon (2002), "Tall Revenue Features: The Genealogy of Modern Blockbuster," in Steve Neale (ed.), *Genre and Contemporary Hollywood*, 11–26, London: British Film Institute.

Hall, Sheldon (2011), *Blockbusters*, New York: Oxford University Press.

Hall, Sheldon and Steve Neale (2010), *A Hollywood History. Epics, Spectacles and Blockbusters*, Detroit: Wayne State University Press.

Hamblin, Sarah and Hugh C. O'Connell (2020), "Blade Runner 2049's Incongruous Couplings. Living and Dying in the Anthropocene," *Science Fiction Film and Television*, 13 (1): 37–58. https://doi.org/10.3828/sfftv.2020.3

Haraway, Donna (2004), "A Manifesto for Cyborgs: Science, Technology and Socialist Feminism in the 1980s," in Sean Redmond (ed.), *Liquid Metal. The Science Fiction Film Reader*, 158–81, London: Wallflower Press.

Hardt, Michael and Antonio Negri (2000), *Empire*. Cambridge: Harvard University Press.

Hark, Ina Rae (2008), *Star Trek*, London: British Film Institute.

Hassler-Forest, Dan (2011), "From Flying Man to Falling Man: 9/11 Discourse in *Superman Returns* and *Batman Begins*," in Véronique Bragard, Christophe Dony and Warren Rosenberg (eds.), *Portraying 9/11: Essays on Representations in Comics, Literature, Film and Theatre*, 134–46, Jefferson and London: McFarland and Company, Inc.

Hassler-Forest, Dan (2012), *Capitalist Superheroes: Caped Crusaders in the Neoliberal Age*, Winchester: Zero Books.

Hassler-Forest, Dan (2016), "Star Trek, Global Capitalism and Immaterial Labour," *Science Fiction Film and Television*, 9 (3): 371–91. DOI: 10.3828/sfftv.2016

Hatfield Charles, Heer Jeet and Kent Worcester (2013), "Introduction," in Charles Hatfield, Jeet Heer and Kent Worcester (eds.), *The Superhero Reader*, xi–xxii. Jackson: University Press of Mississippi.

Hayles, N. Katherine (1999), *How We Became Posthuman. Virtual Bodies in Cybernetics, Literature and Informatics*, Chicago: University of Chicago Press.

Hiscock, John (2009), "James Cameron Interview for Avatar," *The Telegraph*, December 3. Available online: https://www.telegraph.co.uk/culture/film/6720156/James-Cameron-interview-for-Avatar.html (accessed January 11, 2022).

Hodges, Lacy (2009), "Mainstreaming Marginality: Genre, Hybridity, and Postmodernism in *The X-Files*," in J. P. Telotte (ed.), *The Essential Science Fiction Television Reader*, 231–45, Lexington: The University Press of Kentucky.

Hollywood Reporter (2018), "'Black Panther' Represents 'Real Hopes & Dreams' Says Producer Kevin Feige | Close Up," *YouTube*, November 2. Available online: https://www.youtube.com/watch?v=fxku6PW4mdI (accessed February 28, 2022).

Honeycott, Kirk (2011), "Limitless: Film Review," *The Hollywood Reporter*, March 14. Available online: https://www.hollywoodreporter.com/movies/movie-reviews/limitless-film-review-167424/ (accessed June 8, 2021).

Hornaday, Ann (2018), "'Black Panther' Is Exhilarating, Groundbreaking and More than Worth the Wait," *The Washington Post*, February 9. Available online: https://www.washingtonpost.com/goingoutguide/movies/black-panther-is-exhilarating-groundbreaking-and-more-than-worth-the-wait/2018/02/09/5bff1d4c-0916-11e8-94e8-e8b8600ade23_story.html (accessed February 27, 2022).

Huddleston, Tom (2013), "Neill Blomkamp Interview: 'We're Disgusting Organisms,'" *Time Out*, August 22. Available online: https://www.timeout.com/london/film/neill-blomkamp-interview-were-disgusting-organisms (accessed January 12, 2022).

IGN (2008), "Cloverfield: A Viral Guide," *IGN*, January 15. Available online: https://www.ign.com/articles/2008/01/15/cloverfield-a-viral-guide (accessed 19 July, 2021).

Interstellar (2014), [film] Dir. Christopher Nolan, Warner Bros. Entertainment Inc. and Paramount Pictures Corporation.

Itzkoff, Dave (2019), "'Avengers: Endgame': The Screenwriters Answer Every Question You Might Have," *The New York Times*, April 29. Available online: https://www.nytimes.com/2019/04/29/movies/avengers-endgame-questions-and-answers.html (accessed September 7, 2022).

Jakobson, Roman (1960), "Closing Statements: Linguistics and Poetics," in Thomas A. Sebeok (ed.), *Style in Language*, 350–77, Cambridge: MIT Press.

Jameson, Fredric (2005) *Archaeologies of the Future. The Desire Called Utopia and Other Science Fictions*, London and New York: Verso

Jancovich, Mark (2004), "Re-examining the 1950s Invasion Narratives," in Sean Redmond (ed.), *Liquid Metal. The Science Fiction Film Reader*, 325–35, London: Wallflower Press.

Jancovich, Mark and Derek Johnston (2009), "Film and Television, the 1950s," in Mark Bould, Andrew M. Butler, Adam Roberts and Sherryl Vint (eds.), *The Routledge Companion to Science Fiction*, 71–9, London and New York: Routledge.

Jeffords, Susan (1994), *Hard Bodies: Hollywood Masculinity in the Reagan Era*, New Brunswick, NJ: Rutgers University Press.

Jenkins III, Henry (2004), "Star Trek Rerun, Reread, Rewritten: Fan Writing as Textual Poaching," in Sean Redmond (ed.), *Liquid Metal. The* Science Fiction Film Reader, 264–80, London: Wallflower Press.

Johnston, Keith M. (2011), *Science Fiction Film: A Critical Introduction*, Oxford, New York: Berg.

Jones, Nick (2015), *Hollywood Action Films and Spatial Theory*, New York: Routledge.

Kaklamanidou, Betty (2016), *The "Disguised" Political Film in Contemporary Hollywood. A Genre's Construction*, New York: Bloomsbury Academic.

Kaplan, E. Ann (2016), *Climate Trauma: Foreseeing the Future in Dystopian Film and Fiction*, New Jersey: Rutgers University Press.

Kaye, Don (2020), "Josh Trank Talks Where Fantastic Four Went Wrong," *Den of Geek*, May, 13. Available online: https://www.denofgeek.com/movies/josh-trank-talks-where-fantastic-four-went-wrong/ (accessed June 8, 2021).

Kelly, Kevin (2013), "Interview: How Neill Blomkamp Reimagined L. A. as a Wheel in the Sky in 'Elysium,'" *Digital Trends*, August 9. Available online: https://www.digitaltrends.com/movies/elysium-director-neill-blomkamp-on-technology-society-and-the-dystopia-between/ (accessed January 12, 2022).

King, Geoff (2020), "Blade Runner 2049 and the 'Quality' Hollywood film," *Science Fiction Film and Television*, 13 (1): 77–96.

King, Geoff and Tanya Krzywinska (2000), *Science Fiction Cinema: From Outerspace to Cyberspace*, London: Wallflower.

King, Shaun (2018) "Black Panther Is One of the Most Important Cultural Moments in American History," *Medium*, February 20. Available online: https://medium.com/@ShaunKing/black-panther-is-one-of-the-most-important-moments-in-american-history-1fc9166a0972 (accessed October 15, 2021).

Kohn, Eric (2015), "Review: Ridley Scott's 'The Martian' Is the Anti-'Interstellar,'" *Indiewire*, September 11. Available online: https://www.indiewire.com/2015/09/review-ridley-scotts-the-martian-is-the-anti-interstellar-58264/ (accessed September 10, 2021).

Kohn, Eric (2019), "'Avengers: Endgame' Review: A Messy Love Letter to the Biggest Movie Franchise of the Century," *Indiewire*, April 23. Available online: https://www.indiewire.com/2019/04/avengers-endgame-review-1202127374/ (accessed September 8, 2022).

Kragsbjerg, Trine Mærsk (2021), "The Malthusian Alternative and Overpopulation in *Avengers: Infinity War* and *Avengers: Endgame*," *Leviathan: Interdisciplinary Journal in English* 7: 21–31.

Kristeva, Julia (1982), *Powers of Horror. An Essay on Abjection*, Leon S. Roudiez (trans.), New York: Columbia University Press.

Kuhn, Annette (1990), "Introduction: Cultural Theory and Science Fiction Cinema," in Annette Kuhn (ed.), *Alien Zone. Cultural Theory and Contemporary Science Fiction Cinema*, 1–12, London and New York: Verso.

Kuhn, Annette and Guy Westwell (2012), *Oxford Dictionary of Film Studies*, Oxford: Oxford University Press.

La Valley, Albert J. (1985), "Traditions of Trickery: The Role of Special Effects in the Science Fiction Film," in George S. Slusser and Eric S. Rabkin (eds.), *Shadows of the Magic Lamp: Fantasy and Science Fiction in Film*, 141–57, Carbondale and Edwardsville: Southern Illinois University Press.

Lagopoulos, Alexandros Ph. and Karin Boklund-Lagopoulou (2014), "Social Semiotics: Towards a Sociologically Grounded Semiotics," Keynote Speech at 12th World Congress of Semiotics, Sofia, New Bulgarian University, September 16–20.

Lambie, Ryan (2013), "Guillermo Del Toro Interview: Pacific Rim, Monsters and More," *Den of Geek*, July 12. Available online: https://www.denofgeek.com/movies/guillermo-del-toro-interview-pacific-rim-monsters-and-more/ (accessed June 29, 2021).

Landon, Brooks ([1992] 2016), "On a Clear Day You Can See the Horizon of Invisibility: Rethinking Science Fiction Film in the Age of Electronic (Re)production," in Sherryl Vint (ed.), *Science Fiction and Cultural Theory. A Reader*, 200–11, London: Routledge.

Lang, Brent (2019), "How Kevin Feige Super-Charged Marvel Studios into Hollywood's Biggest Hit Machine," *Variety*, April 16. Available online: https://variety.com/2019/film/features/kevin-feige-avengers-endgame-marvel-studios-1203188721/ (accessed September 7, 2022).

Lang Brent and Ricardo Lopez (2018), "Lionsgate Courts Buyers as It Struggles to Compete with Industry Heavyweights," *Variety*, February 27. Available online: https://variety.com/2018/film/features/lionsgate-sale-merger-shares-1202711913/ (accessed January 13, 2022).

Langford, Barry (2005), *Film Genre. Hollywood and Beyond*, Edinburgh: Edinburg University Press.

Lee, Mike (2012), "Christopher Nolan Talks IMAX, 3D, and CGI in Movies," *Screenrant*, April 16. Available online: https://screenrant.com/christopher-nolan-imax-3d-cgi/ (accessed January 12, 2022).

Lenoir, Tim (2000), "All but War Is Simulation: The Military–Entertainment Complex," *Configurations*, 8 (3): 289–335.

Levithan, David (2018), "Suzanne Collins Talks about 'The Hunger Games,' the Books and the Movies," *New York Times*, October 18. Available online: https://www.nytimes.com/2018/10/18/books/suzanne-collins-talks-about-the-hunger-games-the-books-and-the-movies.html (accessed August 9, 2021).

Lewis-Kraus, Gideon (2014), "The Exacting, Expansive Mind of Christopher Nolan," *The New York Times*, October 30. Available online: https://www.nytimes.com/2014/11/02/magazine/the-exacting-expansive-mind-of-christopher-nolan.html (accessed January 12, 2022).

Leydon, Joe (2002), "Steven Spielberg and Tom Cruise. Their 'Minority Report' Looks at the Day after Tomorrow—and Is Relevant to Today," *Moving Picture Show*, June 20. Available online: http://www.movingpictureshow.com/dialogues/mpsSpielbergCruise.html (accessed 19 July, 2021).

Li, Shirley (2014), "'Dawn of the Planet of the Apes' Production Designer on the 'Evolved Thinking' of the Sets," *The Atlantic*, July 21. Available online: https://www.theatlantic.com/culture/archive/2014/07/dawn-of-the-planet-of-the-apes-production-designer-on-films-memorable-look/374773/ (accessed August 9, 2021).

Lodge, Guy (2020), "'Tenet' Review: Christopher Nolan's Grandly Entertaining, Time-Slipping Spectacle Is a Futuristic Throwback," *Variety*, August 21. Available online: https://variety.com/2020/film/reviews/tenet-review-christopher-nolan-1234742936/ (accessed February 17, 2023).

Lubin, Gus (2015), "Tony Stark's Evolution Is the Defining Arc of the Marvel Cinematic Universe," *Business Insider*, May 28. Available online: https://www.businessinsider.in/tony-starks-evolution-is-the-defining-arc-of-the-marvel-cinematic-universe/articleshow/47461693.cms (accessed June 8, 2021).

Magid, Ron (2002), "George Lucas Discusses His Ongoing Effort to Shape the Future of Digital Cinema," *American Cinematographer*, September. Available online: https://theasc.com/magazine/sep02/exploring/index.html (accessed January 11, 2022).

Mair, Jan (2002), "Rewriting the 'American Dream': Postmodernism and Otherness in Independence Day," in Ziauddin Sardar and Sean Cubitt (eds.), *Aliens R Us. The Other in Science Fiction Cinema*, 34–50, London: Pluto Press.

Maslin, Janet (2007), "A World without Humans? It All Falls Apart," *New York Times*, August 13. Available online: https://www.nytimes.com/2007/08/13/books/13masl.html (accessed August 9, 2021).

Masters, Tim (2014), "Oscars: Gravity 'Not Sci-fi', Says Alfonso Cuaron," *BBC*, February 28. Available online: https://www.bbc.com/news/entertainment-arts-26381335 (accessed September 10, 2021).

McCarthy, Todd (2009), "Review: Avatar," *Variety*, December 10. Available online: https://variety.com/2009/film/markets-festivals/avatar-2-1200477897/ (accessed September 26, 2021).

McCarthy, Todd (2012), "Chronicle: Film Review," *The Hollywood Reporter*, February 2. Available online: https://www.hollywoodreporter.com/movies/movie-reviews/chronicle-film-review-286829/ (accessed June 8, 2021).

McCarthy, Todd (2019), "'Avengers: Endgame': Film Review," *Hollywood Reporter*, April 23. Available online: https://www.hollywoodreporter.com/movies/movie-reviews/avengers-endgame-review-1203971/ (accessed September 8, 2022).

McGrath, Charles (2014), "A Circuitous Route to Outer Space," *The New York Times*, January 3. Available online: https://www.nytimes.com/2014/01/05/movies/awardsseason/alfonso-cuaron-discusses-his-films.html (accessed January 12, 2022).

McKagen, Leigh E. (2022), "Colonialism and Imperialism," in Leimar Garcia-Siino, Sabrina Mittermeier and Stefan Rabitsch's (eds.), *The Routledge Handbook of Star Trek*, New York: Routledge.

McMichael, Anthony J. (2004), "Environmental and Social Influences on Emerging Infectious Diseases: Past, present and future," *Philos Trans R Soc Lond B Biol Sci*, 359 (1447): 1049–58.

McSweeney, Terence (2018), *Avengers Assemble! Critical Perspectives on the Marvel Cinematic Universe*, New York: Columbia University Press.

McSweeney, Terence (2020), *The Contemporary Superhero Film: Projections of Power and Identity*, New York: Wallflower Press.

Mendlesohn, Farah (2003), "Introduction: Reading Science Fiction," in Edward James and Farah Mendlesohn (eds.), *The Cambridge Companion to Science Fiction*, 1–12, Cambridge: Cambridge University Press.

Michelson, Annette ([1969] 2016), "Bodies in Space. Film as Carnal Knowledge," in Sherryl Vint (ed.), *Science Fiction and Cultural Theory. A Reader*, 15–27, London: Routledge.

Miéville, China (2009), "Cognition as Ideology. A Dialectic of SF Theory," in Mark Bould and China Miéville (eds.), *Red Planets: Marxism and Science Fiction*, 231–48, Middletown: Weslyan University Press.

Miller, Mat (2019), "The Right-Wing Troll Backlash against HBO's *Watchmen* Is Hilariously Stupid," *Esquire*, October 24, 2019. https://www.esquire.com/entertainment/tv/a29565670/watchmen-hbo-backlash-controversy-white-supremacy/ (accessed February 27, 2022).

Mirlees, Tanner (2014), "How to Read Iron Man: The Economics, Politics and Ideology of an Imperial Film Commodity," *Cineaction: Canada's Leading Film Studies Journal*, 92 (1): 4–11.

Mitchell, Neil (2017), "BFI's '10 Great Sci-Fi Films of the 21st Century," *BFI*, January 17. Available online: https://www2.bfi.org.uk/news-opinion/news-bfi/lists/10-great-sci-fi-films-21st-century (accessed August 9, 2021).

Mittermeier, Sabrina (2021), "Avengers: Endgame," *Science Fiction Film and Television*, 14 (3): 423–9. https://doi.org/10.3828/sfftv.2021.29

Morris, Nigel (2007), *The Cinema of Steven Spielberg. Empire of Light*, London: Wallflower Press.

Morse, Stephen S. (1995), "Factors in the Emergence of Infectious Diseases," *Emerg Infect Dis*, 1 (1): 7–15.

Muller, Christine (2011), "Power, Choice and September 11 in the *The Dark Knight*," in Richard J. Gray II and Betty Kaklamanidou (eds.), *The 21st Century Superhero: Essays on Gender, Genre and Globalization in Film*, 46–59, Jefferson and London: McFarland and Company, Inc.

Nama, Adilifu (2008), *Black Space. Imagining Race in Science Fiction*, Austin: University of Texas Press.

Napier, Susan J. (2016), "When the Machines Stop: Fantasy, Reality and Terminal Identity in *Neon Genesis: Evangelion* and *Serial Experiments: Lain* (2007)," in Sherryl Vint (ed.), *Science Fiction and Cultural Theory*, 294–304, London and New York: Routledge.

Natali, Maurizia (2019), "Empire of Catalandia Science Fiction as the Cinematic Space of the Anthropocene," in Filipa Rosário, Iván Villarmea Álvarez (eds.), *New Approaches to Cinematic Space*, 69–84, New York: Routledge.

Ndalianis, Angela (2009), "Comic Book Superheroes: An Introduction," in Angela Ndalianis (ed.), *The Contemporary Comic Book Superhero*, 3–15. New York and London: Routledge.

Neale, Steve (2000), *Genre and Hollywood*, London and New York: Routledge.

Neale, Steve (2004), "'You've Got to Be Fucking Kidding!': Knowledge, Belief and Judgment in Science Fiction," in Sean Redmond (ed.), *Liquid Metal. The Science Fiction Film Reader*, 11–17, London and New York: Wallflower Press.

Neale, Steve (2012), "Questions of Genre," in Barry Keith Grant (ed.), *Film Genre Reader IV*, 178–202, Austin: University of Texas Press.

Neilson, Toby (2019), "Contemporary Sf Cinema's Imagination of Disaster in the Anthropocene," *Science Fiction Film and Television*, 12 (2): 241–58. https://doi.org/10.3828/sfftv.2019.14

Niessen, Niels (2021), "Black Panther Transmedia: The Revolution Will Not Be Streamed," *JCMS*, 60 (5): 121–49.

O'Falt, Chris (2018), "Roger Deakins' Legacy Is Bigger than an Oscar: A Frank Conversation with the Cinematography Legend," *Indiewire*, February 23. Available online: https://www.indiewire.com/2018/02/roger-deakins-cinematography-oscars-blade-runner-2049-interview-1201931959/ (accessed August 9, 2021).

O'Falt, Chris et al. (2017), "The 25 Best Sci-Fi Movies of the 21st Century, From 'Children of Men' to 'Her,'" *Indiewire*, November 7. Available online: https://www.indiewire.com/feature/best-sci-fi-movies-science-fiction-film-1201817994/3/ (accessed August 9, 2021).

O'Sullivan, Michael (2019), "With Humor and Heart, 'Avengers: Endgame' Is a Fitting Send-off for Marvel's Superheroes," *Washington Post*, April 23. Available online: https://www.washingtonpost.com/goingoutguide/movies/with-humor-and-heart-avengers-endgame-is-a-fitting-send-off-for-marvels-superheroes/2019/04/23/539f3890-6391-11e9-9412-daf3d2e67c6d_story.html (accessed September 8, 2022).

Oldham, Stuart (2009), "Interview: Neill Blomkamp," *Variety*, August 14. Available online: https://variety.com/2009/film/news/interview-neill-blomkamp-1118007279/ (accessed June 29, 2021).

Pak, Chris (2017), "Red Marble," *Science Fiction Film and Television*, 10 (1): 105–14. https://doi.org/10.3828/sfftv.2017.5

Pape, Stefan (2019), "Kevin Feige on Avengers: Endgame: "My Dream Is to Win the Test of Time," *The Hot Corn*, April 9. Available online: https://hotcorn.com/en/movies/news/kevin-feige-on-avengers-endgame-my-dream-is-to-win-the-test-of-time-robert-downey-jr/ (accessed September 7, 2022).

Parikka, Jussi (2010), *Insect Media. An Archaeology of Animals and Technology*, Minneapolis: University of Minnesota Press.

Pascale, Anthony (2009), "Exclusive: Interview with Star Trek Production Designer Scott Chambliss," *Trekmovie.com*, September 12. Available online: https://trekmovie.com/2009/09/25/exclusive-interview-with-star-trek-production-designer-scott-chambliss/ (accessed September 26, 2021).

Patell, Cyrus R. K. (2021), *Lucasfilm: Filmmaking, Philosophy, and the Star Wars Universe*, New York: Bloomsbury Academic.

Pearson, Roberta and Máire Messenger Davies (2014), *Star Trek and American Television*, Berkeley: University of California Press.

Pelkonen, Eeva-Liisa and Donald Albrecht (2006), "Introduction," in Eeva-Liisa Pelkonen and Donald Albrecht (eds.), *Eero Saarinen: Shaping the Future*, 1–12, New Haven and London: Yale University Press.

Penley, Constance (1997), *NASA/Trek: Popular Science and Sex in America*, London and New York: Verso.

Pierson, Michelle (2002), *Special Effects. Still in Search of Wonder*, New York and Chichester: Columbia University Press.

Powell, Corey S. (2016), "Getting under the Alien Skin of the New 'Independence Day,'" *Discover*, June 25. Available online: https://www.discovermagazine.com/the-sciences/getting-under-the-alien-skin-of-the-new-independence-day (accessed June 29, 2021).

Prince, Stephen (2012), *Digital Visual Effects in Cinema. The Seduction of Reality*, New Brunswick: Rutgers University Press.

Proctor, William and Richard McCulloch (2019), *Disney's Star Wars: Forces of Production, Promotion, and Reception*, Iowa City: University of Iowa Press.

Pulver, Andrew (2013), "International Man," *Directors Guild of America*, Summer 2013. Available online: https://www.dga.org/Craft/DGAQ/All-Articles/1303-Summer-2013/Alfonso-Cuaron.aspx (accessed January 12, 2022).

Randell, Karen (2016), "'It Was like a Movie', Take 2: *Age of Ultron* and a 9/11 Aesthetic," *Cinema Journal*, 56 (1): 137–41.

Ressner, Jeffrey (2012), "The Traditionalist," *Directors Guild of America*, Spring 2012. Available online: http://www.dga.org/Craft/DGAQ/All-Articles/1202-Spring-2012/DGA-Interview-Christopher-Nolan.aspx (accessed January 12, 2022).

Rieder, John (2008), *Colonialism and the Emergence of Science Fiction*. Middletown: Wesleyan University Press.

Robbins, Shaw (2019), "Why Superheroes and the Big Screen Experience Still Matter: An Interview with Avengers: Endgame Co-Director Joe Russo," *Boxofficepro*, April 23. Available online: https://www.boxofficepro.com/avengers-endgame-joe-russo-mcu-interview/ (accessed September 7, 2022).

Roeper, Richard (2018), "'Black Panther': One of the Best Superheroes Comes Out of Africa," *Chicago Sun Times*, February 14. Available online: https://chicago.suntimes.com/2018/2/14/18368193/black-panther-one-of-marvel-s-best-movie-superheroes-comes-out-of-africa (accessed 15 October, 2021).

Rogers, Adam (2014), "Wrinkles in Spacetime. The Warped Astrophysics of Interstellar," *Wired*. Available online: https://www.wired.com/2014/10/astrophysics-interstellar-black-hole/ (accessed January 13, 2022).

Rose, Steve (2014), "Sandra Bullock: The Pain of Gravity," *The Guardian*, February 6. Available online: https://www.theguardian.com/film/2014/feb/06/sandra-bullock-pain-gravity-oscars-george-clooney-2014 (accessed September 10, 2021).

Rothkopf, Joshua (2019), "Avengers: Endgame," *Time Out*, April 23. https://www.timeout.com/movies/avengers-endgame-1 (accessed September 8, 2022).

Rotten Tomatoes (n.d.a.), "A. I.: Artificial Intelligence," *Rotten Tomatoes*. Available online: https://www.rottentomatoes.com/m/ai_artificial_intelligence (accessed 19 July, 2021).

Rotten Tomatoes (n.d.b.), "Transformers," Available online: https://www.rottentomatoes.com/franchise/transformers (accessed June 29, 2021).

Rust, Stephen (2013), "Hollywood and Climate Change," in Stephen Rust, Salma Monani and Sean Cubitt (eds.), *Ecocinema Theory and Practice*, 191–211, New York and London: Routledge.

Rust, Stephen A. and Carter Soles (2014), "Living in Fear, Living in Dread, Pretty Soon We'll All Be Dead," *Interdisciplinary Studies in Literature and Environment*, 21 (3): 509–12.

Sager, Mike (2016), "J. J. Abrams Is the Golden Child 'Star Wars' Deserved," *Esquire*, May 13. Available online: https://www.esquire.com/entertainment/a44348/jj-abrams-star-wars/ (accessed January 13, 2022).

Said, Edward W. (2003), *Orientalism*. London: Penguin Modern Classics.

Sawyer, Andy (2009), "Space Opera," in Mark Bould, Andrew M. Butler, Adam Roberts and Sherryl Vint (eds.), *The Routledge Companion to Science Fiction*, 505–9, London and New York: Routledge.

Schauer, Bradley (2007), "Critics, *Clones* and Narrative in the Franchise Blockbuster," *New Review of Film and Television Studies*, 5 (2): 191–210. DOI: 10.1080/174003007014328

Schatz, Thomas (2009), "New Hollywood, New Millennium," in Warren Buckland (ed.), *Film Theory and Contemporary Hollywood Movies*, 19–46, New York and London: Routledge.

Sciretta, Peter (2019), "The Russo Brothers Talk 'Avengers: Endgame', Stan Lee, Lasting Stakes And More [Spoiler-Free Interview]," *Slash Film*, April 23. Available online: https://www.slashfilm.com/565889/endgame-director-interview/ (accessed September 7, 2022).

Scott, A. O. (2010), "This Time the Dream's on Me," *The New York Times*, July 15. Available online: https://www.nytimes.com/2010/07/16/movies/16inception.html (accessed September 10, 2021).

Scott, A. O. (2011), "A Simple Prescription for Superior Powers," *The New York Times*, March 17. Available online: https://www.nytimes.com/2011/03/18/movies/bradley-cooper-as-a-burned-out-writer-in-limitless-review.html (accessed June 8, 2021).

Screenrant (2014), "Guardians of the Galaxy Set Interview: James Gunn Talks Cameos and Working with Marvel," *Screenrant*, n.d. Available online: https://screenrant.com/guardians-of-the-galaxy-set-interview-james-gunn/3/ (accessed September 26, 2021).

Sharf, Zack (2020), "'Tenet' Divides Critics: Nolan's Latest Called a 'Monumental Spectacle' and 'Head-Scratching' Dud," *Indiewire*, August 21. Available online: https://

www.indiewire.com/2020/08/tenet-critics-divided-christopher-nolan-1234581611/ (accessed September 10, 2021).

Sharf, Zack (2021) "Neill Blomkamp Confirms Long-Planned 'District 9' Sequel Is Now Being Written: 'It's Coming,'" *Indiewire*, February 26. Available online: https://www.indiewire.com/2021/02/neill-blomkamp-district-9-sequel-written-1234619653/ (accessed June 30, 2021).

Short, Sue (2005), *Cyborg Cinema and Contemporary Subjectivity*, Hampshire and New York: Palgrave Macmillan.

Silberman, Steve (2005), "George Lucas on Star Wars, Fahrenheit 9/11 and His Own Legacy," *Wired*, May 1. Available online: https://www.wired.com/2005/05/lucasqa/ (accessed January 11, 2022).

Silvio, Carl and Tony M. Vinci (eds.) (2007), *Culture, Identities, and Technology in the Star Wars Films: Essays on the Two Trilogies*, Jefferson and London: McFarland and Company, Inc.

Sims, David (2019), "What It Was like Making the Biggest Movie of 2019," *The Atlantic*, May 7. Available online: https://www.theatlantic.com/entertainment/archive/2019/05/russo-brothers-interview-avengers-marvel-endgame/588832/ (accessed September 7, 2022).

Smith, Gavin (2014), "Interview: Alfonso Cuarón," *Film Comment*, February 27. Available online: https://www.filmcomment.com/blog/interview-alfonso-cuaron/ (accessed January 12, 2022).

Smith, Sean (2013), "'Elysium': Future Shock," *Entertainment*, July 26. Available online: https://ew.com/article/2013/07/26/elysium-future-shock/ (accessed August 9, 2021).

Sobchack, Vivian (1987), *Screening Space: The American Science Fiction Film*, New Brunswick: Rutgers University Press.

Sobchack, Vivian (2004), "Cities on the Edge of Time: The Urban Science Fiction Film," in Sean Redmod (ed.), *Liquid Metal. The Science Fiction Film Reader*, 78–87, New York: Wallflower Press.

Sontag, Susan (1965), "The Imagination of Disaster," *Commentary* 65: 42–8.

Spitznagel, Eric (2012), "Q+A: Ridley Scott's Star Wars," *Esquire*, June 4. Available online: https://www.esquire.com/entertainment/interviews/a14300/ridley-scott-prometheus-interview-9423167/ (accessed January 11, 2022).

Staiger, Janet (2012), "Hybrid or Inbred: The Purity Hypothesis and Hollywood Genre History," in Barry Keith Grant (ed.), *Film Genre Reader IV*, 203–17. Austin: University of Texas Press.

Stam, Robert, Robert Burgoyone and Sandy Flitterman-Lewis (1992), *New Vocabularies in Film Semiotics. Structuralism, Post-Structuralism and Beyond*, London and New York: Routledge.

Stefanopoulou, Evdokia (2021), "The Rhetoric of Ecology in the Post-apocalyptic Cinematic Landscape," *Res Rhetorica*, 8 (2): 38–54. DOI: https://doi.org/10.29107/rr2021.2.3

Stevens, Dana (2019), "Waiting for Thanos. Avengers: Endgame Is like Samuel Beckett with Superheroes," *Slate*, April 24. Available online: https://slate.com/

culture/2019/04/avengers-endgame-review-marvel-movie-samuel-beckett.html (accessed September 8, 2022).

Stewart, Garrett (2016), "The 'Videology' of Science Fiction," in Sherryl Vint (ed.), *Science Fiction and Cultural Theory. A Reader*, 177–87, London: Routledge.

Suvin, Darko (1972), "On the Poetics of the Science Fiction Genre," *College English*, 34 (3): 377–82.

Tapley, Christopher (2015), "Ridley Scott Tapped for Visual Effects Society's Lifetime Achievement Award," *Variety*, October 27. Available online: https://variety.com/2015/film/awards/ridley-scott-visual-effects-society-lifetime-achievement-award-2-1201627907/ (accessed January 11, 2022).

Tartaglione, Nancy (2021), "'Avatar' Overtakes 'Avengers: Endgame' as All-Time Highest-Grossing Film Worldwide; Rises To $2.8B Amid China Reissue—Update," *Deadline*, March 13. Available online: https://deadline.com/2021/03/avatar-overtakes-avengers-endgame-highest-grossing-film-all-time-worldwide-box-office-china-james-cameron-disney-1234713788/ (accessed September 26, 2021).

TED (2010), "TED Talk: James Cameron: Before Avatar ... A Curious Boy," *TED*, February. Available online: https://www.ted.com/talks/james_cameron_before_avatar_a_curious_boy?language=en (accessed January 11, 2022).

Telotte, J. P. (2001), *Science Fiction Film*, Cambridge: Cambridge University Press.

Telotte, J. P. (2008a), "Introduction: The Trajectory of Science Fiction Television," in J. P. Telotte (ed.), *The Essential Science Fiction Television Reader*, 1–34, Lexington: The University Press of Kentucky.

Telotte, J. P. (2008b), "Serenity, Cinematisation and the Perils of Adaptation," *Science Fiction Film and Television*, 1 (1): 67–80.

Telotte, J. P. (2016), *Robot Ecology and the Science Fiction Film* (Routledge Focus on Film Studies) Taylor and Francis, Kindle Edition.

Today (2005), "'War of the Worlds' Draws on 9/11 Anxieties," *Today*, June 28. Available online: https://www.today.com/popculture/war-worlds-draws-9-11-anxieties-wbna8381687 (accessed June 30, 2021).

Todorov, Tzvetan (1975), *The Fantastic. A Structural Approach to a Literary Genre*, Richard Howard (trans.), Ithaca, New York: Cornell University Press.

Travers, Peter (2005), "War of the Worlds," *Rolling Stone*, July 6. Available online: https://www.rollingstone.com/tv-movies/tv-movie-reviews/war-of-the-worlds-250033/ (accessed June 30, 2021).

Travers, Peter (2009), "Transformers: Revenge of the Fallen," *Rolling Stone*, June 24. Available online: https://www.rollingstone.com/movies/movie-reviews/transformers-revenge-of-the-fallen-122384/ (accessed June 30, 2021).

Travers, Peter (2018), "'Black Panther' Review: Marvel's History-Making Superhero Movie's a Masterpiece," *Rolling Stone*, February 6. Available online: https://www.rollingstone.com/movies/movie-reviews/black-panther-review-marvels-history-making-superhero-movies-a-masterpiece-198071/ (accessed 15 October, 2021).

Trumbore, Dave (2012), "Writer Max Landis Talks CHRONICLE 2 Featuring the World's First Super-Villain; Comments on Possibility of Josh Trank Directing the Sequel," *Collider*, April 29. Available online: https://collider.com/chronicle-2-sequel-max-landis/(accessed June 8, 2021).

Tsing, Anna, Swanson Heather, Gan Elaine and Nils Bubandt (2017), "Introduction: Haunted Landscapes of the Anthropocene," in Anna Tsing, Swanson Heather, Gan Elaine and Nils Bubandt, *Arts of Living on a Damaged Planet. Ghosts and Monsters of the Anthropocene*, 1–17, Minneapolis: University of Minnesota Press.

Tuan, Yi-Fu (1977), *Space and Place. The Perspective of Experience*, Minneapolis: University of Minnesota Press.

Turan, Kenneth (2018), "Review: 'Black Panther' Is a Royally Imaginative Standout in the Marvel Cinematic Universe," *Los Angeles Times*, February 6. Available online: https://www.latimes.com/entertainment/movies/la-ca-mn-black-panther-review-20180206-story.html (accessed February 27, 2022).

Turnock, Julie A. (2015), *Plastic Reality. Special Effects, Technology and the Emergence of 1970s Blockbuster Aesthetics*, New York: Columbia University Press.

Vidler, Anthony (2000), *Warped Space. Art, Architecture and Anxiety in Modern Culture*, Cambridge: MIT Press.

Vint, Sherryl (2009), "Simians, Subjectivity and Sociality: *2001: A Space Odyssey* and Two Versions of *Planet of the Apes*," *Science Fiction Film and Television*, 2 (2): 225–50. DOI: 10.3828/sfftv.2009.3

Vint, Sherryl (2010), *Science Fiction and the Question of the Animal*, Liverpool: Liverpool University Press.

Vishnevetsky, Ignatiy (2018), "The Entertaining and Ambitious Black Panther Breaks from the Marvel Formula," *The A.V. Club*, February 14. Available online: https://www.avclub.com/the-entertaining-and-ambitious-black-panther-breaks-fro-1822976016 (accessed February 27, 2022).

Wallace, Carvell (2018), "Why 'Black Panther' Is a Defining Moment for Black America," *New York Times Magazine*, February 12. Available online: https://www.nytimes.com/2018/02/12/magazine/why-black-panther-is-a-defining-moment-for-black-america.html (accessed 15 October, 2021).

Wallace, Lewis (2009), "Secrets of District 9's Grungy Alien Realism," *Wired*, August 14. Available online: https://www.wired.com/2009/08/secrets-of-district-9s-grungy-alien-realism/ (accessed June 10, 2019).

Wasielewski, Marek (2009), "Golden Age Comics," in Mark Bould, Andrew M. Butler, Adam Roberts and Sherryl Vint (eds.), *Routledge Companion to Science* Fiction, 62–70, London and New York: Routledge.

West III, Thomas J. (2019), "Going Ape: Animacy and Affect in *Rise of the Planet of the Apes* (2011)," *New Review of Film and Television Studies*, 17 (2): 236–53. DOI: 10.1080/17400309.2019.1602980

Westfahl, Gary (2003), "Space Opera," in Edward James and Farah Mendlesohn (eds.), *The Cambridge Companion to Science Fiction*, 197–208, Cambridge: Cambridge University Press.

Wetmore, Kevin, Jr. (2005), *The Empire Triumphant: Race, Religion and Rebellion in the Star Wars Films*, Jefferson and London: McFarland and Company, Inc.

Wetmore, Kevin, Jr. (2022), "Avenging the Anthropocene. Returning the Dead to Life while Destroying the Planet in the Avengers films," in Simon Bacon (ed.), *The Anthropocene and the Undead: Cultural Anxieties in the Contemporary Popular Imagination*, 133–46, Lanham, Maryland: Lexington Books.

Whitten, Sarah (2021), "The 13 Highest-grossing Film Franchises at the Box Office," *CNBC*, January 31. Available online: https://www.cnbc.com/2021/01/31/the-13-highest-grossing-film-franchises-at-the-box-office.html (accessed June 29, 2021).

Williams, Trey (2018), "Fox and Disney Shareholders Vote to Approve $71.3 Billion Merger," *The Wrap*, July 27. Available online: https://www.thewrap.com/fox-disney-shareholders-vote-approve-merger/ (accessed January 13, 2022).

Wolfe, Cary (2010), *What Is Posthumanism?*, Minneapolis: University of Minnesota Press.

Wolfe, Jennifer (2015), "'Interstellar' VFX Team Helps Science Build a Better Black Hole," *AWN.com. Animation World Network*, February 20. Available online: https://www.awn.com/news/interstellar-vfx-team-helps-science-build-better-black-hole (accessed January 13, 2022).

Yahr, Emily (2015), "Does 'Jurassic World' Remind You of 'Blackfish'? How a Dinosaur Movie Tackled Animal Rights," *The Washington Post*, June 15. Available online: https://www.washingtonpost.com/news/arts-andentertainment/wp/2015/06/15/does-jurassic-world-remind-you-of-blackfish-how-a-dinosaur-movie-tackled-animal-rights/ (accessed 19 July, 2021).

YouTube (2009), "Avatar Exclusive-Behind the Scenes (The Art of Performance Capture)," Youtube, December 16. Available online: https://www.youtube.com/watch?time_continue=2&v=P2_vB7zx_SQ (accessed June 11, 2019).

Żaglewski, Tomasz (2019), "Infinite Narratives on Infinite Earths. The Evolution of Modern Superhero Films," *Panoptikum*, 22 (29): 158–72.

Zeitchik, Steven (2015), "For Matt Damon Movie 'The Martian,' Lots of Research—and a Watery Coincidence," *Los Angeles Times*, September 29. Available online: https://www.latimes.com/entertainment/movies/moviesnow/la-et-mn-the-martian-movie-mars-water-matt-damon-20150929-story.html (accessed September 10, 2021).

Zornado, Joseph and Sara Reilly (2021), "Fantasies of the Anthropocene," in Joseph Zornado and Sara Reilly (eds.), *The Cinematic Superhero as Social Practice*, 83–120, Cham: Palgrave Macmillan.

Index

Abbott, Stacey 46
Abrams, J. J. 46, 51–2, 84
The Abyss (1989) 50
Action Comics 63
action films 35–6, 47, 64, 105, 108, 149, 152, 179, 185
Adams, Douglas 170
adaptations 35, 41–2, 62–3, 79, 130–1, 156, 170
Ad Astra (2019) 138
Aditya, R. P. 176
The Adjustment Bureau (2011) 138, 153
Aeon Flux (2005) 120, 128, 191 n.12
Afrofuturism 135, 182–6
After Earth (2013) 42, 120, 132–3
Age of Extinction (2011) 92
A. I. Artificial Intelligence (2001) 98, 106–7, 111–12, 114
Alien (1979) 2, 49, 94, 105, 144–5
Alien: Covenant (2017) 49, 138, 144–5
alien encounters cycle (SF bodies square) 6–7, 18, 21, 35, 57, 79, 97–8, 100, 105, 139
  common people and experts 81–7
  films 80–1 (*see also specific alien counters cycle films*)
  good/bad alien opposition 81, 87–96
Aliens (1986) 50
Alien Vs. Predator films (2004, 2007) 80, 86–7
  Alien Vs Predator: Requiem (2007) 83–4
Alita: Battle Angel (2019) 120, 128
alternate realities 20, 28, 147, 154, 175–6, 181
Altman, Rick 4–5, 27, 56, 57–8, 155
  "A Semantic/Syntactic Approach to Film Genre" 4
  semantic/syntactic/pragmatic approach 4, 175
Amazing Stories 2, 188 n.1
American exceptionalism 69, 96

American Ultra (2015) 35
The Animal (2001) 62, 72, 192 n.5
animation/animation techniques 28, 51, 101, 189 n.10
Annihilation (2018) 138, 145–6
Anthropocene 7, 57, 119–20, 127–8, 133, 136, 176–7
  climate change 134
Apollo 18 (2011) 43, 138, 144–5
Arrival (2016) 21, 81, 88, 90, 92–5, 191 n.9
audience discourses 179–80, 184, 187
Avatar (2009) 1, 28, 42, 50–1, 157, 159–60, 172, 191 n.9
Avatar: The Way of Water (2022) 193 n.4
Avengers films (2012, 2015, 2018, 2019) 62
  Avengers: Endgame (2019) 1, 7, 63, 68, 159, 175–81, 183, 186, 191 n.2, 194 n.1
  Avengers: Infinity War (2018) 68, 176–8, 191 n.2

Babylon 5 (1994–8) 156
Back to the Future film series (1985, 1988, 1989) 147, 176–8
Ballistic: Ecks vs. Sever (2002) 35
Barthes, Roland 188 n.1
Batman films (1989–97) 63
Battle: Los Angeles (2011) 80, 86, 89
Battle Royale (2000) 123
Battleship (2012) 42, 80, 86
Battlestar Galactica (1978–9) 156
Bay, Michael 90
The Beast from 20,000 Fathoms (1953) 98
Being John Malkovich (1999) 111
Benash, W. Richard 182
Berney, Jim 131
Bicentennial Man (1999) 107
Big Six Hollywood studios 40, 43, 173, 190 n.5. *See also* Columbia; Disney; Paramount Pictures; 20th Century Fox; Universal Pictures; Warner Bros.

Blackfish (2013) 101
Black Panther (2018) 7, 120, 134–6, 175–6, 181–7, 191 n.9, 192 n.4
Blade II (2002) 33
Blade Runner (1982) 2, 49, 124–5, 126–7
Blade Runner 2049 (2017) 120, 126–7, 129
blaxploitation films 182–3
blockbusters 1, 40–2, 46–7, 62–3, 76–7, 80, 99–100, 152, 162, 170, 190 nn.3–4
Blomkamp, Neill 46, 54–5, 93–4, 113, 125–6
Bloodshot (2020) 62, 66, 191 n.1, 192 n.5
B-movies 2, 88, 99
Boden, Anna 191 n.12
Boklund-Lagopoulou, Karin 11
Booker, M. Keith 162, 165–6, 193 n.6
Bould, Mark 25, 191 n.11
Box Office Mojo 27–8, 43
Bradshaw, Peter 177, 183
Brooker, Will, *Star Wars* 193 n.5
Buckland, Warren 150, 191 n.11
Buck Rodgers in the 25th Century (1979–81) 156
Buck Rogers (1939) 156
budgets, films 42, 49, 70, 73, 130, 141, 189 n.9
 big-budget films 2, 42–3, 63, 73, 76–7, 88, 92–3, 99, 105, 126, 142, 147, 170
 medium- and low-budget films 1, 42–3, 62, 71, 77, 93, 99–100, 105–6, 170
Buell, Lawrence 129
Bukatman, Scott 15, 17, 64, 191 n.11
Bumblebee (2018) 80, 87
Burger, Neil 71
The Butterfly Effect (2004) 36

Cameron, James 1, 28, 42, 46, 50–1, 149, 159
Campbell, John W., "Who Goes There?" 86
Canavan, Gerry 129, 182
Captain America films (2011, 2014, 2016) 62, 66, 75
 Captain America: Civil War (2016) 68
 Captain America: The First Avenger (2011) 67
Captain Marvel (2019) 62, 67, 191 n.12

Captain Video (1949–56) 156
Carpenter, John 86
cerebral blockbusters 52, 147
Chambliss, Scott 167
Chappie (2015) 54, 98, 106–7, 111, 113–14
Chiang, Ted, "Story of Your Life" 94
Children of Men (2006) 53–4, 120–2, 191 n.9
Chinlund, James 132
Chronicle (2012) 62, 73–4, 76, 192 n.5
The Chronicles of Riddick (2004) 33–4
cinema of attractions 45
climate-centered narratives 177
Clockstoppers (2002) 36
Close Encounters of the Third Kind (1977) 2, 46–7, 80, 82, 84
Cloud Atlas (2012) 120, 191 n.12
Cloverfield (2008) 51, 98, 105–6
cognition effect 6, 12, 23–7, 33–4
cognitive estrangement, literature of 3, 24
Cold War paranoia 79–80, 83, 162
Collins, Suzanne, *The Hunger Games* 41, 123
Colossus: The Forbin Project (1970) 107
Columbia 190 n.5
computer-generated imagery (CGI) 28, 40, 46, 50–3, 161
concept-authors 47
Conglomerate Hollywood 6, 39–44, 47, 55–6, 62–3, 68, 71, 77, 85, 88, 91, 96, 99, 159–60, 162, 173–5
 economic strategies of 176
 imperatives of 62, 159
 post-auteur author of 50
 tactics of 71, 73
Connolly, Derek 100
Conquest of Space (1955) 140
Coogan, Peter 64, 66
Cooper, Bradley 71–2
The Core (2003) 137, 144
Cornea, Christine 3–4, 69
corpus of films 5–6, 27–8, 33–7, 41–4, 49, 51, 54, 62, 79, 157, 163, 173–5, 189 n.8, 190 n.5, 191 n.12
 broad corpus 27
 final corpus (2001–20) 28, 29–33
 initial corpus, criteria 6, 28

Cowboys & Aliens (2011) 80, 87, 191 n.13
Creature from the Black Lagoon (1954) 98
creatures cycle (SF bodies square) 6–7, 21, 57, 61–2, 85, 97, 99, 104
    films 98 (*see also specific creatures cycle films*)
    machinic 107–14
    organic 98–106
Crutzen, Paul J. 119
Csicsery-Ronay, Istvan, Jr. 157
Cuarón, Alfonso 46, 53–4, 121, 139–40
cultural logic of ecology 119, 131, 136
cyborgs 16, 69

The Darkest Hour (2011) 80, 190 n.7
Dark Skies (2013) 43, 80
Dawn of the Planet of the Apes (2014) 129, 131–2. See also Planet of the Apes film series (2001, 2014, 2017)
The Day after Tomorrow (2004) 120–1, 128, 133–4
Daybreakers (2009) 120, 190 n.7
The Day the Earth Stood Still (1951) 2, 79, 89
The Day the Earth Stood Still (2008) 80
Death Race 2000 (1975) 123
Death Race (2008) 35
de Balzac, Honoré, "Sarrasine" 188 n.1
Debruge, Peter 177, 183
deep structure (SF) 6, 12, 14–15, 20, 57, 173
Déjà Vu (2006) 138, 153
Deleyto, Celestino 5
Del Toro, Guillermo 85
Demon Seed (1977) 107
De Niro, Robert 71
Destination Moon (1950) 140
digital technology/techniques 28, 39, 41, 48, 156, 174
Dimension Films 43, 190 n.8
Discovery, Inc. 189 n.1
Disney 43, 190 n.5
District 9 (2009) 21, 54, 80–1, 87–8, 90, 92–4, 113, 191 n.9
Divergent film series (2014, 2015, 2016) 120, 125, 190 n.7
Dixon, Leslie 71

Doctor Strange in the Multiverse of Madness (2022) 194 n.1
dominant 21, 58, 65, 69, 79, 83, 96, 179, 181, 188 n.4
Donner, Dick 183
Doom (2005) 137, 144–5
Dowd, A. A. 177
Downsizing (2017) 120, 128
Dragonball Evolution (2009) 33–4
Dreamcatcher (2003) 80, 84, 87
Dredd (2012) 35
Dune (1984) 156
dystopia/utopia cycle (SF worlds square) 6–7, 18, 22, 41, 54, 57, 112, 117–19, 137, 138, 158, 175, 187, 192 n.1, 192 n.4
    films 120 (*see also specific dystopia/utopia cycle films*)
    future city *vs.* postapocalyptic wasteland 120–36

Earth to Echo (2014) 43, 80–1, 84, 92
Ebert, Roger 48
Ebiri, Bilge 73
Edelstein, David 177
Edge of Tomorrow (2014) 20, 22, 138, 153
Ehrlich, David 183
Elsaesser, Thomas 45, 148, 159–60
Elysium (2013) 19, 42, 54, 113, 120, 125–6, 144
Empire 157–8, 168
    technoscientific 160, 163–72
Ender's Game (2013) 157, 190 n.7
Escher, M. C. 168
Eternal Sunshine of the Spotless Mind (2004) 36
E.T. the Extraterrestrial (1982) 36, 47, 80, 82, 84
Eve of Destruction (1991) 107
Everything Everywhere All at Once (2022) 194 n.1
Evolution (2001) 80, 87
exo-semiotic 6, 11, 37, 39, 45, 174

Fahrenheit 9/11 (2004) 83
Fancher, Hampton 126
Fantastic Four films (2005, 2007, 2015) 62, 73, 76

fantastic worlds cycle (SF worlds square) 6–7, 18, 20, 22, 28, 34, 41–2, 58, 139, 155, 191–2 n.2
  cosmic spaces of technoscientific Empire 158–72
  films 157 (*see also specific fantastic worlds cycle films*)
Fargo (2014–) 178
Feige, Kevin 178–9, 183–4
The Fifth Element (1997) 156
The 5th Wave (2016) 81, 83–4, 87
film genres/genre theory 1–2, 4–7, 39–40, 46, 48, 57, 62, 70, 74, 96, 107–8, 118, 126, 138, 162, 173, 175–6, 178, 180, 183, 186, 188 n.1, 189 n.9, 190 n.3, 194 n.1. See also *specific film genre*
  genre mixing 5
  genre purity 5
filmmakers and technology 44–56, 131
Firefly (2002–3) 170
Fisher, Mark 148
Flash Gordon film serials (1936, 1938, 1940) 107, 156
Fleck, Ryan 191 n.12
Fleury, James 43
Focus Features 40
Forbidden Planet (1956) 2, 138
The Forgotten (2004) 35
Fourier, Charles 117
The Fourth Kind (2009) 80
Fox Searchlight 40
franchise 1, 40, 41–2, 44, 47–9, 62, 65, 70, 73, 85, 90–1, 101, 109, 127, 157, 159, 162, 165–6, 170, 172–3, 179–80, 190 n.2, 193 n.3, 193 n.7
  and serialization 190 n.2
Freedman, Carl 24
Friedman, Josh 79

Galaxy Quest (1999) 156
Game of Thrones (HBO, 2011–19) 178
Gamer (2009) 120, 190 n.7
Garland, Alex 145
Gemini Man (2019) 35–6
Geostorm (2017) 42, 120–1, 129, 133–4
Geraghty, Lincoln 162
Gernsback, Hugo 188 n.1

Ghidorah, the Three-Headed Monster (1964) 85
Ghost in the Shell (2017) 120, 128
Ghost of Mars (2001) 33
G.I. Joe: Retaliation (2013) 35
G.I. Joe: the Rise of Cobra (2009) 35
The Giver (2014) 43, 120, 128
Glass (2019) 33–4
global capitalism 139, 144, 158, 160, 166, 168
Godzilla film series (1954, 2014, 2019) 85, 98, 102–4
Goldsman, Akiva 130
grammar roles (Subject/Object, Helper/Enemy, Sender/Receiver) 23–4, 26, 36–7, 65–6, 68, 71, 81, 99–105, 108–11, 120, 138, 140, 151, 154
Grant, Barry Keith 191 n.11
Gravity (2013) 26, 42, 53, 138, 139–43, 146, 191 n.9
Green Lantern (2011) 62, 73
Green, Michael 126
Greimas, Algirdas J. 6, 11–12, 23–4, 188 n.2, 189 n.6
  On Meaning. Collection of Selected Writings in Semiotic Theory 14
  Sémantique Structurale 12
Groundhog Day (1993) 147
Guardians of the Galaxy series (2014, 2017) 157, 164, 168–9
Gunn, James 168

Hablin, Sarah 127
Hall, Sheldon 190 n.3
The Happening (2008) 120–1, 129, 133–4
Haraway, Donna 69
Hardt, Michael 166
Hardware (1990) 107
Hartzheim, Hikari 43
Hassler-Forest, Dan 64, 69, 166
Heisserer, Eric 94
Her (2013) 98, 107, 111, 114, 191 n.9
heterogeneity 5
Hitchcock, Alfred 147
The Hitchhiker's Guide to Galaxy (2005) 157, 170–1

Hollywood 1, 48, 56, 68, 76, 94, 161–2, 187. *See also* Conglomerate Hollywood
  classical 5, 94, 149
The Hollywood Reporter 71, 177
Honeycutt, Kirk 71
Hornaday, Ann 182
horror film 3, 33–5, 43, 74–5, 99, 105, 130, 144
horse opera 193 n.1
The Host (2013) 43, 80, 83, 87
Hot Tub Time Machine (2010) 36
Hulk films (2003, 2008) 62, 67–8
human/alien opposition 35, 81, 87–9, 92–6
human-animal relationship 16, 75, 99–101, 103–5, 132
human exceptionalism 102–3, 108–10, 113
human/technology opposition 14–18, 20, 27, 56, 61, 65–6, 69–70, 72, 76, 108, 173, 174, 188 n.3
The Hunger Games film series (2012, 2013, 2014, 2015) 120, 124–5, 129, 190 n.7

I Am Legend (2007) 120, 129–32
I Am Number Four (2011) 33–4
I, Frankenstein (2014) 33–4
Iger, Bob 179
ILM (Industrial Light and Magic) 48
imaginary worlds 7, 18, 24, 57, 118, 174
IMAX screens 44
IMDb 1, 5, 27–8, 43, 179–80, 184–6, 189 n.7, 189 n.10
imperialism and colonialism 79, 157, 159, 162–3, 166, 171
Inception (2010) 22, 42, 52, 138, 146–50, 152, 191 n.9
The Incredible Hulk (2008) 67. *See also* Hulk films (2003, 2008)
Independence Day (1996) 80, 87–8
Independence Day: Resurgence (2016) 21, 81, 87, 90
Interstellar (2014) 42, 52–3, 138–9, 141–4, 147, 191 n.14
In Time (2011) 120, 128
The Invasion (2007) 80, 83–4
Invasion of the Body Snatchers (1956) 79–80, 84
I, Robot (2004) 120, 128

Iron Man films (2008, 2010, 2013) 62, 67–9, 176
The Island (2005) 42, 120, 128
It's a Wonderful Life (1946) 147

The Jacket (2005) 36
Jackson, Peter 93
  The Lord of the Rings trilogy 177
Jaffa, Rick 100, 103
Jakobson, Roman 188 n.4
Jameson, Fredric 14, 17, 24–5, 117, 119
Jancovich, Marc 80
Japanese animated films (anime) 28, 85
Japanese giant monster films 85
Jason X (2002) 35
Jaws (1975) 101
John Carter (2012) 33–4
Johnson, Rian 151
Johnston, Derek 80
Johnston, Keith M. 4
Jones, Duncan 149
Jonze, Spike 111
Jumper (2008) 33–4
Jupiter Ascending (2015) 42, 157, 191 n.12
Jurassic Park/Jurassic World film series (1993, 2003, 2015, 2018) 47, 98, 100–4, 106, 191 n.13
Just Imagine (1930) 118
Just Visiting (2001) 33

Kaklamanidou, Betty 27
King, Geoff 3, 80
King, Shaun 134
Kirkpatrick, Karey 170
Koepp, David 79
Kohn, Eric 178
K-PAX (2001) 33
Kragsbjerg, Trine Mærsk 177
Kristeva, Julia 75
Krzywinska, Tanya 3, 80
Kubrick, Stanley 112
Kuhn, Annette 2, 45
Kusama, Karyn 191 n.12

Lagopoulos, Alexandros Ph. 11
Landon, Brooks 46
Lang, Fritz 147
language, functions 188 n.4

The Last Man on Earth (1964) 130
The Last Mimzy (2007) 138
Last Starfighter (1984) 156
Lawrence, Francis 130
Lazan, David 130
The Lazarus Effect (2015) 62, 74–5, 190 n.7, 192 n.5
Life (2017) 138, 144–5
Limitless (2011) 62, 71–2, 192 n.5
Lionsgate Films 43, 190 n.6
live action cinema 28, 101, 189 n.10
Logan (2017) 62, 191 n.9
Loki (2021–) 194 n.1
Looper (2012) 20, 22, 138, 147, 151–2
Lost (2004–10) 178
Lucas, George 46–51

machinic creations 97–8, 106–14
Mamber, Stephen 43
The Manchurian Candidate (2004) 35
Man of Steel (2013) 75
Markus, Christopher 177–8
Mars Attack (1996) 80
The Martian (2015) 19, 49, 138–9, 142–3, 146, 191 n.9
Marvel Cinematic Universe (MCU) films 63, 66–9, 176–8, 182–4, 192 n.3, 194 n.1
Marvel Studios 134–5, 176, 178–9, 185
Matheson, Richard 130–1
Matrix trilogy 19, 89, 191 n.12
　The Matrix Reloaded (2003) 120
　The Matrix Revolutions (2003) 120
The Maze Runner film series (2014, 2015, 2018) 120, 125
McCarthy, Todd 73
McFeely, Stephen 177–8
McKagen, E. Leigh 166
McSweeney, Terence 63–4, 69, 182
media conglomerates 189 n.1
The Meg (2018) 98
Méliès, Georges 45, 92
Men in Black films (2002, 2019) 80, 87, 191 n.13
　Men in Black 3 (2012) 138, 153
　Men in Black (1997) 80
Metropolis (1927) 107, 118
Michelson, Annette 17

Miéville, China 25
militaristic SF films 86, 102
millennial films 6, 27, 47, 49–50, 63–4, 68–9, 80, 85, 87, 89, 92, 96, 107, 109, 118–19, 127, 139, 147, 156–7, 166, 170
mind-game films 111, 148–9
Minority Report (2002) 18, 120, 128
Miramax Films 190 n.8
Mirlees, Tanner 69
Misek, Richard 149
The Mist (2007) 43, 98, 105
Moore, Michael 83
More, Thomas, *Utopia* 117
multimedia 40
multiverse 176, 194 n.1

narrative grammar 6, 12, 23
　cognition effect as actant 23–7
　grammar roles (*see* grammar roles (Subject/Object, Helper/Enemy, Sender/Receiver))
nature *vs.* technology opposition 103, 188 n.3
Ndalianis, Angela 63
Neale, Steve 4, 191 n.11
Negri, Antonio 166
neo-space opera 156
New Film History 39
New Hollywood 2, 63
New Line Cinema 40
new millennium 39, 43, 56, 57–8, 96, 98, 119, 136, 172, 174, 193 n.3
The New Mutants (2020) 62
Next (2007) 33–4
Nielson, Toby 133
Niessen, Niels 182
9/11 attacks 63–4, 83, 105
Nolan, Christopher 46, 52–3, 141, 147, 152. *See also* cerebral blockbusters

Oblivion (2013) 120, 133
O'Connell, Hugh C. 127
The Omega Man (1971) 130–1
The One (2001) 35
organic creatures 97–106, 108–9. *See also* creatures cycle (SF bodies square)
O'Sullivan, Michael 178

Pacific Rim films (2013, 2018) 42, 80–2, 85–6, 88–9
Pak, Chis 143
Pandorum (2009) 19, 138, 144, 190 n.7
Paramount Pictures 94, 190 n.5
Passengers (2016) 42, 138, 144
Paul (2011) 36
Paycheck (2003) 138, 153
Phantom Empire (1935) 107
Pierson, Michelle 46, 191 n.11
Pixar 40
place
    definition of 19
    space/place opposition 14, 17–20, 27, 117, 136, 155, 172–3
Planet of the Apes film series (2001, 2014, 2017) 100, 103–4, 120, 131–3
popularity (of films/cycles) 63, 172, 176, 189 n.9
post-structuralism 11, 188 n.1
Power Rangers (2017) 62, 190 n.7
The Predator (2018) 80, 86–7
Predators (2010) 138, 144–5
The Prestige (2006) 36
Prince, Stephen 191 n.10
Project Almanac (2015) 138, 153
Prometheus (2012) 49–50, 138, 144–5
Propp, Vladimir 23, 189 n.6
Protosevich, Mark 130
Pulse (2006) 33–4
Purdy, Jenna 89
The Purge (2013) 35
The Purge: Anarchy (2014) 35
The Purge: Election Year (2016) 35
Push (2009) 62, 190 n.7

quality films 94, 180
A Quiet Place (2018) 33–4

racial themes 7, 57, 81, 87–93, 95, 134–5, 182
Rampage (2018) 42, 98, 103
Randell, Karen 64
Rastier, François 12
Ray, Billy 123
Ready Player One (2018) 120, 128
Reagan, Ronald 69, 193 n.6

reality/social reality 3–4, 11, 14, 18–19, 52, 56, 72, 74, 107, 122–3, 125, 131, 134–6, 148, 153–5, 160, 168, 183
Reeves, Matt 105
Reilly, Sara 177
Relativity Media 43, 71
Repo Men (2010) 120
Resident Evil film series (2002, 2004, 2007, 2010, 2012) 120, 128
retro-futurism 124, 127
Riddick (2013) 33–4
Rieder, John 162
Ripley, Ben 149
Rise of the Planet of the Apes (2011) 98, 100, 103–4, 106, 132. *See also Planet of the Apes* film series (2001, 2014, 2017)
Robocop (1987) 69
Robocop (2014) 62
Rodan (1956) 85
Rodenberry, Gene 165
Rollerball (2002) 35
Ross, Gary 123
rotoscoping technique 189 n.10
Rotten Tomatoes 179–80, 184–6
Run, Lola, Run (1998) 147
Running Man (1987) 123
Russo, Anthony 178, 180
Russo, Joe 178, 180

Saarinen, Eero 167
A Scanner Darky (2006) 189 n.10
Schatz, Thomas 189 n.1
    "New millennium, New Hollywood" 39–40
Schauer, Bradley 193 n.5
Schneider, Rob 72
Schwarzenegger, Arnold 109–10
science fiction (SF) film 1, 3–4, 45–6, 50, 54–5, 63–4, 71, 74, 77, 99, 118, 130, 140, 165, 177, 185, 188 n.1. *See also specific science fiction genre films*
Science Wonder Stories 188 n.1
scientifiction 188 n.1
Scott, A. O. 72
Scott, Ridley 46, 49–50, 142, 145
Screen Gems 40
Self/Less (2015) 62, 72, 192 n.5

semiotics 11
    methodology/theory 5, 37
    semiotic systems and exo-semiotic sphere 11 (*see also* exo-semiotic)
semiotic square 6, 12, 14, 26–7, 35–6, 58, 61, 81, 96–7, 99, 117, 136, 155, 158, 168, 173–4, 191 n.2, 194 n.1
    abstract model of 12
    deep structure 6, 12, 14–15, 20, 57, 173
    imaginative worlds 6–7
    other-than-human ontologies 6–7
    SF bodies 6–7, 14–17, 20, 57, 174 (*see also specific SF bodies cycle*)
    SF worlds 6–7, 15, 17–20, 57, 117, 174 (*see also specific SF worlds cycle*)
    syntax and cycles 15, 20–3, 28, 37, 56–8, 97, 117, 119, 134, 155, 158, 173
sequels/prequels/reboots/remakes 41, 43, 88, 100, 123, 128, 159
Serenity (2005) 157, 170–1
Seven Days (1998–2001) 147
Shelley, Mary 192 n.6
Signs (2002) 80, 83
silent cinema 190 n.2
Silent Running (1972) 138
Silver, Amanda 100, 103
Simone (2002) 98, 107, 110–11
Sky Captain and the World of Tomorrow (2004) 138, 154
Skyline (2010) 80, 83
Sliders (1995–2000) 147
Sliding Doors (1998) 147
soap opera 156, 193 n.1
Sobchack, Vivian 15, 77, 99, 118, 138, 191 n.11
    Screening Space: The American Science Fiction Film 3
social semiotics 5, 11, 173
Solaris (2002) 137
Sontag, Susan, "The Imagination of Disaster" 85, 134
Sony Pictures 94
Source Code (2011) 20, 22, 138, 146–7, 149–51, 190 n.7
spaceship 84, 88–9, 93, 138–9, 144–5, 156, 163, 167, 171, 194 nn.8–9

space, space zones 17–19, 120, 122–3, 125, 128, 137–47, 150, 155, 158, 160–1, 163, 165–6, 168. *See also* place, space/place opposition
    films 137–8 (*see also specific space zones films*)
    vast space 20, 155–6, 158, 163, 168
special effects 4, 7, 28, 39, 44–8, 50–1, 55, 63, 156, 162, 168, 191 n.11
Spider-Man films (2002, 2004, 2007, 2012, 2014, 2017, 2019, 2021) 26, 40, 62, 63, 65–6, 194 n.1
Spielberg, Steven 46–51, 82–3, 86, 90, 101, 112
Splice (2009) 62, 74–5, 192 n.5
Staiger, Janet 5
Starship Troopers (1997) 156
Star Trek series (2002, 2009, 2016, 2013) 18, 51, 89, 156, 157, 162, 165–6, 169, 170, 172, 178, 193 n.3, 193 n.7
Star Trek Beyond (2016) 164, 167, 194 n.9
Star Trek into Darkness (2013) 51
Star Trek: The Original Series (1966–9) 165–6
Star Wars series (2002, 2005, 2015, 2016, 2017, 2018, 2019) 138, 157, 162–3, 165, 172, 178, 193 n.3, 193 nn.5–7
Star Wars (1977) 2, 46, 48–9, 89, 156
Star Wars: Episode II- Attack of the Clones (2002) 48
Star Wars: Episode VII-The Force Awakens (2015) 51, 157, 163–4, 170
state-of-the-art effects (special effects) 140–1, 156, 158
Stealth (2005) 42, 98, 107, 110
The Stepford Wives (2004) 62, 70, 72
Stevens, Dana 177
structuralism 11, 188 n.1
Sunshine (2007) 137–8, 144
Super 8 (2011) 51, 80, 84, 92, 191 n.13
superhero narratives/films 41, 62–70, 73–7, 134–5, 168, 175–6, 179–87, 192 n.4. *See also specific superhero films*
    basic traits of 64
    millennial 68–9
    technological body 68, 75 (*see also* techno-body)

Superman films (1978, 2006, 2013, 2016, 2017) 62–3, 65–6, 183
surface structure (SF) 6, 12, 23–4, 57, 66, 68, 81, 99–100, 104, 108, 120, 140, 142, 146, 154
Surrogates (2009) 120
Suvin, Darko 3, 24–5, 117, 119
syntax and cycles 15, 20–3, 28, 37, 56–8, 97, 117, 119, 134, 155, 158, 173. See also specific SF cycles

techno-body 62, 70, 73–7
techno-humans cycle (SF bodies square) 6–7, 16, 21, 41, 57, 61, 97–8, 108, 135, 175, 181, 192 n.4, 194 n.1
    and artificial beings 61
    ordinary body 70–7
    superhero body (*see* superhero narratives/films)
technology 6–7, 18, 39, 44, 66, 143–4, 152, 159–60, 164–7, 174, 181
    filmmakers and 44–56
    human/technology opposition 14–16, 20, 27, 61, 65–7, 69–70, 72–4, 76, 97, 108, 173–4, 188 n.3
technoscientific sublime 168–9
television shows 43–4, 165, 170
Telotte, J. P. 46
Tenet (2020) 42, 52, 138, 147, 152–3
Terminator film series (1984, 2003, 2015, 2019) 50, 69, 98, 107, 109, 176
    Terminator: Dark Fate (2019) 110
    Terminator Genisys (2015) 109
    Terminator 2: Judgment Day (1991) 50, 107, 109
    Terminator 3: Rise of the Machines (T3) 109
    Terminator Salvation (2009) 120, 192 n.1
Them! (1954) 98
theoretical model (of the SF film) 7, 57–8, 174–6, 181, 186–7, 194 n.1
The Thing (2011) 80, 86
The Thing from Another World (1951) 80
Things to Come (1936) 118
Thorne, Kip 191 n.14
3D cinematography 159, 161
thriller/mystery 35–6, 43, 70–2, 184

time heist 178–80
Timeline (2003) 138, 153–4
The Time Machine (2002) 138, 153
time zones 20, 22, 128, 137–8, 146–54
    films 138 (*see also specific time zones films*)
    time-loops (loops) 20, 137, 147, 149–53
    time-travel 33, 36, 147, 151–4, 175–81
Todorov, Tzvetan 3
Tom Corbett, Space Cadet 156
Tomorrowland (2015) 138, 153
Tony Stark (comic book character, *Iron Man*) 67
Total Recall (2012) 120, 128
Trank, Josh 73, 76
Transcendence (2014) 42, 98, 107, 111, 113–14
Transformers film series (2007, 2009, 2011, 2014, 2017) 80–1, 85, 87–8, 90–1, 191 n.13
    Transformers: Revenge of the Fallen (2009) 89, 92
transmedia 41–2, 55, 173–4, 182
Trevorrow, Colin 100–1
Tron Legacy (2010) 120
Tuan, Yi-Fu, *Space and Place: The Perspective of Experience* 17–19
Tucker, Wilson 156
Turnock, Julie A. 46, 191 n.10
The Tuxedo (2002) 35
Twelve Monkeys (1995) 147
20th Century Fox 73, 76, 159, 189 n.1, 190 n.5
2001: A Space Odyssey (1968) 2, 138, 140
2012 (2009) 120–1, 128, 133–4

Ultraviolet (2006) 120
Universal Pictures 190 n.5
Utopia/Anti-Utopia 24, 118

Venom (2018) 62
verisimilitude (social and generic) 14, 18, 25, 100, 135, 175
Verne, Jules 183, 188 n.1
V for Vendetta (2006) 120
Victor Frankenstein (2015) 62, 74–5, 192 n.5

Villeneuve, Denis 94, 126
visual effects 46, 48–52, 54, 71, 191 n.10, 191 n.14
voice-over narration 86, 88, 133, 166, 194 n.8

Wachowski, Lana 191 n.12
Wachowski, Lily 191 n.12
Wallace, Carvell 134
Walt Disney Company 179, 189 n.1
Warner Bros. 189 n.1, 190 n.5
WarnerMedia 189 n.1
War of the Worlds (1953) 83
War of the Worlds (2005) 79–82, 86
Weinstein, Bob 190 n.8
The Weinstein Company 43, 190 n.8
Weinstein, Harvey 190 n.8
Weir, Andy 142
Welles, Orson 79, 147
Wells, H. G. 79, 81–3, 153
Western colonialism 79–80
Western expansionism 140–1
Westworld (1973) 107
Wetmore, Kevin J., Jr. 162, 176
Whedon, Joss 170
When Worlds Collide (1951) 138
The Wolverine (2013) 36–7
The World's End (2013) 80, 89
Wyatt, Rupert 103

The X-Files franchise
    The X-Files (Fox, 1993–2002 & 2016–18) 84
    The X-Files: I Want to Believe (2008) 35
X-Men film series (2003, 2006, 2009, 2011, 2014, 2016, 2019) 36, 62, 65
    X-Men (2000) 40, 63
    X-Men: Dark Phoenix (2019) 73

Żaglewski, Tomasz 176
zombie cycle 130
zones cycle (SF worlds square) 6–7, 19, 22, 57, 137, 158, 194 n.1. *See also* space, space zones; time zones
    space zones 137–46
    time zones 137–8, 146–54
Zornado, Joseph 177

www.ingramcontent.com/pod-product-compliance
Lightning Source LLC
Chambersburg PA
CBHW052037300426
44117CB00012B/1857